W9-BZE-820

# RHETORIC IN INTERCULTURAL CONTEXTS

# INTERNATIONAL AND INTERCULTURAL COMMUNICATION ANNUAL

**Volume XXII** 1999

## Co-Editors

Alberto González
*Bowling Green State University*

Dolores V. Tanno
*California State University, San Bernardino*

## Editorial Assistant

Cory Young
*Bowling Green State University*

## Consulting Editors for Volume XXII

Donal Carbaugh
*University of Massachusetts*

Fernando Delgado
*Arizona Sate University West*

Donald Enholm
*Bowing Green State University*

Mary Garrett
*Ohio State University*

M. Cristina Gonzalez
*Arizona State University*

Janice King
*Missouri State University*

Wenshu Lee
*San Jose State University*

Casey Lum
*William Peterson University*

Ringo Ma
*State University of New York
College at Fredonia*

Mark McPhail
*University of Utah*

Richard Morris
*University of Northern Illinois*

Tarla Peterson
*Texas A & M University*

William Starosta
*Howard University*

Patricia Sullivan
*State University of New York
College at New Paltz*

INTERNATIONAL AND INTERCULTURAL COMMUNICATION ANNUAL
VOLUME XXII                                                    1999

# RHETORIC IN INTERCULTURAL CONTEXTS

edited by
# Alberto GONZÁLEZ
# Dolores V. TANNO

Published in cooperation with
National Communication Association
International and Intercultural Division

Sage Publications, Inc.
*International Educational and Professional Publisher*
Thousand Oaks ▪ London ▪ New Delhi

EMERSON COLLEGE LIBRARY

HM
258
.R38
2000

Copyright © 2000 by the National Communication Association

All rights reserved. No part of this book may be reproduced or utilized in any form or by any means, electronic or mechanical, including photocopying, recording, or by any information storage and retrieval system, without permission in writing from the publisher.

*For information:*

Sage Publications, Inc.
2455 Teller Road
Thousand Oaks, California 91320
E-mail: order@sagepub.com

Sage Publications Ltd.
6 Bonhill Street
London EC2A 4PU
United Kingdom

Sage Publications India Pvt. Ltd.
M-32 Market
Greater Kailash I
New Delhi 110 048 India

Printed in the United States of America

*Library of Congress Cataloging-in-Publication Data*

ISBN 0-7619-2103-6 (cloth)
ISBN 0-7619-2104-4 (pbk.)
ISSN 0270-6075

This book is printed on acid-free paper.

00   01   02   03   10   9   8   7   6   5   4   3   2   1

| | |
|---|---|
| *Acquiring Editor:* | Margaret H. Seawell |
| *Editorial Assistant:* | Sandra Krumholz |
| *Production Editor:* | Diana E. Axelsen |
| *Editorial Assistant:* | Victoria Cheng |
| *Indexer:* | Virgil Diodato |

# Contents

## PART IV: FORUM ON DEVELOPING FRAMEWORKS FOR INTERCULTURAL RHETORICAL ANALYSIS

# Acknowledgments

We would like to recognize the special efforts of those who helped to make this volume possible. We would like to thank Margaret Seawell, developmental editor at Sage, for her patience and encouragement. We wish to recognize the following for their assistance in the preparation of this edition: Marie Kuesel, Alycia R. Humphrey (and all the other office staff workers across the country who took our calls and answered our questions), and the consulting editors whose names appear opposite the title page of this book. Special thanks go to Rosalinda Cantú, Sandy Schmidt, and Cory Young.

# I

# INTRODUCTION: RHETORIC
# AT THE INTERCULTURES

# 1

# Rhetoric at the Intercultures

ALBERTO GONZÁLEZ • *Bowling Green State University*

DOLORES V. TANNO • *University of Nevada,*
*Las Vegas*

> Perhaps there will be so many alternative spaces that they will no longer be
> called alternative.
>
> *—Guillermo Gomez-Peña (1993, p. 63)*

As recent scholarship attests, intercultural considerations of rhetoric inevitably appear at the wall of Greco-Roman traditions. Whether these traditions
of rational argument, deliberation, speaker credibility, and careful speech
delivery are used as a point of reference (Kennedy, 1998) or as a point of
departure and contestation (Falk, 1999), the wall assumes an unfortunate
presence that is intimidating and dominating.

And so Gomez-Peña's diversity dream for the next millennium is unreal-
ized. What Ron Jackson II (1999) states about the study of whiteness and
white privilege is true also of intercultural study: "It awakens emotions and
issues which conjure frustration, guilt, pain, hostility, antipathy, and dis-
cord" (p. 51). The wall represented safety as well as constraint.

But the push to explore beyond the wall is well under way. Though they
write from very different interpretive and critical perspectives, rhetoric as an
explicitly cultural activity has been introduced by several communication
ethnographers. Gerry Philipsen (1973), for example, explores the persuasive
options available to urban men in a Chicago neighborhood. He calls their
use of intermediaries a "rhetoric of connections" (p. 19). Dwight Conquergood
(1992) writes, "Ethnographers have responded productively to the invitation
to recognize their consubstantiality with rhetoricians" (p. 80). Indeed, Donal
Carbaugh's (1993) study of the play between then-Soviet and U.S. cultural
discourses in a television talk show and Jennifer Willis's (1997) study of the
performances of Latino and Latina identity in an Anglo community are
further instances of rhetorical perspectives that are brought to examinations

of intercultural interactions. But what are the connections among the study of culture, cultures interacting, rhetoric, and criticism? What are the implications of these connections for intercultural research? These are the questions that inspire this collection of essays.

## OVERVIEW OF CHAPTERS

The authors in this annual are united in two respects. First, they view interactional practices as significant outgrowths of the beliefs and values of particular cultural communities. Second, these authors are interested in understanding what happens when people negotiate interests (Carbaugh and Wolf; Peterson and Pauley), align their relationships (Gareis), and compose their organizational environments (Dixon and Shaver)—in other words, when people act rhetorically—and their diverse cultural assumptions and understandings suddenly are apparent. The authors explore in this volume the critical and theoretical possibilities that derive from examining rhetoric in intercultural contexts.

The six chapters in Part II examine past and current relationships between rhetoric and culture. These chapters also present visions for future criticism of intercultural rhetoric. The four chapters in Part III are varied examples of intercultural rhetorical criticism. The final section of this annual is an exchange on "Developing Frameworks for Intercultural Rhetorical Analysis."

### *Part II: Perspectives on Rhetoric and Intercultural Communication*

Robert Shuter (Chapter 2) makes the case that "culture and rhetoric are inseparable—a critique of discourse is a critique of the culture that produced it." He draws contrasts between Confucian and Aristotelian discourse traditions and shows how the tendency of any discourse tradition to universalize its tenets potentially "blinds" an adherent to the rhetorical relevancies of other cultures. Shuter proposes a "grounded" approach to rhetorical criticism as a remedy for universalizing critical claims and constructs.

Using the vocabulary derived from ethnography of communication research, Carbaugh and Wolf (Chapter 3) examine "how single occasions can create culturally distinctive exigencies." They outline the complexities evident in the "rhetorical contests" over Mount Graham, a site in Arizona that is both a location for a telescope observatory and a place of Apache sacred knowledge. Like Shuter, Carbaugh and Wolf reveal the intercultural limitations of prevailing models of communication—in this instance, Toulmin's model of argument. The central components of the Toulmin model—data, claims, and warrants—are of little use in understanding the argumentative preferences—

based in circular reasoning and silence—of the Apache people. Carbaugh and Wolf offer and describe a notion of "cultural discourse" as a way to understand and appraise the "deep intelligibilities" present in argument across cultures.

Ronald L. Jackson II (Chapter 4) outlines the premises and critical pre-scriptions of Africalogical rhetorical criticism. Jackson states that Africalogical critical methods "are not limited to the rhetorical texts of Afri-cans or African Americans." Hence, he encourages critics to accept Africalogical criticism but also to understand the spiritual and cultural per-spective that is brought to language use and communication generally. Jackson's crucial challenge to rhetorical critics "is to attempt to think in a non-Western manner, to avoid categorizing, splicing, reducing, and univer-salizing human phenomena."

Raymie E. McKerrow's challenge (Chapter 5) is equally crucial and no less difficult. For McKerrow, ". . . the task is to write rhetoric out of the lived experience of women and people of color, and thereby produce their history, rather than to merely write their efforts into the history of rhetoric as already constructed." The end result, he argues, is a postmodern rhetoric "that does not privilege, at the outset, any one singular means of achieving goals."

Vanessa B. Beasley (Chapter 6) approaches intercultural rhetoric by "ask-ing new questions of our 'old' subjects." She views U.S. presidential rheto-ric as a useful site for exploring the tensions between multi- and monoculturalism in U.S. public address. Beasley expects that an intercul-tural approach to presidential rhetoric may reveal that "chief executives speak under a much more complicated set of constraints than we have previously considered."

Drawing upon her programmatic research on Chinese rhetoric, Mary M. Garrett (Chapter 7) describes how Chinese culture and discourse escape easy Western preconceptions. Westerners' elevation of Confucian thought at the expense of Buddhist "disputation" and narrative discourse, a similar preoc-cupation with Daoist influences upon expression, and the tendency to flatten Chinese approaches into a single temporal and dogmatic character all work, Garrett argues, to maintain Western superiority and Eastern exoticism. Garrett recommends to critics of intercultural rhetoric, as does Shuter in Chapter 2, a rigorous intracultural knowledge: "There is no reason to abandon," she states, "the trained skepticism that characterizes, with its demands for suffi-ciency of evidence, appropriate credentialing of authorities, awareness of bias and underlying ideological commitments, and so on."

## Part III: Rhetoric in Intercultural Contexts

The United Nations Conference on Environment and Development (com-monly known as the "Earth Summit"), held in Rio de Janeiro in June 1992, was a very visible example of international and intercultural rhetorical conflict. The attendance of U.S. President George Bush was significant, because Bush "was in a position to further invigorate world opinion in support of environmentally sound development policies." Instead, Tarla Rai Peterson and Kathi Lynn Pauley (Chapter 8) argue that Bush's "imperialist agenda" clashed with the cooperative discourse of the conference. Their analysis details the series of messages by which U.S. participation came to be viewed as intransigent and self-centered.

Elizabeth Gareis (Chapter 9) examines the "rhetorical aspects of [intercultural] friendship formation." Gareis begins by showing how differing cultural definitions of the word "friend" set the stage for misaligned expectations in intercultural friendships. Gareis identifies key rhetorical moments in friendship initiation and in established friendships and concludes by providing several helpful strategies for aiding friendship formation.

Ringo Ma (Chapter 10) applies Western conceptualizations of metaphor and identification to examine the prescriptive power of water-related terms in the *Meng Tzu*. In Chapter 11, Linda Dee Dixon and Paul M. Shaver examine how organizational members in a medical clinic create a "language culture" through architectural composition that is at odds with the cultural sensibilities of the Native American clientele.

### Part IV: Forum on Developing Frameworks
### for Intercultural Rhetorical Analysis

The Forum brings together several authors of varied critical perspectives. The Forum section in this volume makes explicit the vulnerability created when a scholar embarks on an innovative path of research. William J. Starosta (Chapter 12) describes the twists and turns in his 25-year effort to broaden the parameters of intercultural communication research. He begins with his realizations that the corporate-friendly communication concepts that have prevailed in speech communication did not reflect all that he witnessed in his study of "development" communication in India. The critical repositioning of government initiatives in rural India and elsewhere, from informing to persuading, led Starosta to conceptualize the intercultural interaction as rhetorical. His subsequent models for intercultural rhetoric produced some of the most innovative speech analyses of the 1980s and 1990s. John C. Hammerback's reply to Starosta (Chapter 13) adds four considerations to an intercultural research framework: the rhetor's role in shaping intercultural discourse, history as a context for understanding intercultural action, mediated messages as frequent means and sites of intercultural interaction, and research centers as vehicles for promoting intercultural communication research.

In Chapter 14, Raka Shome replies to Starosta by agreeing that Starosta's open struggle to come to terms with the culture-privileging questions and methods of prevailing research frameworks was largely ignored in intercultural communication research. The tendency to ignore issues of power and ideology, Shome argues, is "symptomatic not just of the state of intercultural communication but of the larger field of communication in general." Shome extends Starosta's framework for intercultural research by elaborating the notion and implications of researcher privilege.

The Forum concludes with Starosta's brief rejoinder to the two responses (Chapter 15). The irony is heavy—an area of communication dedicated to intercultural understanding and dialogue occasionally has made outcasts of those seeking new ways to understand and dialogue.

## REFERENCES

Carbaugh, D. (1993). "Soul" and "self": Soviet and American cultures in conversation. *Quarterly Journal of Speech, 79,* 182-200.

Conquergood, D. (1992). Ethnography, rhetoric, and performance. *Quarterly Journal of Speech, 78,* 80-123.

Falk, E. (1999). Jewish laws of speech: Toward multicultural rhetoric. *Howard Journal of Communications, 10,* 15-28.

Gomez-Peña, G. (1993). *Warrior for Gringostroika.* Saint Paul, MN: Greywolf Press.

Jackson, R. L., II. (1999). White space, white privilege: Mapping discursive inquiry into the self. *Quarterly Journal of Speech, 85,* 38-54.

Kennedy, G. (1998). *Comparative rhetoric: An historical and cross-cultural introduction.* New York: Oxford University Press.

Philipsen, G. (1973). Speaking "like a man" in Teamsterville: Culture patterns of role enactment in an urban neighborhood. *Quarterly Journal of Speech, 61,* 13-22.

Willis, J. L. (1997). "Latino Night": Performances of Latino/a culture in northwest Ohio. *Communication Quarterly, 45,* 335-354.

# II

## PERSPECTIVES ON RHETORIC AND INTERCULTURAL COMMUNICATION

# 2

# The Cultures of Rhetoric

ROBERT SHUTER • *Marquette University*

In the past decade, a select group of communication scholars has challenged the rhetorical literature of the 20th century, arguing that because the literature has been generated by Western critics, it is therefore grounded in Western culture and, hence, of limited value beyond a Western context (Chang & Holt, 1991; Garrett, 1993a, 1993b; Lu, 1993; Xiao, 1995). Xiaousui Xiao (1995) argues, for example, that because the "west has tended to see its logic as inevitable and universal," it has "demanded that other cultures understand its doctrines in the way westerners do" (p. 83). This Western bias has prompted some rhetoricians to deny the existence of ancient Eastern rhetoric, according to Lu and Franke (1993), who cite James Murphy's ethnocentric conclusion that "there is no evidence of an interest in rhetoric in the ancient civilization of Babylon and Egypt, [and] for instance neither Africa nor Asia to this day produced rhetoric" (quoted in Lu & Franke, p. 447). East Asian scholars and some Western researchers have shattered the myth of Western rhetorical supremacy by exploring Asian rhetoric, principally Chinese argumentation. This exploration has enhanced rhetorical criticism and theory and, at the same time, drawn attention to the limitations of established rhetorical frameworks (Jensen, 1987; Oliver, 1971). Mary Garrett's (1993a, 1993b) research is noteworthy both in terms of its analysis of the Western roots of *logos* and *pathos* and of Bitzer's rhetorical situation—cherished rhetorical concepts—and in terms of its examination of Chinese discourse and the challenges it poses for Western critics.

This essay explores research trends in intercultural rhetoric, discusses limitations of the research, and offers an intracultural approach to rhetorical analysis that situates discourse within the culture that produced and nurtured it. Although I have not established a reputation as a rhetorician, the insights offered in this essay spring from my cultural critiques of interpersonal, small group, intercultural, and organizational research, critiques coming from a critical perspective that digs for unarticulated and often unseen national cultural axioms that drive every nuance of the research process, from questions asked to methods used (Shuter, 1990, 1998, 2000; Shuter & Turner, 1997).

## THE INSEPARABILITY OF CULTURE AND RHETORIC: THE CASE OF ARISTOTLE

Culture and rhetoric are inseparable—a critique of discourse is a critique of the culture that produced it. This is evidenced in the few cultural critiques of Aristotelian criticism. Jane Sutton (1986) argues that the dichotomy between *logos* and *pathos*—hallmarks of Aristotelian rhetoric—has fragmented rhetoric, privileging logical appeals and diminishing the value of *pathos*, *ethos*, and style. Such emotions are characterized as irrational, sometimes uncontrollable, and George Kennedy (1980) considers them "secondary rhetoric," subordinate to logical proofs, which are primary appeals.

Placing logic and reason above emotion has its roots in Western culture, where the separation of mind and body is central to Judeo-Christian tradition. Only human beings possess an intellect, according to this perspective, and that intellect elevates humankind above animals and nature. Because reason is central to free will, ethical discourse must emphasize logical arguments so that listeners can make reasoned choices when exposed to a message. Emotion short-circuits the intellect and appeals to baser instincts related to the body.

Reflecting the dualism of his era, Aristotle's preoccupation with *logos* may be incompatible with Eastern thought, particularly Confucianism, which values a heart-mind (*hsin*) approach to determining the appropriateness of behavior.

Confucian thought does not elevate reason and logic to an ideal; on the contrary, it places the heart—the essence of human nature—at the center of ethical behavior. It is the heart and mind—the total human being—that can judge ethical behavior, and by extension, ethical messages (Shuter, 2000).

Mary Garrett (1993a) argues that the distinction between emotion and reason in Chinese thought is "a matter of degree not essence." In fact, she points out that in ancient China, human emotions were thought to distinguish people from animals and lead to humanness. Although the Chinese believed that uncontrolled emotions could produce dysfunctional behavior, affect was considered central to human nature and equally important as reason.

Chinese rhetoric challenges an Aristotelian framework. The bifurcation of reason and emotion—so central to Aristotle's rhetoric—is incompatible with Confucianism and, hence, can be expanded through a unitary concept of rhetorical appropriateness that values equally the affective and cognitive domains. Extending rhetorical appropriateness to emotional appeal requires replacing the mind-body separation of Western philosophy with a holistic view of human nature that integrates feeling and thought. This reconceptualization requires the rhetorical critic to weigh with a neutral eye the persuasive value and appropriateness of argument, privileging neither logical nor emotional appeals.

Clearly, cultures have discourse traditions that shape the generation and interpretation of argument. This is reflected cogently in the research of Xiaosui Xiao (1995, 1996), who examined the rhetorical processes for communicating a work that is influential in one culture to a different cultural audience for which it was not intended. Referred to as intercultural rhetoric, this line of inquiry is rarely pursued by communication scholars, according to Xiao, who examined the introduction of Darwin's ideas in China through Aldous Huxley's *Evolution and Ethics,* which was interpreted by Yan Fu and presented in his *Heavenly Ethics.* In his compelling analysis, Xiao concludes that because Huxley's work was significantly adapted to Chinese culture by Yan Fu, the success of foreign ideas in a culture may result from the interpretation and modification of those ideas by native interpreters.

Like Confucianism, Indian rhetoric and philosophy also challenge Aristotelian emphasis on reason and the subordination of emotion. *Moksha,* which is roughly translated as liberation or salvation, is central to Hinduism and is among the most important pursuits of its adherents (Crawford, 1974). There are a range of pathways to reach *moksha,* but all of them require the involvement of the emotional domain. Subconscious connection through yoga and deep spiritual reflections is more effective in reaching truth and enlightenment than is reason, which is a "temporal tool to be used in social relations, but limited in utility and scope" (Shuter, 2000). As Robert Oliver noted in 1971, Indian philosophy provides a unitary view of human nature, harmonizing cognition and affect rather than compartmentalizing them as is done in Western philosophy.

This unitary view of human nature affects Indian rhetoric through its emphasis on truthfulness—the foremost goal of ancient Indian speech (Kirkwood, 1989; Oliver, 1971). Truthfulness extends far beyond the Western concept of honesty and is intimately tied to knowing Brahman—"an absolute, unchanging reality which transcends all dualities" (Coward, 1989, p. 10). To know about Brahman is insufficient, for one must experience Brahman, which is often achieved through meditative silence. This profound understanding—the key to spiritual fulfillment—is integral to truthfulness. When those who are in touch with Brahman reveal their thoughts, it is the truth that is being revealed.

Clearly, Aristotle's rhetorical framework is not culturally compatible with non-Western rhetorics. For that matter, all rhetorical critics, their criticism, and the analytical frameworks they use are reflections of the cultures that produced them. Through an exploration of feminist criticism and cocultural rhetoric, the next section reveals the subtle ways in which rhetorical critics and their criticism reflect culture.

## BEYOND ARISTOTLE: THE CULTURES OF RHETORICAL CRITICS AND CRITICISM

Rhetorical critics are not neutral vessels—they are imbued with their own personal values that influence their criticism both consciously and unconsciously. Although this is not a profound statement, few if any critics present their own personal and cultural profile in their research or explain how their criticism may have been influenced by their backgrounds. Consider feminist criticism.

Feminist criticism is as American as apple pie—its assumptions, goals, and critical perspectives are linked to American culture. According to Sonya Foss (1989), feminist criticism rests on the central belief "that men and women should have equal opportunities for self expression" (p. 151). As a result, feminist critics not only uncover male biases in language and argument but also give voice to women's experience and rhetoric.

Equality—a cherished American ideal—is strongly rooted in individualism, the belief that speakers, regardless of their gender, ethnicity, race, or social class, ought to have equal opportunity for self-expression and access to information. This belief is fundamentally at odds with Hinduism, for example, where the Varna Dharma prescribes caste- and class-related duties and even defines the communicative relationship between castes (Walker, 1986). Similarly, Hinduism defines the roles of men and women quite clearly in Dharma and Yoga Sutras and obligates communicators to interact differently with each sex (Coward, 1989). Hence, individuals from lower castes and women in general are not supposed to receive the same information as men or people from higher castes. Similarly, Confucian philosophy values receivers differently, privileging men and older persons in communication encounters. Therefore, feminist critics and their criticism would impose an American perspective on Eastern discourse.

The influence of culture on critics and their criticism can also be found within a society. Consider the analysis of cocultural discourse (i.e., ethnicity, race, social class) within the United States and the recent concerns raised by scholars like Orbe (1995), Rigsby (1993), and González (1989) that Mexican American and African American voices have been muted or distorted by Eurocentric rhetorical critics and criticism. These researchers have implied that the unarticulated biases of rhetorical critics and their criticism have subtly shaped the selection of minority discourse, its analysis, and the conclusions drawn from the criticism. Rigsby points out that the type of African American rhetoric selected for analysis in the 1970s focused on angry black men and women protesting on the streets of America. When protests waned, rhetorical scholars, writes Rigsby, appeared to have little interest in African American rhetoric, given the scarcity of this type of research in the 1980s.

Orbe's (1995) research reveals the subtle ways in which an analysis of African American communication is influenced by culture. For example, the Eurocentric bias of researchers is revealed in such research habits as the creation of stereotypical generalizations about blacks, which eliminate diversity within the culture, and in the repeated comparisons of European Americans and African Americans, as though black culture cannot be analyzed independently of white America. González (1989) echoes Rigsby and Orbe's concerns in terms of Mexican Americans when he calls for rhetorical research on the culture of Mexican Americans that will help explain "how cultural understandings inform rhetorical choices" (p. 409).

Criticism of interethnic exchanges within America can reveal in subtle ways the influence on criticism of a critic's cultural background, sometimes even when the critic is rhetorically sensitive to culture. In Starosta and Coleman's (1986) analysis of Jesse Jackson's "Hymietown" apology, they argue that interethnic rhetoric should be analyzed in six stages:

1. the delineation of historical relations between the speaker's culture and that of the audience,
2. identification of those elements of a speaker's culture that normally determine the speaker's style of discourse,
3. the specification of any prior image the speaker may have among members of the audience culture,
4. the enumeration of public expectations concerning the address,
5. message analysis in light of the preceding factors, and
6. analysis at the level of interethnic rhetoric. (Starosta & Coleman, p. 118)

For some reason, they omit from their framework how the background of the critic strongly influences the rhetorical analysis in each of these stages. For example, in Starosta and Coleman's (1986) analysis, traces of their own backgrounds may be reflected in their essay when they refer to Jews as a "race" (p. 118). Judaism is a religion, not a race, and to refer to Jews as a race conjures up negative historical images. One wonders in what other ways the authors' backgrounds may have affected their analysis, in terms of both marshaling and interpreting the facts.

Consider Starosta and Coleman's (1986) statement that Jews have remained silent on racism and slavery, which has "left a bitter taste in the mouths of twentieth-century blacks" (p. 119). Except for an allusion to "Jewish individuals" in the 1920s and 1930s who opposed racism and the mention of Rabbi David Einhorn's antislavery position, the authors do not examine the considerable involvement of Jewish civil rights activists and Jewish religious and community groups in the civil rights movements for African Americans in the 19th and 20th centuries. Clearly, the selection of facts in support of an argument may be influenced consciously and unconsciously by a critic's background.

## AN INTRACULTURAL APPROACH TO
## RHETORICAL CRITICISM

This essay has explored some of the challenges of doing rhetorical criticism across cultures. Not only are rhetorical frameworks culturally biased, but critics themselves are embedded in cultures, which inevitably affects their criticism. How, then, can a critic more accurately analyze discourse within and across cultures?

I propose an intracultural approach to rhetorical criticism that includes the following characteristics:

1. It is based on the assumption that rhetoric and its critics are wedded to culture.
2. It relies on grounded analysis to do criticism rather than establishing rhetorical frameworks and approaches.
3. It challenges critics to immerse themselves intellectually in the culture of the community being studied.
4. It requires that rhetorical critics explore and explain possible effects of their personal backgrounds on the criticism.
5. It resists comparative rhetorical criticism, opting instead for discourse analysis within a country or coculture.

Because rhetoric and culture are inseparable, an intracultural perspective uses a grounded approach to explore discourse rather than using culturally biased rhetorical frameworks. A grounded approach allows the discourse to reveal itself to the critic, rather than having the critic "squeeze" rhetoric into the predetermined categories and schemes—all steeped in sociocultural assumptions—that are inherent in any traditional rhetorical framework. To enhance this process, the critic should approach the analysis with a deep understanding of the culture that produced the discourse. With this understanding, the critic may observe nuances in the discourse—language devices and arguments endemic to the culture—that may be invisible to the uninformed critic. However, because critics are a product of their own cultures, it is important that critics critique themselves, exploring and explaining possible background effects on their criticism.

With an intracultural perspective, rhetorical scholars may be able to generate criticism that reflects more accurately and sensitively the rhetorical repertoire of the community being studied. Clearly, some of the critics examined in this essay are approaching this goal, particularly Xiao (1995, 1996), Garrett (1993a, 1993b), Lu (1993), González (1989), and Katriel (1987)—this last critic is a rhetorical scholar who uses a grounded approach in her brilliant criticism of Israeli rhetoric. With sufficient grounded studies, rhetorical scholars may be able to develop rhetorical theory about additional countries and cocultures beyond China, where most of the cross-national rhetorical studies have focused for the past decade.

# REFERENCES

Chang, H. C., & Holt, G. R. (1991). More than relationship: Chinese interaction and the principle of Kun-Hsi. *Communication Quarterly, 39,* 251-257.

Coward, H. G. (1989). Purity in Hinduism. In H. Coward, J. Lipner, & K. Young (Eds.), *Hindu ethics* (pp. 9-40). Albany: State University of New York Press.

Crawford, S. C. (1974). The evolution of Hindu ethical ideals. Calcutta, India: Firma K.L. Mudhopadhyay.

Foss, S. (1989). *Rhetorical criticism: Exploration and practice.* Prospect Heights, IL: Waveland Press.

Garrett, M. (1993a). Pathos reconsidered from the perspective of classical Chinese rhetorical theories. *Quarterly Journal of Speech, 79,* 19-39.

Garrett, M. (1993b). Wit, power, and oppositional groups: A case study of "pure talk." *Quarterly Journal of Speech, 79,* 303-318.

González, A. (1989). Participation at WMEX-FM: Intercultural rhetoric of Ohio Mexican Americans. *Western Journal of Communication, 53,* 398-410.

Jensen, J. V. (1987). Rhetorical emphasis on Taoism. *Rhetorica, 5,* 219-229.

Katriel, T. (1987). Rhetoric in flames: Fire inscriptions in Israeli youth movement. *Quarterly Journal of Speech, 73,* 444-459.

Kennedy, G. (1980). *Classical rhetoric and its Christian and secular traditions from ancient to modern times.* Chapel Hill: University of North Carolina Press.

Kirkwood, W. (1989). Truthfulness as a standard for speech in ancient India. *Southern Communication Journal, 54,* 213-234.

Lu, Y. (1993). The theory of persuasion in Fan Fei Tzu and its impact on Chinese communication behavior. *Howard Journal of Communication, 5,* 108-122.

Lu, Y., & Franke, D. (1993). On the study of ancient Chinese rhetoric/Bian. *Western Journal of Communication, 57,* 445-463.

Oliver, R. (1971). *Communication and culture in ancient India and China.* New York: Syracuse University Press.

Orbe, M. (1995). African American communication research: Toward a deeper understanding of interethnic communication. *Western Journal of Communication, 59,* 61-78.

Rigsby, E. (1993). African American rhetoric and the profession. *Western Journal of Communication, 57,* 191-199.

Shuter, R. (1990). The centrality of culture. *Southern Communication Journal, 55,* 237-249.

Shuter, R. (1998). The centrality of culture revisited. In J. Martin, T. Nakayama, & L. Flores (Eds.), *Readings in intercultural communication* (pp. 38-48). Belmont, CA: Mayfield Press.

Shuter, R. (2000). Ethics, culture, and communication. In L. Samovar & R. Porter (Eds.), *Intercultural communication* (pp. 443-449). Belmont, CA: Wadsworth.

Shuter, R., & Turner, L. (1997). African American women and European American women in the workplace: Perceptions of conflict communication. *Management Communication Quarterly, 11,* 74-96.

Starosta, W., & Coleman, C. (1986). Jesse Jackson's "Hymietown" apology: A case study of interethnic rhetorical analysis. In Y. Y. Kim (Ed.), *Interethnic communication: Current research* (pp. 117-135). Newbury Park, CA: Sage.

Sutton, J. (1986). The death of rhetoric and its resurgence in philosophy. *Rhetorica, 4*(2), 200-216.

Walker, B. (1986). *Hindu world: An encyclopedic survey of Hinduism.* London: Allen and Unwin.

Xiao, X. (1995). China encounters Darwinism: A case of intercultural rhetoric. *Quarterly Journal of Speech, 81,* 83-99.

Xiao, X. (1996). From the hierarchical Ren to equalitarianism: A case of cross-cultural rhetorical mediation. *Quarterly Journal of Speech, 82,* 38-54.

# 3

# Situating Rhetoric in Cultural Discourses

DONAL CARBAUGH • *University of Massachusetts*

KAREN WOLF • *Oregon State University*

Mount Graham is situated in southeastern Arizona, about 70 miles from Tucson and the University of Arizona. Its height is greater than 10,000 feet, and the region's arid climate provides the massif with a variable blanket of mesquite, scrub oak, and ponderosa pine. The climate also situates the mountain with a lot of dry air and clear skies, two qualities that are very attractive to astronomers.

Since the early 1980s, Mount Graham has been the subject of a complicated public controversy. Because of its close proximity to Tucson's university and because of its climate, the mountain was proposed as the site of a major observatory. Supported by the University of Arizona, Germany's Max Planck Institute of Radioastronomy, an astrophysical laboratory in Italy, and the Vatican Observatory, a plan to build a complex of telescopes atop Mount Graham was begun, with initial construction now under way.

Mount Graham is also situated about 20 miles south of the border of the San Carlos Apache Indian Reservation. According to some members of the Apache Reservation, Mount Graham is like all sacred places and spiritual things: a living part of nature, a revered, living place that can be consulted for wisdom and that can be a source for increasing one's understanding.

For the past decade, rhetorical contests have resulted as *Mount Graham* has been verbally pitched on the one hand as *a site for an observatory,* and, alternatively, as *a sacred place.* How shall this mountain be conceived, as a legal or a cultural place? Which human activities shall be deemed most proper in this place? Astroscientists have claimed that knowledge about the origins of stars and planets, as well as various technical innovations, could be advanced if this place became a scientific observatory. The Apache, however, have some different things to say.

One Apache who has much to say on the matter is Ola Davis, a 70-year-old grandmother who is head of the Apache Survival Coalition. About Mount Graham, she says:

> This is our Apache sacred mountain. Us Native American Indians, we have no building. We pray outside on a mountain. This is the way we are. We have not one door—we have open doors all around us. Mount Graham is just as sacred as this church. If I try to destruct this church, I know something terrible will happen to me. That's exactly how my Apache tribe feels about Mount Graham. (quoted in Bordewich, 1996, p. 206)

The complexities in these matters can run very deep. A discussion of the issue in Bordewich (1996, pp. 217-218) includes the following quotes. In March 1992, during public meetings at the University of Arizona concerning the telescopes on Mount Graham, Apache speakers were asked by others to "explain precisely what it is about Mount Graham that is sacred." One response was this:

> Ordinarily, these matters are not spoken about at all. It is very likely that there are only a few Apache who know what is sacred about Mount Graham, and that if they did and were asked, a truly traditional Apache might very well not answer or admit to knowing. (quoted in Bordewich, pp. 217-218)

A second response was as follows:

> In order [for you, white people] to understand . . . you would have to know how to show respect [in the Apache way] to this place. Why should we try to explain why the telescopes are a terrible thing to do to the mountain, if you will use what is said disrespectfully? (quoted in Bordewich, pp. 217-218)

An expert on Apache language and culture was quoted as saying "deferential avoidance in word and deed" was being used here by the Apaches, that is, silence was being used to preserve and respect this spiritual place and its traditional forms of life. Further, if particular Apaches were willing to "explain" the sacredness of the place, it was highly questionable whether they would do so to outsiders, especially to those who allegedly were unable to respect the place in the proper Apache way.

This Apache response—speaking of a culturally rooted unspoken dynamic and enacting that very dynamic in this public scene—was quite irritating to others, especially to some white people, who thought and spoke about these matters differently. One such observer characterized the Apache responses as "maddeningly vague," with a "dizzying circularity" that resulted in an incredible, "stunning argument." At the heart of this reaction were two beliefs: the belief of these white people that one must speak verbally in order to be heard and the belief that silence is simply a way of saying nothing and knowing nothing. One astonished observer commented in disbelief about this Apache response: "To say nothing was to say everything; to appear to know nothing was to know it all" (Bordewich, 1996, p. 218).[1]

How is it that a single occasion like this can produce variable exigencies, with each invoking deeply different rhetorical discourses? This is the main question we want to propose and to briefly address with our remarks. Just as an Apache response of silence can speak volumes to Apaches about a mountain, the union of material and spiritual worlds, ancestral wisdom, and historical events, so it can also confuse those who expect a different, albeit more Western, scientific, verbal response. Our purpose here is to invite reflection upon these types of rhetorical situations in which single occasions precipitate dramatically different rhetorical acts. Our proposal is developed with the concept of cultural discourses and with one of its main conceptual entailments, spheres of consciousness.

Recent rhetorical and cultural studies have carefully explored intercultural moments like these. For example, Keith Chick (1990) has examined the ways in which suasory discourse in South African classrooms exhibits different cultural forms of rhetorical action. Yousef Griefat and Tamar Katriel (1989) have examined how Arab and Israeli discourses celebrate different styles for discussing and being. Gerry Philipsen (1992) has examined public speech of the late Mayor Daley of Chicago and demonstrated how its production by Daley and its reception by the dominant news media exhibited different communication codes. Televised discourse has also been analyzed regarding the cultural rituals, rules, and premises that Americans and Russians used upon a single communicative occasion (Carbaugh, 1993). These studies, like the exchange between the Apaches and the scientists, suggest to us how single occasions can create culturally distinctive exigencies and how each such exigence can motivate radically different rhetorical responses, with each response, in its own terms, being nearly unintelligible to the other.

## THE TWIN PROBLEMS OF COHERING AND COMMUNING

This recent wave of rhetorical and cultural study turns its attention to complex multicultural occasions and suggests two fundamental problems with which we must wrestle. One has to do with mutual intelligibility—the shared, common, and publicly active meanings that can be presumed to be the basis for practical rhetorical action. What meanings do people presume as conditions for producing the very forms of discourse they produce? The presumption and social utility of mutual intelligibility exhibits a kind of meaningfulness about people and their world, about civic character, about what is intelligible and appropriate to do, and what is not. Any occasioned action is selected from the available features of some common culture as a way of verbally casting the scene into a meaningful event that is deemed appropriate to the occasion. Mutually intelligible action, like civic character, is thus presumed and constructed through the largely unspoken premises that communicate a common culture (Scruton, 1979).

This kind of intellectual problem is of course evident in our opening drama. Ola Davis presents a verbal claim, that Mount Graham "is just as sacred as this church" (quoted in Bordewich, 1996, p. 206). In so doing, she associates *mountain* and *church* in a way that deeply links land and spirit, the place being, for Apaches, a sacred site for reflection and worship. The mountain is thus symbolized as a powerful cultural scene, like a church, where spiritual living is keenly active. Using a different channel for rhetorical action on this occasion, other Apaches enacted and discussed a nonverbal act of silence— a deep watching, listening, hearing, smelling—this being a deeply traditional way of knowing such places, a proper way of gaining knowledge within them and of conveying knowledge about them. Each such act, of verbal claims about the mountain-church and nonverbal acts pertaining to it, is deeply intelligible to these Apache people. Each activates beliefs about people and place and morals about proper living, which are part of the sacred meanings of this common culture that are active upon this occasion.

Of course for others, what was desired was "a precise explanation" of the mountain's sacredness. When told by the Apaches that those who know the answer best are precisely the ones least likely to speak about the matter, these others accused the Apaches of being vague and circular in their argument. For these others, an intelligible response would perhaps be more of a verbal argument, with claims stated explicitly, supported by exacting data, and, above all, couched in clearly explicated definitions of concepts and premises, because this pattern is a deeply rooted and intelligible rhetorical form of their common culture.

The problem of intelligibility is related to, although not solely reliant on, a cultural construction of argument. Take for example Stephen Toulmin's (1958) model of argument, which suggests that through claims, data, and warrants, one can make a sound argument. Toulmin's model is applicable to an array of communicative situations. However, the consequence of adhering to a model of argument is apparent when certain peoples—like the Apache—use the communicative form of silence to support their claims, consequently falling outside of the boundary of what some people deem a legitimate argument.

For each, a legitimate argument is dramatically different. For example, what is deemed intelligible and appropriate as ways of discussing Mount Graham, what is a principal exigence to be addressed (for example, building an unwanted observatory or allegedly unintelligible Apache people), what rhetorical response is most fitting (for example, silent acts or verbal arguments), and what ends are sought (for example, the mountain as a spiritual end in itself or as an instrumental means to an end) varies in each case on this occasion.

A second, related problem that needs to be addressed in such discourse is the problem of community. How do people conceive and evaluate membership in human groups? What levels of shared identification and division are activated on occasion?[2] In one sense, community can be tightly linked to one standard of and for communication, as an ordered system of more or less uniform beliefs and morals, with this standard being used to conceive and evaluate membership in a group. Community, in this sense, is wedded explicitly to a shared identity and to shared means for conceiving and evaluating members as such. Alternately, community can organize a diverse range of standards and provide for various beliefs and morals. Community, in this sense, explicitly embraces various shared identities and various means for conceiving and evaluating them.[3] The communication of a community thus raises complex questions about membership, how it is conceived and evaluated, as well as the various levels and ways of identifying with group(s) that are being conducted and (de)legitimated.

By raising the problem of community, we do not want to imply that one conceptualization is necessarily better than the other on all occasions. We want simply to invite thought about the relationship, in such discursive occasions, between mutually intelligible actions, community life, and the variety of levels of identification that are possible. Upon any one occasion, weight can be placed more upon action within, or division among, social groups, amplifying some levels of identification above others and valorizing certain beliefs and values over others, with all of this presumed for the rhetorical action to be enacted the way it is. And it is this, a focus on actual situated rhetorical actions, and the problems of (in)cohering and (ex)communing in them, that we want to invite reflection upon and to bring more centrally into view.

The problems of coherence and community relate to our opening example in at least the following ways. First, we focus on coherence: Given a public occasion for describing Mount Graham, what means of rhetorical action can be used and properly understood as meaningful by those present, especially those in positions to make policy decisions? In addition to verbal arguments, could prayers, chants, and songs, or even silence, be intelligibly used? If so, by whom, and what meanings would be active on this occasion for those rhetorical means of expression? Further, we focus on problems of community: How are the means of expression used linked to levels of identification? Do the means signal participation in a publicly identifiable group (for example, concerning American citizens), or do they symbolize something else, perhaps an uncooperative citizen or an incoherent outsider (for example, white vs. Apache people)? What sense of community, what model for legal, political, and cultural action is being presumed and used given the way the rhetorical occasion unfolds? How does it relate those who are active on this occasion? Given our opening example, are the Apache people to be affirmed as legitimately active members—politically, economically, legally, and culturally—in this occasion? Or are they to be ruled as outside the boundaries of this "community" and its range of intelligible actions and morals? Perhaps they can even be seen as sovereign actors from a different—Apache—Nation?

By posing these two basic problems, of cohering and communing, or likewise of incohering and excommuning, we want to invite reflection upon basic features of these and of other similarly situated rhetorical actions. How are rhetorical actions—occasions, exigencies, responses, and ends—such as these conceived and evaluated by actors, and how do they create standards for civic character and community living? One construct that we find helpful in developing responses to these problems is the concept of cultural discourse.

## RHETORIC AND CULTURAL DISCOURSE

We define cultural discourse as a complex expressive system of terms, topics, forms, and their meanings that people use on occasions to help shape and organize social lives. By cultural, we focus on the basic premises of belief and value that people share in public life in order to recognize who they are and of what they are a part; by discourse, we have a pragmatic focus in mind, referring to expressive practices being used in specific social scenes. In referring to terms and topics, we refer to the actual words, phrases, and images (verbal and nonverbal) that people use and the domains of meaning these bring into play; by forms, we refer to recognizable means of expression, from individual acts such as requests to complex sequences of acts such as rituals; and by meanings, we refer to basic concepts and premises about being, acting, relating, feeling, and dwelling that people recognize as part of their common life.[4] As a complex construct, cultural discourse draws attention to the specific resources that people use to make meanings, by explicating the expressive system of which these resources are a part.

With regard to rhetoric, our argument is this: Cultural discourses radically differ with regard to the conception and evaluation of rhetorical occasions, exigencies, fitting actions, and goals. If rhetoric is, as Aristotle argued and as Thomas Farrell has recently advanced, a discovery procedure through which available means and meanings of persuasion come into view, then the concept of cultural discourse suggests one discovery procedure through which communal means and meanings of communication can be explicated. That is, it offers a way these can be discovered, described, interpreted, and critically assessed in each case.[5]

Considering the Apache comments above, we can use our construct of cultural discourse to notice the terms being used and how they are arranged, such as the linking of land and church, the topics addressed, and how these move from science to spirituality. We can also notice the forms of expression used, especially silence as a way of knowing a place and showing that one knows in the proper way. Through these terms, topics, and means of expression, a meaningful system of cultural premises is activated, which says that a person is one who lives with a spiritually infused natural world, that one should act so as to become attuned with that spiritual world, and that one can best become attuned with it through silence. Further, common Apache premises suggest that feeling extends through physical senses and animals, not just into people alone, such that one dwells in a world of intimately interconnected things, animals, spirits, and people: This is One Whole, not separate things.

Our summary here is offered simply as a suggestive application of the concept of cultural discourse, which is by no means comprehensively applied here. What it points to, we think, is a kind of cultural analysis of deep intelligibilities that are active in these terms, topics, and forms, a system of beliefs about what the social and natural world is, how it operates, and how people should act within it. It is this combination of the means of expression through terms, topics, forms, and their cultural meanings in premises for being, acting, feeling, and dwelling that has guided our primary application here.[6]

The Apache discourse used upon this occasion brings into play, for Apache hearers, a way of being and feeling in the world, a *sign-set* leading to a *mind-set,* which makes some of nature's objects, such as mountains, important channels of spiritual messages, if one can listen and hear properly. Such a discourse, when properly active in an Apache way, brings into being a kind of consciousness, a way of living in the world where objects, animals, and other things, as well as people, become sources of messages. Note here, with this cultural discourse system, that consciousness is not contained within an individual exclusively, but permeates animals and things, infusing the world with a unity that can speak if only consulted and heard in a proper way.[7] We might call this way of attuning in the world, in which all things are spirited and sources of nontrivial messages, a sphere of natural consciousness.

Another cultural discourse runs counter to that of the Apache on this occasion. It is crafted through terms that link land with development and the creation of an observatory and with topics linking science to the progress of knowledge; furthermore, these linkages are active in particular forms of expression, especially in deliberative verbal arguments. These terms, topics, and means of expression rely for their force upon common premises: People are best when rational, and people should think rationally about the world; the world does not know or feel in any real sense, but people do; people create knowledge verbally and should do so explicitly and reasonably; and people dwell in a world that can be used for the advancement of human objectives.

From the vantage point of this discourse system, human activity is separated from nature's objects, and mountains are not conveyors of messages, but humans are, with the human mind being the site of conscious activity. Note here how the consciousness that derives from and is elaborated in this discourse is contained within individual people and does not extend easily into the nonhuman world. We might call this a sphere of individual consciousness.

A third cultural discourse system is also identifiable, but not active in this scene. It uses terms, topics, and forms of expression that valorize collective activity, with cultural premises coupling unique human qualities with humanwide capacities. For example, in some Russian discourse, issues are discussed through terms of collective being, human morals, and passions, with this realm of uniquely moral feeling belonging distinctly to the human spirit and thus being sharply separated from the natural world. As a result, uniquely human feeling and spirit is active only across people and does not extend into the realm of animals or into nature's objects. We might call this a sphere of transpersonal consciousness.[8]

## CULTURAL DISCOURSE AND CONSCIOUSNESS

What we draw attention to with our brief discussion can be summarized in this way: The concept of cultural discourse can provide a discovery procedure that addresses problems of mutual intelligibility and community; such problems are largely presumed in traditional approaches to rhetoric or glossed with presumptions of a culturally homogeneous audience; explorations of cultural discourse can unveil distinctive systems of terms, topics, and forms of expression that presume and recreate common premises of being, acting, relating, feeling, and dwelling; and each such system presumes and elaborates a particular sphere or spheres of consciousness.

Our concept of sphere of consciousness has been proposed with a particular methodology implied. Through it, one moves from explorations of situated communicative scenes, to the explication of cultural discourse(s) within them, to positing spheres of consciousness that are activated in that cultural discourse. The concept is intended to invite explorations of at least the following dimensions of consciousness: (a) the generative force(s) motivating the scene (is it a person, spirit, animals, or people collectively?); (b) the loci or site of conscious activities (is it an individual *I,* an integral spirit-nature, or a relational *We*?); (c) the basic themes being elaborated (are they personal, religious, or social structural?); and (d) the scope of community (is it personal circumstances, cosmic connectedness, or collective morality?).[9]

The three general spheres of consciousness typified above and demonstrated in distinctive cultural discourses illustrate these basic dimensions.[10] The pan-natural consciousness is generated through a Great Spirit of all people and things, the locus of which is ubiquitously interperson and interobject, with basic themes being the holistic and interrelated union of the world. The individual consciousness is generated through the person's human will, the locus of which is an individual human organism, with basic themes being human, personal, and individual. The transindividual consciousness is generated through a humanwide spirit, the locus of which is the shared, uniquely human world, with basic themes being human, moral, and communal.

Through cultural discourses, spheres of consciousness come into play. In the process, historically based forces, activities, and themes become active, or possibly deactivated (see Morris, 1997). We thus propose our concept of cultural discourse and its entailment, consciousness, as a procedure for exploring deeply rooted means and meanings of rhetorical action, in the hope that it can provide a way (a) to describe how rhetorical actions get played into culturally complicated occasions, (b) to interpret the meaningfulness of this action within expressive systems, and (c) to critically assess the role of such action in our local and global lives.

Our approach is related to those of others. With regard to Thomas Farrell's (1993) focus on rhetorical culture, we share several commitments, especially the emphasis upon practice (pp. 10, 62), particularity (p. 9), the active audience, and concerns for civic character and a dynamic rhetorical forum (pp. 282, 288). Further, we find our focus amplified by Farrell in his discussion of what he calls the "mediated rhetorical occasion" (p. 281). In such occasions, he emphasizes "collisions among our cultural norms" (p. 281). However, our readings of Farrell's treatise suggest that he is very attentive to normative guides for public discourse, and perhaps less attentive to radically different cultural conceptions of its very nature and use. We thus propose our concept of cultural discourse as a complement to, not a replacement of, the concepts of "venue, grounds and space" discussed by Farrell (see pp. 277-288). Farrell's explication of the rhetorical form provides a way to understand how what is deemed "cultural" can be questioned, challenged, and discussed (p. 285). We want to take this notion further by suggesting that there also exist rhetorical occasions—such as the one we describe with the Apache—wherein a culture's cognitive constructions are inaccessible because the participants' argument styles are unintelligible to one another. In short, this state of unintelligibility limits the discussion that can ensue—for example, if silence is not deemed valid to the other, then one cannot engage in a logical discussion with the other.

Our hope is to embrace the radically different notions of rhetorical action that peoples bring to specific occasions. Similarly, we hope our approach offers one way of contextualizing our studies suggested by Lee (1993) and can serve as a basis for addressing Wander's (1996) lament: "As a field, we do not know many of the peoples who fall within America's 'sphere of influence'" (p. 408). We hope that, in time, we can help develop our understanding of the culturally distinctive discourses various peoples produce, in the United States and elsewhere. Along the way, we must strive to cohere and understand with others the worlds we consciously inhabit and reproduce. Our ability to live together and to forge robust versions and sustainable visions of community hangs in the balance.

## NOTES

1. The events discussed above draw primarily from Chapter 6, "Predators, Victims, and Mother Earth," in Bordewich (1996); but also from Basso (1990) and from some of Carbaugh's (e.g., Carbaugh, in press) work with the Blackfeet.

2. Our language here invokes the rhetorical theory of Kenneth Burke (1965), especially his discussion of orientation and of trained (in)capacity.

3. We invoke here Dell Hymes's (1972) sense of community as "an organization of diversity" as well as Philipsen's (1987) idea of "cultural communication" as the creation and affirmation of shared identity.

4. The approach summarized here builds on Hymes (1972), Philipsen (1987), and Carbaugh (1988, especially p. 178 and Chapter 11). A recent explication and demonstration appears in Carbaugh, Gibson, and Milburn (1997).

5. We draw attention here to Aristotle's discussion in *The Art of Rhetoric* about the purpose of rhetoric: "its function is not so much to persuade, as to find out in each case the existing means of persuasion" (1926, p. 13), or similarly, "Rhetoric then may be defined as the faculty of discovering the possible means of persuasion in reference to any subject whatsoever" (p. 15). Discussing his approach to rhetorical culture, Farrell (1993) reminds us repeatedly of the normative agencies of audiences and the role of the rhetor in engaging them. But this relies focally on seeing rhetoric as a "kind of discovery which enables us to come as near to persuasion as the case allows" (p. 68; see especially pp. 61-83). The present approach builds upon rhetoric as a discovery procedure, but it does so with a radical ethnographic turn, with the currently available means of persuasion requiring critical reflection upon the faculties foregrounded by both Aristotle and Farrell.

6. The interested reader will find more detailed applications elsewhere (e.g., Carbaugh, 1988, 1993; Griefat & Katriel, 1989; Philipsen, 1992).

7. Our formulation here relies upon literatures about American Indian communication, including Basso (1990) and Carbaugh (in press).

8. This description is based upon Wierzbicka (1989) and Carbaugh (1993).

9. We deliberately do not refer to Anthony Giddens's (1984) notions of discursive and practical consciousness here, mainly because our studies suggest that consciousness cannot be neatly divided into these types. For example, some enactments of a practical consciousness (e.g., a silent communicativeness) rely heavily upon a particular discursive

formation for their shape and meaning.

10. Considerations of the scope of the typical spheres would run into affordances and limits inherent in these typical spheres of consciousness, especially the cultural entailments about what is coherent and what constitutes community. Because of the complexities inherent in this fourth dimension, we do not discuss its relation to the three posited typical spheres.

# REFERENCES

Aristotle. (1926). *Art of rhetoric* (J. H. Freese, Trans.). Cambridge, MA: Harvard University Press.

Basso, K. (1990). *Western Apache language and culture.* Tucson: University of Arizona Press.

Bordewich, F. (1996). *Killing the white man's Indian: Reinventing Native Americans at the end of the twentieth century.* New York: Doubleday.

Burke, K. (1965). *Permanence and change.* Indianapolis, IN: Bobbs-Merrill.

Carbaugh, D. (1988). *Talking American: Cultural discourses on DONAHUE.* Northwood, NJ: Ablex.

Carbaugh, D. (1993). "Soul" and "self": Soviet and American cultures in conversation. *Quarterly Journal of Speech, 79,* 182-200.

Carbaugh, D. (in press). "Listening" as a Blackfeet form of communication. In C. Barbisio (Ed.), *Narrative psychology and landscape.* Torino, Italy: University of Torino Press.

Carbaugh, D., Gibson, T., & Milburn, T. (1997). Communication as cultural pragmatic action: "Discussing" at school and "deciding" at a Puerto Rican Center. In B. Kovacic (Ed.), *Emerging perspectives on human communication* (pp. 1-24). Albany: State University of New York Press.

Chick, J. K. (1990). The interactional accomplishment of discrimination in South Africa. In D. Carbaugh (Ed.), *Cultural communication and intercultural contact* (pp. 225-252). Hillsdale, NJ: Lawrence Erlbaum.

Farrell, T. (1993). *Norms of rhetorical culture.* New Haven, CT: Yale University Press.

Giddens, A. (1984). *The constitution of society: Outline of the theory of structuration.* Cambridge, MA: Polity Press.

Griefat, Y., & Katriel, T. (1989). Life demands "Muusayra": Communication and culture among Arabs in Israel. *International and Intercultural Communication Annual, 13,* 121-138.

Hymes, D. (1972). Models of the interaction of language and social life. In J. Gumperz & D. Hymes (Eds.), *Directions in sociolinguistics: The ethnography of communication* (pp. 35-71). New York: Holt, Rinehart & Winston.

Lee, W. S. (1993). On not missing the boat: A processual method for inter/cultural understanding of idioms and lifeworld. *Journal of Applied Communication Research, 22,* 141-161.

Morris, R. (1997). Educating savages. *Quarterly Journal of Speech, 83,* 152-171.

Philipsen, G. (1987). The prospect for cultural communication. In L. Kincaid (Ed.), *Communication theory: Eastern and Western perspectives* (pp. 245-254). New York: Academic Press.

Philipsen, G. (1992). *Speaking culturally.* Albany: State University of New York Press.

Scruton, R. (1979). The significance of common culture. *Philosophy, 54,* 51-70.

Toulmin, S. E. (1958). *The uses of argument.* Cambridge, U.K.: Cambridge University Press.

Wander, P. (1996). Marxism, post-colonialism, and rhetorical contextualism. *Quarterly Journal of Speech, 82,* 402-426.

Wierzbicka, A. (1989). Soul and mind: Linguistic evidence for ethnopsychology and cultural history. *American Anthropologist, 91,* 41-58.

# 4

# Africalogical Theory Building

## Positioning the Discourse

RONALD L. JACKSON II • *Pennsylvania State University*

*Afrocentricity* and *Africalogy* are two terms that have consistently ignited much controversy throughout various disciplines whenever they are spoken in conservative scholarly circles. Africalogical theory building is a needed paradigmatic renovation among rhetorical-critical approaches. For me, it is more than an intellectual gesture or exercise—it is an enduring venture, the objective of which is to clarify and demonstrate what it means to be African and what it means to epistemologically locate and define oneself within discourse(s) and the analyses of the discourse(s).

What is often identified as "good rhetorical criticism" is usually determined by the perspective of the rhetorical critic within the ongoing conceptual debate regarding the superiority of audience-centered versus speaker-centered criticism. It has been argued that audience-centered criticism is superior because it measures the efficacy and inducement of the message by placing the emphasis on the audience. However, speaker-centered criticism is considered by some to be more valuable, because the intent and identification efforts of the speaker provide worthwhile information regarding the history and production of the text. On the one hand, it is rather surprising that a relatively sharp group of intellectuals would allow themselves to be eased into a battle of futility that ultimately resists what we know to be critical thought. For an intellectual, it should be apparent at some point that every inquiry does not deserve a simple yes or no and every evaluation a simple good or bad, but that sometimes there is a continuum. The Africalogical method is holistic; consequently, it does not conform to either a speaker-centered or an audience-centered perspective. It is word centered, audience centered, and speaker centered. Because I have already elaborated elsewhere (Jackson, 1995) the centrific nature of the word, audience, and speaker within the method, I will not spend much time here on this issue. The primary objective of this chapter is to express my position on rhetorical theory building and to challenge readers to recondition their minds and redefine the range of rhetorical methods in order to embrace Africalogical theory building. This is not an apologia for Africalogy, nor is it an attempt to dismiss Western approaches. It is an opportunity to further consider a non-Western approach or method among other viable rhetorical paradigms. The chapter begins with a few basic concerns regarding the nature of rhetorical theory building. This is followed by an explanation of Africalogical rhetorical approaches, a cursory glance at doing Africalogical criticism, and the issuing of a challenge to rhetorical scholars. Finally, a few suggestions for future rhetorical theoretical directions are provided.

## SOME BASIC CONCERNS

Whenever I begin writing to explain the Afrocentric-Africalogical rhetorical method, I find myself feeling compelled to justify Afrocentricity, because Afrocentric thought has been so widely criticized. Furthermore, I am also admonished by those of my colleagues who are also Afrocentric thinkers that apologia is unnecessary and a waste of energy. Yet I am too frequently confronted by master's and doctoral students who are initially interested in using the Afrocentric method in their theses and dissertations but are then discouraged by their advisers on the grounds that Afrocentricity is unsystematized or incoherent. In other words, it is not considered traditional or classical; however, I would argue that every culture has a different interpretation of classical thought.

*Classical* is a culturally relative variable. Within the past century, scholars throughout the various disciplines have begun to seriously consider African philosophy and traditions. Anthropologists, linguists, sociologists, psychologists, musicologists, and theologians are but a few of those who have intensely studied the Africalogical worldviews. The communication discipline has yet to fully consider the theoretical dimensions of African cosmological structures. The buzzword is *nommo* among scholars privy to the Afrocentric paradigm. At one National Communication Association national meeting a couple of years ago, a young scholar, who apparently wanted to appear knowledgeable on the topic, placed *nommo* in the title of his paper. Because it seemed so awkwardly insignificant to his paper, I asked him during the question-and-answer period to explain or define what *nommo* means. He confessed that he didn't really have any idea what it meant. "I just thought it sounded appropriate for this study," he replied. Although that moment must have been embarrassing for him, there are several other scholars I have discovered since then who are equally ill prepared to discuss Afrocentricity and Africalogical thought.

## THE APPROACH

Africans are notoriously religious, and each people has its own religious system with a set of beliefs and practices. Religion permeates all the departments of life so fully that it is not always easy or possible to isolate it. A study of these religious systems is, therefore, ultimately a study of the peoples themselves in all the complexities of both traditional and modern life (Mbiti, 1990, p. 1).

Paradoxically, Afrocentricity is both complicated and parsimonious, young and antiquated, culturally particular and yet useful for examining other cultures. Afrocentric methods intend to expand the repertoire of human perspectives on knowledge (Asante, 1990). They are not limited to the rhetorical texts of Africans or African Americans. The conceptual foundation of these methods includes a recognition of the connectedness of all things in the universe. Consistent with African philosophy, Afrocentric paradigms clearly envelop the notion that the universe is sacred in origin. Even the word has life within it. The spoken word is not seen as an utterance that is the consequence of skillful manipulation. It is seen as *nommo,* a life-giving mystical force or vivacity offered through verbal and vocal discourse (Asante, 1987). The *magara* principle is a companion concept to *nommo.* Jahnheinz Jahn (1961) defines *magara* as "the system in which one force can inwardly strengthen or weaken another and in which the individual growth can take place" (p. 111). Essentially, the effective presentation of the word is evidence of a spiritual substance enacted within a rhetorical event. African cultures place high value upon the establishment, maintenance, and continuity of relationships. As a result, the effectiveness of African-influenced orature is measured by the response from the audience, the articulate and dynamic presentation of the word, and the moral intent and character of the orator. As John Mbiti (1990) suggests, by studying the African-influenced word-text, one gains insight into the culture of the orator. This is true for Western orators as well. If one studies the manner in which the message-text within film, TV, sitcoms, music, and other mass media is produced, one will also be studying the people themselves. For example, the linear nature of most American films, progressing from the introduction of characters to the clear distinction between hero and villain, is indicative of Platonic dialogic thinking. It is also interesting to note that the American sense of maleness or masculinity is reinforced at the end of movies where the "good guy wins the girl" theme is reenacted. An Africalogical rhetorical paradigm becomes especially useful in adding clarity to the unorthodox film production technique of Spike Lee. In each of his films, Spike Lee never really tells his audience what to do, nor does he make it simple to identify the heroes and the villains.

It is precisely this interconnectedness, this observance of circularity, harmony, and dialectic that was taught to Plato by Socrates. As we know, Plato was inclined to use dialogues, for dialogues hinted at circularity. The basic argument has more than one side or one dimension, so by offering a juxtaposed set of contentions, one is systematically able to examine more than one side of an issue. The term *dialectic* does not, from an Afrocentric standpoint, suggest opposites. Africalogical scholars prefer synthesis over dichotomy. As a result, it is practically a reflex to challenge dichotomous thinking wherever it is discovered, simply because there is the possibility that other factors, alternatives, and rationales may be excluded. Essentially, it is characteristic of the Afrocentric epistemology to explore, uncover, and use codes, paradigms, symbols, motifs, and circles of discussion that reinforce the centrality of African ideals and values as a valid frame of reference for acquiring and examining data (Asante, 1990).

There is no doubt that Afrocentric inquiry diverges from mainstream methodological approaches. This divergence is what cosmologically distinguishes and heuristically privileges this paradigm. But both sets of theory, traditional and nontraditional, European and African influenced, do seek to define certain parameters within which scholars choose to investigate human behavior, whether communicative or otherwise. Certainly, the disciplinary and subdisciplinary perspectives of the modern theorists facilitate increasingly controversial discussions of Afrocentricity as method. By the nature of the terms being used, traditional and nontraditional, the latter must distinguish itself in some way from the former. The kaleidoscopic nature of metatheory is a bit misleading when discussing the nontraditional method of Afrocentricity. Whereas a metatheory is defined as a formulated paradigm that outlines how a given set of theories should be structured, much more is frequently expected of the Afrocentric metatheory. Afrocentricity is so broad a concept that it can be adopted as a theoretic label for intercultural, interpersonal, mass, intergroup, organization, or rhetorical communication theories. One must understand, however, that Afrocentricity is a metatheory that guides the discussion of Africalogical rhetorical theory building just as *The Rhetoric of Western Thought* (Golden, Berquist, & Coleman, 1997) guides the discussion of modern analogic paradigms (i.e., fantasy theme analysis, dramatism, narrative analysis). From the way *cultural criticism* is defined in contemporary rhetorical theory textbooks, Africalogical theory building can not neatly fit as a rubric. According to Rybacki and Rybacki (1991), "All other [traditional] approaches in this book differ from cultural approaches by their linkage to communication theory rather than to values or ideologies" (p. 134). Chapter 7 in their book, which is devoted to cultural approaches, suggests that much of cultural criticism is related to what might otherwise be labeled pop-cultural or feminist criticism as opposed to composite nativistic cultural criticism. In order to include Africalogical rhetorical theories under the heading of cultural approaches, scholars will need to reconsider the possibility that cultural rhetorical criticism does envelop communication theory. The introduction of feminist communication theories by Julia Wood (1996), Lana Rakow (1992), and Marsha Houston Stanback (1988) has already begun to challenge the notion that cultural approaches are devoid of communication theory.

## DOING AFRICALOGICAL CRITICISM

Rhetorical criticism is the business of identifying the complications of rhetoric and then explaining them in a comprehensive and efficient manner. Rhetorical critics must make arguments to perform these functions. "[For example,] feminists argue that articles in popular magazines demean women. While a few of us speak poetry day to day all of us, as Moliere reminded us, speak prose . . . rhetorical criticism is criticism of life itself, of our own participation in the experience of living" (Hart, 1997, pp. 23-26).

The beauty of the modern rhetorical methods is in their multiple and textured perspectives on the lived rhetorical text. Although several of the modern approaches are analogically defined, each still offers important commentary on the criticism of life itself. If Roderick Hart (1997) is correct in postulating that all rhetorical critics are arguers, then the next logical question refers to what the principal argument for the Afrocentric-Africalogical critic is. An Afrocentrist would respond with the claim that all rhetoric is meaning centered and that meaning is derived from culture. Furthermore, all rhetorical criticism is grounded in the individual critic's and rhetorician's cultural interpretations of the text's meaning. I use the words *individual* and *cultural interpretation* neither to exclude the notion of community nor to confuse the reader, but to accent the influence of the community in forming individualized perspectives on knowledge and experience. In short, the Afrocentric critic considers it erroneous for one to think that he or she has escaped culture in the process of analyzing the text, or as Hart (1997) says, in the criticism of life itself.

Before commenting on doing Africalogical rhetorical criticism, it is imperative that criticism be defined and understood. Roderick Hart's (1997) definition of rhetorical criticism, as mentioned before, is relatively consistent with definitions found within reputable rhetorical theory texts in the discipline. Rybacki and Rybacki (1991), for instance, suggest that rhetorical criticism is the analysis of the development and use of verbal and visual symbols that function to persuade an audience. Ultimately, the authors contend, rhetorical criticism is a quest for meaning within the rhetorical act. Criticism is theoretically driven yet encapsulated in pragmatic experiences. The norm for effective criticism has been to systematize the observation of ideas, circumstances, attitudes, histories, language, and meaning so that the text yields insight about the nature of human events. The critic maintains a certain reflexivity between theory (that is, a set of predictions about the substance of the text) and systematized observation, so that the rhetorical method becomes the instrument used to determine whether the text is consonant with a given set of theoretic predictions. For example, Kenneth Burke's pentadic method is named in *The Rhetoric of Western Thought* as a rhetoric-as-motive paradigm. That is, Burke's model assists the critic in analyzing the motive(s) of the orator. Golden et al. (1997) remind us that Burke's idea of motive is a reference not to causal tendencies, but rather to the completed action. Therefore, the analysis of the orator's motive is really the analysis of a completed rhetorical act. The prediction is that all human action is situated in symbols that reflect "guilt," "conflict," and "victimage." The method is useful in explaining and justifying completed actions that are considered applicable to these themes. Each method, no matter how it is presented, is an interpretation of the human condition. The Africalogical approach enlists the themes of community, liberation, and relational ethics in order to discuss the human condition. Relational ethics reinforces what is meant by community. Each cultural community creates and maintains its ethical standards, and the value placed upon the standards emphasizes relationships with others.

In analyzing the typical public-speaking situation, the critic (by using the Afrocentric method) is able to uncover the cultural worldviews of the orator and the audience, because all rhetoric is meaning centered, and meaning is derived from culture. A few of the terms that represent the paraphernalia of Africalogical rhetorical method when doing rhetorical criticism are as follows: (a) *nommo* and *magara,* (b) "The Manifestations of *Nommo*" (a phrase coined by Jeffrey Woodyard), (c) the seven senses, and (d) the logoforms. Each of these four terms can be used separately as critical devices, and they are all based on three methodological premises. First, all rhetoric is culturally self-reflexive, because rhetoric is meaning centered, and meaning is derived from culture. Second, audiences are the barometers of effective oratory. Third, rhetorical criticism is at its optimum when it considers all of the following: pretext, text, and context. Fourth, in analyzing the "word" or the text, logoforms (that is, signification, indirection, metonymy, substitution, codifying, etc.) are the guiding discursive elements to be used. Finally, all rhetoric is relational, and therefore the work, speaker, and audience are interconnected.

There are a few investigative questions that should be asked by the critic (this list is not conclusive): Because the speaker is never said to use the work, to what extent does the presentation of the work engage audience? For whom is the message intended? What are the circumstances that led to the production of the text? How does the audience engage the speaker? How does one or more of the manifestations of *nommo* affect the vivacity of the word? Where is the principle of community found in the rhetorical act? Does the speaker use the *magara* principle in influencing the audience? How and by whom is *nommo* produced within the rhetorical act? And finally, what does the text inform about liberation?

When doing Africalogical rhetorical criticism, the critic must be familiar with the paraphernalia, methodological premises, and investigative questions. Each of these aids in using the paradigm for rhetorical criticism. Beyond applying the method, however, there is an even greater challenge.

## THE CHALLENGE

The challenge is to attempt to think in a non-Western manner, to avoid categorizing, splicing, reducing, and universalizing human phenomena. Naturally, this is antithetical to covering law models such as Berger and Calabrese's (1975) uncertainty reduction theory and Sherif and Hovland's (1961) social judgment theory, which claim that all humans impulsively categorize environmental stimuli. One point of reference that elucidates the challenge is the scholarly definition of communication. Most professors walk into their classrooms and teach their students that all communication is either verbal or nonverbal, vocal or nonvocal. These instructors are willing to admit that there are combinations of these terms that can exist simultaneously, but essentially they have reduced all human interaction to dichotomous pairs. I propose that communication has an aggregate continuum from pretalk to nontalk. There are at least five points on the continuum—preverbal, verbal, epiverbal, subverbal, and nonverbal. The preverbal has much to do with both sociocultural history and body politics. For example, my skin color conjures certain feelings, apprehensions, and insecurities for some persons. Race as biologistic construct is social and physiognomic, because it carries with it a memory of a set of experiences or episodes. Before I begin to converse, these preverbal elements intercede because of my undivorceable personal history.

Then, there is verbal communication (exchange of words), during which epiverbality takes place. Epiverbal communication is that which exists—"on top of the communication"—the context or what we might call the "rhetorical situation." Subverbal communication is the underlying meaning of the message as communicated at any of the points on the continuum. One form of this is signification, and metonymy would be another. All of these points can occur simultaneously, except the preverbal.

Nonverbal communication has already been defined and extensively studied. Terms like *objectics, paralanguage, chronemics, kinesics,* and *proxemics* are concepts produced to facilitate the discussion of these communicative dimensions. Perhaps it could be argued that postverbal communication also exists and relates to subsequent relationship renewal, repair, and initiation. This continuum is yet another dynamic to the holistic nature of Africalogical rhetorical theory and is considered to be part of the previously mentioned logoforms. It is evident that preverbality and epiverbality can be studied independently to determine how the pretext or context affects production and dissemination of the text. These pairs, among the others, can provide insight about the word meaning, orator, and the audience.

James Baldwin asserts that the Black intellectual is a "bastard of the West" (quoted in West, 1993, p. 85)—an illegitimate offspring developed and sustained by standards that are foreign but that are nevertheless treated as familiar. The objective of Africalogical thought is to reintroduce the composite African cultural personality to mainstream scholarly discourse. Martin Bernal (1996) explains his version of the Afrocentric scholarly continuum:

> The label of "Afrocentrist" has been attached to a number of intellectual positions ranging from 'all good things come from Africa' . . . to my own shared position that maintains that Africans or peoples of African descent have made many significant contributions to world progress and that, for the past two centuries, these have been systematically played down by European and North American historians. (p. 86)

Clearly, since its rise in the 1960s, Africalogical research has been met with intense resistance by the most unlikely critics—white women, Black women, and Black men. Some of the individuals who have led the national conversation in opposition to Afrocentricity are Mary Lefkowitz (1996), Cornel West (1993), and Stanley Crouch (1995/1996). Among the popular proponents defending Afrocentricity are Molefi Asante (1987, 1988, 1990, 1993, 1996), Martin Bernal (1996), G. G. M. James (1992), Marimba Ani (1994), Wade Nobles (1991), E. A. Wallis Budge (1994), Na'im Akbar (1991), and the entire Temple School of Africalogists. The arguments have become so inflammatory that Lefkowitz refused to include Bernal's response to her latest polemic in her forthcoming book *Black Athena Revisited.* Nonetheless, the debate on Afrocentricity between Bernal and Lefkowitz was moved to the Internet in May of 1997, sponsored by Lefkowitz's publisher, HarperCollins.

## DIRECTIONS FOR RHETORICAL THEORY BUILDING

Rhetorical theorists are an interesting brand of communication scholars. We don't want to use the argot of the staunch and rigid quantitative statisticians and researchers. Yet we are not so quick to embrace the interpretivists either. The jargon of rhetorical communication is specific to rhetorical theorists and critics, yet what we study is ever growing. It seems that it is fitting that our methods also be ever growing to accommodate the perspectives that modern approaches are not adequately equipped to discuss. Perhaps there should be a metaphysical rhetoric that assists the critic in properly analyzing religio-spiritual texts. I am particularly leery of any paradigm approach that claims to have all the answers to human behavior, for if you claim to know everything, then it is probably more accurate to say that you know nothing. In 1998, I attended a family reunion and heard a relative confess that when she was younger, she thought she knew it all, but as she has grown older and more mature, it has become crystal clear to her that she knows nothing at all. For rhetorical theorists who have studied classical Greek rhetoric, this anecdote draws an obvious parallel to Socrates's defense in the trial at Athens. It was there that he stated as a line of defense that he should be exonerated because of his superior ethical, intellectual, and experiential position of acknowledging his ignorance, something his opposition was not so willing to do.

As rhetorical scholars, we must be willing to invite new perspectives, to experiment with nontraditional ideological paradigms in order to progress. Humanistic inquiry is guided by the need to understand the human condition. Rhetorical scholars are invested in analyzing rhetorical acts to gather information about human behavior, events, and phenomena. Every direction in which rhetorical theory is driven must move us (as humans) forward. Kenneth Burke, in devising his concept of identification, explained:

> Identification is compensatory to division. If men were not apart from one another, there would be no need for the rhetorician to proclaim their unity. If men were wholly and true of one substance, absolute communication would be of man's very essence. (Burke, 1950, p. 22)

Humans are cultural beings with values, morals, beliefs, standards, ideologies, practices, and norms. Consequently, if we are ever to understand human behavior, we must focus on culture. Our students, who are culturally diverse, appreciate the recognition by their instructors that culture is central to their everyday lives. The test of whether it is worthwhile to use the proposed Africalogical or Afrocentric method is whether it allows us to acquire further knowledge about the discursive manifestations of human behavior while accenting culture. We must ask if methods of this sort are useful in critically assessing rhetorical acts and meaning that is culturally grounded. As with any theory, to determine its heuristic value, it must be tested to determine if it can actually do what it purports to do. One Africalogical method has been proposed, and the challenge to rhetorical scholars has been issued. It is time to test and continue the development of Africalogical communication methods to be employed within and beyond rhetorical studies.

**REFERENCES**

Akbar, N. (1991). *Chains and images of psychological slavery.* Jersey City, NJ: New Mind Productions.

Ani, M. (1994). *Yurugu.* Trenton, NJ: Africa World Press.

Asante, M. K. (1987). *The Afrocentric idea.* Philadelphia: Temple University Press.

Asante, M. K. (1988). *Afrocentricity.* Trenton, NJ: Africa World Press.

Asante, M. K. (1990). *Kemet, Afrocentricity, and knowledge.* Trenton, NJ: Africa World Press.

Asante, M. K. (1993). *Malcolm X as cultural hero & other Afrocentric essays.* Trenton, NJ: Africa World Press.

Asante, M. K. (1996). The principal issues in Afrocentric inquiry. In M. K. Asante & A. Abarry (Eds.), *African intellectual heritage* (pp.256-261). Philadelphia: Temple University Press.

Berger, C. R., & Calabrese, R. (1975). Some explorations in initial interactions and beyond: Toward a developmental theory of interpersonal communication. *Human Communication Research, 1,* 99-112.

Bernal, M. (1996, Spring). The Afrocentric interpretation of history: Bernal replies to Lefkowitz. *Journal of Blacks in Higher Education,* 86-94.

Budge, E. A. W. (1994). *The Egyptian book of the dead.* Brooklyn, NY: A & B Books.

Burke, K. (1950). *Rhetoric of motives.* New York: Prentice Hall.

Crouch, S. (1995/1996, Winter). The Afrocentric hustle. *Journal of Blacks in Higher Education,* 77-82.

Golden, J., Berquist, G., & Coleman, W. (1997). *The rhetoric of Western thought.* Dubuque, IA: Kendall/Hunt.

Hart, R. (1997). Modern rhetorical criticism (2nd ed.). Boston: Allyn & Bacon.

Houston Stanback, M. (1988). What makes scholarship about Black women and communication feminists communication scholarship? *Women's Studies in Communication, 11,* 28-31.

Jackson, R. L., II. (1995). Toward an Afrocentric methodology for the critical assessment of rhetoric. In L. A. Niles (Ed.), *African American rhetoric: A reader* (pp. 148-157). Dubuque, IA: Kendall/Hunt.

Jahn, J. (1961). *Muntu.* New York: Grove Press.

James, G. G. M. (1992). *Stolen legacy.* Trenton, NJ: Africa World Press.

Lefkowitz, M. (1996). *Not out of Africa: How Afrocentrism became an excuse to teach myth as history.* New York: Basic Books.

Mbiti, J. S. (1990). *African religions and philosophies* (2nd ed.). Portsmouth, NH: Heinemann.

Nobles, W. (1991). African philosophy: Foundations of Black psychology. In R. L. Jones (Ed.), *Black psychology* (pp. 47-64). Berkeley, CA: Cobb and Henry.

Rakow, L. (1992). *Women making meaning: New feminist directions in communication.* New York: Routledge.

Rybacki, K., & Rybacki, D. (1991). *Communication criticism: Approaches and genres.* Belmont, CA: Wadsworth.

Sherif, M., & Hovland, C. (1961). *Social judgement: Assimilation and contrast effects in communication and attitude change.* Westport, CT: Greenwood.

West, C. (1993). *Keeping faith.* New York: Routledge.

Wood, J. (Ed.). (1996). *Gendered relationships.* Mountain View, CA: Mayfield.

Woodyard, J. L. (1995). Locating Asante: Making use of the Afrocentric idea. In D. Ziegler (Ed.), *Molefe Kete Asante and Afrocentricity: In praise and criticism* (pp. 27-43). James C. Winston: Nashville, TN.

# 5

## Opening the Future

### Postmodern Rhetoric in a Multicultural World

RAYMIE E. McKERROW • *Ohio University*

My purpose in this chapter is to comment on three themes: first, rhetoric's orientation to the critical analysis of discourse in a multicultural world; second, the significance of a postmodern perspective on that rhetoric; and finally, what *opening the future* means in terms of training future critics. As an initial caveat, whatever our focus of study, we need to approach the future with far less arrogance than has been our past practice. As critics fully subjected to and qualified within a Western culture, we need to remind ourselves constantly that ours is not the only way, much less the best way, in which critical conclusions might be drawn.

To that end, I have argued for a re-visioning of rhetorical theory—a retheorizing that moves us beyond the strictures of what is otherwise a hegemonic view of rhetoric's nature and practice. We need to conceptualize a rhetoric that does not privilege, at the outset, any one singular means of achieving goals (McKerrow, 1995). Until and unless we are successful in reworking our theoretical assumptions, we will forever be mired in a narrow, provincial perspective that automatically consigns some rhetoric to the world of the irrational, regardless of how its practitioners perceive its utility. The task before us is not simply to include more new subjects into our present way of thinking, but to change our way of thinking. As a specific illustration, the challenge is not simply to write the missing into our history, for to do so is merely to provide them a place in our already constructed present (Ballif, 1992). Rather, the challenge is to write history into the lived experience of those who are currently missing. To be more precise, the task is to write rhetoric out of the lived experience of women and people of color, and thereby produce their history, rather than to merely write their efforts into the history of rhetoric as already constructed. Only through such a reconceptualization shall we find freedom from the privilege that currently dominates the rhetorical landscape. The sense of rhetoric that we bring to the table is constrained if we start from preconceived notions of what it must be—we need to recognize that rhetoric is ever an open-textured term and is therefore constantly open to change.

Merely re-visioning rhetoric is not enough, in terms of orienting ourselves to the practice of criticism in a multicultural world. Andreas Huyssen (1990) provides a rationale for considering the significance of the postmodern, in terms of its critical reception in our present world:

> Time and again postmodernism has been denounced and ridiculed in recent debates, both by neoconservatives and the cultural Left in the United States. If such ridicule were all that could be said about postmodernism . . . then it would not be worth the trouble of taking up the subject at all. I might just as well stop right here and join the formidable chorus of those who lament the loss of quality and proclaim the decline of the arts since the 1960s. My argument however will be a different one. (p. 234)

For those firmly ensconced in a modern world, the postmodern impulse seems the epitome of an excessive tolerance of the irrelevant. When people view the postmodern as a pastiche of the irresponsible, the indeterminable, and the undecidable, they view it as the worst that is in us and forgo the chance at rehabilitation: There can be no reconciliation with such an incommensurable world. For such critics, the task is not to reconstitute rhetoric in terms that acknowledge its indeterminacy, for that is to reject their own worldview. As they perceive the postmodern critic, they are prone to ask, "What can you tell us we don't already know?" Their question reveals what is otherwise concealed: a hegemonic posture expressing condescension toward lesser humans. To attempt to respond from a postmodern orientation to such a question is to fall prey to the trap that has been set; there is no answer that will satisfy the critic's presumptive question. All that an "answer" achieves, from the perspective of the questioner, is the confirmation that no answer could satisfy and hence that there is no value in the enterprise being interrogated. Were the world as black and white, as simply constructed, as those asking of the postmodern "What is your value?" believe it to be, we might well despair of ever crossing the incommensurable worlds and conversing about matters—in this case the reconstitution of rhetoric. Lyotard (1984) would say that we have an invitation to silence.

There is a position that denies the incommensurability thesis, provided both sides are willing to inhabit its space. First, one must recognize that postmodernism is neither wholly continuous with modernity, as though the shift were gradual, nor wholly discontinuous, as in the sense of rupture. Rather, the relation is more properly constituted as a *both/and:* In some senses the shift is transformational, and in others it is clearly disjunctive. Hence, one creates a space for the relation, in Bernstein's (1992) terms, as a "constellation" or juxtaposition. In this context, the expression *modernity/postmodernity* may be positive ground from which to explore the nuances that are presently inscribed as differences. In reconstituting rhetoric as postmodern, the point is that there is value in both enterprises, just as there is danger in the excessive reliance on either to the exclusion of the other. Modernity needs the postmodern to keep it off balance; postmodernism needs modernity to recenter itself from time to time.

In the case of rhetoric, taken to an extreme in a "modern" world, where universal rules are at the apex of decision making, there would be no need for deliberation—one would simply apply the universal rule. At the furthest extreme of the postmodern, there would likewise be no need for rhetoric, as the fragmentation would be so total as to deny the possibility of communication between and among the fragments. Rhetoric requires relationality—it must have the ability to "construct" a reality from diverse fragments in order to provide a commensurable world in which communication can occur.

Given this orientation toward the postmodern, how is rhetoric changed as the equation shifts to a constellation of forces? Wenzel (1993) argued that, in a postmodern context, argument would still be argument, that is, it would still play by the same rules. But would it? Or, even if it still does, because of the inertia underlying shifts in discourse conventions, must it? Should it? These are the critical questions that must be dealt with in the broader context of a re-visioned rhetoric. To simply affirm that the future will resemble the past, especially with respect to the conventions constraining discourse options, is to obviate the need to contemplate a future.

Closer to the mark, consider rhetoric's potential—conceived in a modernist universe, dominated by a specific form of rationality, oriented toward systematic appraisal leading to predictive power, and culminating in the perfectibility of whatever its object might be—for addressing those cultures that share not at all in these visions. The task of reconstitution is not demanded because the postmodern has arrived on the scene—it only serves as one, albeit potent, manifestation of the need to reconsider how discourse operates and what conventional practices must be altered or expanded to allow for the discourse of the Other to be heard—and not only heard, but heeded.

Science fiction novelist Anne McCaffrey (1978) has solved the problem of travel by reference to an "in-between"—an absence of space wherein time and distance disappear. What I am suggesting is, in metaphorical terms, a similar nonspace space—an in-between wherein one might interrogate both modernism and postmodernism, wherein one might be neither wholly in one nor wholly in the other, and wherein time and distance are not factors limiting one's ability to land where one wishes. Although such a fictional space may not be essential to the task of reconstruction, it is nevertheless precisely where the action must take place if the task is to be accomplished. To operate within either domain to the total exclusion of the other is to privilege the characteristics of rhetoric that work in that domain alone, and thereby to limit the opportunity to transport other ideas across time and space. It is, I believe, a given that reconstitution of rhetoric for a postmodern, multicultural world is essential. That one cannot privilege any facet of either modernity or postmodernity also is a given.

What emerges from the struggle will determine the power of a people to change their own lives. As Chantal Mouffe (1993) has argued, politics is not simply about reaching consensus. It is, rather, about the possibility of maintaining dissensus within the framework of an established agreement on how to conduct affairs. In that framework, the goal is to accommodate the Other in the space between our worlds.

If we are to open the future with an orientation other than that which dominates the present, what will that critical analysis entail? The litany of possible visions is not likely to be objectionable. Nevertheless, the challenge is to ensure that our students see themselves in our teaching: If we are teaching rhetoric's history from present resources, such as Conley (1990), Golden, Berquist, and Coleman (1989), or Foss, Foss, and Trapp (1991), we should note that women and people of color are notably absent, or if present only minimally so. African Americans in a graduate rhetorical history course can say, with conviction, that they are absent and hence rendered invisible—that apparently the history that would render them visible is not accounted as critical or important. The same could be said for Native Americans or Asian Americans, and the list goes on. Although our graduate education has begun to respond more directly to these issues, as in the case of Bizzell and Herzberg's (1990) text, think how little we have to say to our undergraduates about the richly textured multicultural history that should be our past. Revisioning rhetoric is not in itself the end goal; it is rather a means to get us thinking about what is not present in our teaching, and what must yet be accomplished if we are to bring new students of rhetoric into the fold.

With respect to those same students, accommodation has a price. The politics of preservation within the academy being what they are, the mantra that "the last great teacher was Jesus, hence you better write if you are to survive" remains firmly entrenched. This shifts the focus from reconstituting rhetoric to the potential for also reconstituting how those who function as critics within the academy are to survive. The power of disciplining, in Foucault's sense, has been eloquently noted. The chilling effect that our conventional processes may have on who is allowed to speak need not be recounted here (Bach, Blair, Nothstine, & Pym, 1996; Blair, Brown, & Baxter, 1994). In countering these forces, it is important to ask, "Where is there room for scholarship that is at the margins?" What happens when that scholarship is routinely pummeled, reshaped into appropriate or "proper" venues of analysis, such that it ceases to exist as "marginal" except when rejected? What happens when one at the margins publishes outside the field, only to learn that influence is based on what one does for the field from the inside? These are the critical issues that, along with reconstituting rhetoric, we need to address if critics are to engage multicultural issues in ways that will be received by the academy.

Reconstitution, with this in mind, thus has two vectors: One is to reconstitute it in terms that acknowledge the culturally diverse world in which we live, and the other is to reconstitute it such that divergent voices become valued. That there already are voices calling for opening up the discipline—changing the boundaries of what constitutes acceptable research and writing—offers hope to those who represent divergent voices within the discipline. Many of those voices represent the already tenured and thereby provide a lifeline to the future. I remain optimistic that reconstitution in the senses articulated above will move forward; the future is too important to leave in the hands of inaction and silence.

## REFERENCES

Bach, T. E., Blair, C., Nothstine, W. L., & Pym, A. (1996). How to read "how to get published." *Communication Quarterly, 44,* 399-422.

Ballif, M. (1992). Re/dressing histories; Or, on re/covering figures who have been laid bare by our gaze. *Rhetoric Society Quarterly, 22,* 91-98.

Bernstein, R. J. (1992). *The new constellation: The ethical-political horizons of modernity/postmodernity.* Cambridge: MIT Press.

Bizzell, P., & Herzberg, B. (1990). *The rhetorical tradition: Readings from classical times to the present.* Boston: Bedford Books.

Blair, C., Brown, J. R., & Baxter, L. A. (1994). Disciplining the feminine. *Quarterly Journal of Speech, 80,* 383-409.

Conley, T. M. (1990). *Rhetoric in the European tradition.* Chicago: University of Chicago Press.

Foss, S. K., Foss, K. A., & Trapp, R. (1991). *Contemporary perspectives on rhetoric* (2nd ed.). Prospect Heights, IL: Waveland Press.

Golden, J. L., Berquist, G. F., & Coleman, W. E. (Eds.). (1989). *The rhetoric of western thought* (4th ed.). Dubuque, IA: Kendall/Hunt.

Huyssen, A. (1990). Mapping the postmodern. In L. J. Nicholson (Ed.), *Feminism/postmodernism* (pp. 234-237). London: Routledge.

Lyotard, J. F. (1984). *The postmodern condition: A report on knowledge* (G. Bennington & B. Massumi, Trans.). Minneapolis: University of Minnesota Press.

McCaffrey, A. (1978). *Dragonflight.* New York: Ballantine.

McKerrow, R. E. (1995). Re-visioning rhetoric in a culturally diverse world. In J. Hauser (Ed.), *New dimensions in communication: Proceedings of the 52nd Annual Conference: Vol. 7* (pp. 1-10). Syracuse: New York State Speech Communication Conference.

Mouffe, C. (1993). *The return of the political.* London: Verso.

Wenzel, J. W. (1993). Cultivating practical reason: Argumentation theory in postmodernity. In R. E. McKerrow (Ed.), *Argument and the postmodern challenge: Proceedings of the eighth SCA/AFA conference on argumentation* (pp. 1-7). Annandale, VA: Speech Communication Association.

# 6

## Asking New Questions of Old Texts

### *Presidential Rhetoric and the Demands of Multiculturalism*

VANESSA BOWLES BEASLEY • *Texas A&M University*

Contemporary politics all boils down to the "need, sometimes the demand, for recognition," according to political theorist Charles Taylor (1994, p. 25). Battles waged in all sorts of public and private institutions in the United States over the past few decades seem to support this observation. Corporations and governmental agencies continue to wrangle over hiring practices, religious groups splinter over gender and sexual politics, and colleges and universities struggle over whom and what they should teach. Indeed, as Amy Gutmann (1994) has noted, today it would be difficult to find any democratic organization "that is not the site of some significant controversy over whether and how [it] . . . should better recognize the identities of cultural and disadvantaged minorities" (p. 3).

The field of speech communication is no exception. Although it hardly seems an issue in a volume such as this one, the question of whether there should be recognition of people and practices previously ignored in communication research remains controversial in some halls. Yet even when people agree on this matter, questions of how this recognition might occur prove to be much more nettlesome. How should communication scholars investigate cultural differences? How might we conceptualize identity in order to acknowledge different "types" of it without falling back into the ontological traps of days past? And even if we could achieve some conceptual clarity on such matters, how should we talk and write about them?

Queries like these are often answered with the same pluralistic optimism with which they are asked: Communication scholars should welcome a wide variety of diverse approaches. They should study people and processes that they have never studied before, and, perhaps more important, they should search for new methodologies and theories that help explain a more complete range of communication behaviors and philosophies than we have previously known.[1] Such prescriptions are based on political realism (for example, an awareness of the material consequences of what happens when different types of people are not recognized) as well as the more time-honored academic mission of expanding knowledge. To be sure, both of these impulses are important. Yet the assumption that only completely new methodologies are appropriate for this research may have an unfortunate side effect. In short, this inclination may encourage communication scholars to ignore our own well-worn paths, and to do so at our own peril.

Specifically, we may assume that communication phenomena that we know well—dyadic exchanges between Midwestern college-aged subjects, for example, or newcomer strategies within organizations—have little relevance to more timely matters of multiculturalism and intercultural communication. Some of us may feel that communication scholars have simply exhausted these topics, that there is nothing new to be found in such old data, or that too many journal pages have already been dedicated to these old chestnuts to revisit them for any purpose. I disagree, however, and suggest that we can learn a great deal about cultural diversity and its political implications by asking new questions of our "old" subjects. What role did cultural differences play in the interaction between those Midwestern sophomores, for example? And how does ethnicity or gender, say, impact organizational entry? Leaving these studies to colleagues in interpersonal and organizational communication, in this chapter, I suggest that public-address scholarship is also well suited for such investigations.

By asking new questions of old texts, the rhetorical critic can produce insights into the communicative processes and practices that have historically withheld political recognition from certain groups of people in the United States. Likewise, rhetorical criticism can provide excellent analytical tools for investigating how democratic leaders have responded to such demands in the past, and, perhaps more importantly, why these calls have still not been sufficiently answered. Given the interrelationship between democratic politics and public speech, such questions seem imperative in an increasingly diverse society.

## DEMOCRACY, DIVERSITY, AND PUBLIC ADDRESS IN THE UNITED STATES

Speech making, almost all public-speaking manuals agree, is vital to democracy. In our classrooms and textbooks, most communication educators trace the political significance of oratory back to ancient Greece and argue that the birth of popular sovereignty necessitated the need for public address. Although this historical nod is certainly warranted, it typically ignores some basic facts: that the audiences for these early classical orations were remarkably homogeneous and small and that the speakers themselves were almost certainly demographic ringers for their listeners (see Dahl, 1989). Robert Dahl reports that the ancient democratic city-states were of "modest size" so that citizens could all know one another and could "meet together in the assembly and thus act as rulers of the city" (p. 16). Political speech making, along with the representative government it facilitated, was therefore easier in ancient Greece than it is in the United States today. Pericles could speak with far more certainty on his audience's common experiences and assumptions—and with far less risk of a "politically incorrect" slip of the tongue—than can Bill Clinton thousands of years later.

Indeed, in the time that has passed between the time of Pericles's predecessors and Clinton's day, we have learned that large-scale democracy is difficult. It is difficult to learn and practice, as eastern Europeans have discovered, and it is even difficult to remember, a fact evidenced by the dismal voting behaviors of the American people. Whatever other reasons there may be for this difficulty, modern-day democracy is hard because it requires emotional fortitude of the most strenuous kind. It demands faith and patience— faith that the common good will be served and patience that one's own needs will be considered at some point as part of that process.

These feelings are especially hard to sustain in a demographically diverse society in which membership is not based exclusively on hereditary ties such as ethnicity. In the United States, for example, where almost all citizens come from very different backgrounds and heritages, people may have to be persuaded that they are connected at all, with such appeals being based in "idioms of social identity," in Edwin Black's (1992, p. 18) words, reflecting symbolic, situated constructions of shared self-definition of the social unit's "composite character" (Black, p. 22). Whatever its additional constitutive parts, then, social identity in the United States can be viewed as a rhetorical construct. Interlocutors must constantly articulate their common bonds— that is, "who we are"—as well as their disassociations—that is, "who we are not." If public discourse was vital to the small, homogeneous, democratic political systems of ancient Greece, just imagine how important it is within a large, heterogeneous society, in which even the most basic assumptions about identity must constantly be articulated, argued for, and negotiated over time.

These articulations, arguments, and negotiations are themselves complex, especially within political discourse aimed at a national audience. U.S. politicians must proceed carefully on such matters. They must be neither too broad, lest their comments appear overgeneralized and platitudinous (e.g., "What makes us all Americans is our love for the flag"), nor too specific, lest their appeals seem too narrowly cast toward one particular demographic group (e.g., "What makes us all Americans is the color of our skin"). Both of the previous examples represent ridiculous extremes, of course—very few speakers would risk sounding so boorish or bigoted. Yet the challenge of finding a middle way—a rhetoric that speaks specifically enough to recognize differences among citizens while also speaking broadly enough to keep alive some sense of a common good—is tremendous. Rhetors who would meet it must find a way of affirming a social identity that is at once multicultural and monocultural, two perspectives that may seem mutually exclusive.

## MULTICULTURALISM AND MONOCULTURALISM: PRESIDENTIAL RHETORIC AS A CASE STUDY

However difficult it may seem, this balance between multiculturalism and monoculturalism has become increasingly necessary within American politics. The legacies of immigration, women's suffrage, and the civil rights movements have caused the emergence of different groups of citizens than existed during the country's founding, with the relative strengths of these coalitions varying across time. In order to be elected, national leaders have had to convince these groups that they have had the groups' particular interests in mind, even if groups' needs have at times conflicted with those of other groups. But leaders have also had to affirm the notion of a common good, a national agenda more abstract and arguably more important than the needs of individual citizens and their cohorts. Such rhetors have thus had to acknowledge difference (multiculturalism) while also affirming some level of similarity (monoculturalism). We can learn more about the nature and limitations of both of these demands, as well as the political compromise leaders have historically found between them, by looking at presidential rhetoric in new ways.

First, we can learn more about the political and symbolic realities of the American people's differences as they have been imprinted onto this discourse. The demands of a diverse democracy have meant that presidential rhetoric has often been intercultural communication. Some individual politicians have clearly put more effort into appealing to minority groups than others have, to be sure, but in general, as their constituents have become more diverse and more vocal about their differences, these rhetors have increasingly had to step outside of their own cultural heritages and assumptions to express an interest in those of others. Increasingly, a president's speaking schedule may thus reflect the sociology of the day, with audiences as varied as National Association for the Advancement of Colored People members, Knights of Columbus, soccer moms, and so on. Ironically, then, instead of being merely the province of the mostly dead, all-white males who have occupied the White House, presidential rhetoric can be viewed as evidence of the ongoing politics of diversity in the United States. What have presidents or candidates said to such groups? Which groups have they most commonly addressed, and which have they ignored? When they have addressed such groups, how have they discussed each audience's perceived uniqueness? How have they designed their messages to accommodate an audience's felt needs?

Second, we can learn more about the seemingly monolithic models of American culture and identity that national leaders have also worked hard to endorse. If presidents attend too much to their constituents' differences, they might dismantle the perceived unity of U.S. citizens; in the worst case, they would keep themselves from having an "American people" to lead at all. In order to avoid these pitfalls, presidents must affirm a conservative definition of American identity that is broad enough to include all comers. In recent research, I have found that presidents from Cleveland to Bush have defined American identity by bypassing discussions of background or biology and focusing instead on quintessential American beliefs (Beasley, 1996). However, although such a definition of citizenship may appear to be inclusive, it may also encourage exclusion, especially if certain groups of citizens are perceived as inherently less loyal to these ideals. Are there other representations of a monocultural American identity in presidential speech? If so, what do these models look like? What rhetorical strategies or practices do presidents use to endorse such monolithic ideals in spite of the very real differences among their constituents? Do these practices enhance or hinder citizens' demands for recognition? How?

Last, we can also learn more about the significance of the choices presidents have made as they have tried to incorporate both multicultural and monocultural themes into their discourse. Like all democratic politicians, chief executives must navigate the waters between the Scylla of naked pragmatism, motivating them to embrace cultural differences if only to get votes, and the Charybdis of ideological idealism, leading them to insist that ethnic and racial differences do not matter in the United States. These constraints pit American reality against its mythology, and by viewing presidents' talk as the result of a forced choice between the two, we can learn much about the relative significance of these impulses to any leader and at any point in time. Perhaps more important, because presidential rhetoric presumably tells its audience what the audience wants to hear, we can also gain a sense of when and how often the American people have themselves demanded to be recognized, reassured, or both. By answering these questions and charting such trends across time, rhetorical critics could develop a road map of the symbolic impact of diversity among the American people as well as on their leaders' talk.

Viewing presidential rhetoric in these ways is not necessarily the typical modus operandi within public-address studies. Indeed, in order to take this view, one has to problematize some of the basic assumptions that characterize more traditional approaches to studying presidential discourse. One can hold presidents accountable for their words, for example, but also realize that the nature of a diverse democracy may also mean that chief executives speak under a much more complicated set of constraints than we have previously considered. Because these constraints presumably bind would-be activists as well as their elected leaders, we would profit by learning more about them. Similarly, one may have to look more closely at these old texts to understand what is not being said in addition to what is and to see if and how these absences still haunt American discourse on these topics. What Andrew Johnson did not say during Reconstruction, for instance, might have something to do with the nature of race relations in the United States today.

These are important questions, especially because the demand for recognition shows no signs of abating within contemporary politics. These are also questions that rhetorical critics are uniquely poised to answer, using traditional approaches and methodologies as starting points for asking new questions and uncovering new answers. Diversity and its problems are not new to the United States, nor are they new to presidential rhetoric. When presidents call for national conversations about race relations, as Bill Clinton did in 1997, students of American public address can inform such efforts by showing where such talk has gotten presidents and their constituents in the past. To ignore such studies is to risk remaking old mistakes and to potentially overlook the opportunity to discover potential alternatives for the future.

## NOTE

1. For elaboration of these sentiments, see the proceedings from the National Communication Association's 1997 Summer Conference (Moreale & Jones, 1997).

## REFERENCES

Beasley, V. B. (1996). *You, the people: Diversity and citizenship in presidential rhetoric.* Unpublished doctoral dissertation, University of Texas, Austin.

Black, E. (1992). *Rhetorical questions.* Chicago: University of Chicago Press.

Dahl, R. A. (1989). *Democracy and its critics.* New Haven, CT: Yale University Press.

Gutmann, A. (1994). *Multiculturalism.* Princeton, NJ: Princeton University Press.

Moreale, S. P., & Jones, A. A. (Eds.). (1997). *Racial and ethnic diversity in the 21st century: A communication perspective.* Annandale, VA: National Communication Association.

Taylor, C. (1994). The politics of recognition. In A. Gutmann (Ed.), *Multiculturalism* (pp. 25-73). Princeton, NJ: Princeton University Press.

# 7

## Some Elementary Methodological Reflections on the Study of the Chinese Rhetorical Tradition

MARY M. GARRETT • *Wayne State University*

### INTRODUCTION

The Chinese population is now estimated to be about 1.2 billion people. China has been a prominent cultural influence in East Asia for centuries, and it continues to be a leading political player on the world stage. All this creates a prima facie case for the importance of studying this culture, both its past and its present. But as the classicist Arnaldo Momigliano (1975) remarked:

> Hellenism still affects our attitude toward ancient civilizations. . . . The average knowledge of an educated modern man about India is not superior to that which is to be found in Greek and Roman writers. Even now there is no obligation in our traditional curriculum to know anything about China because the Greeks and the Romans knew nothing or almost nothing about it. (pp. 11-12)

This same melancholy observation extends to the rhetorical tradition of the culture; little is known about Chinese rhetoric, and of that, a surprising amount is false or misleading.

How has this state of affairs come about, and what can be done about it? In this chapter I will maintain that the study of Chinese rhetoric is peculiarly vexed methodologically, standing as it does at the intersection of a number of methodological issues, some of them common to cross-cultural studies, some of them peculiar to or exacerbated by a focus on rhetoric, and others endemic to studies of China. Although this methodological situation is vexed, it is not doomed. After outlining some of the pitfalls, I will suggest ways to circumvent them—or at least, to not fall in quite so deeply. Although I concentrate on China, many of these issues recur in other cross-cultural rhetorical contexts, so that this analysis may well be applicable in other cases as well, mutatis mutandis.

## "RHETORIC IS, AFTER ALL, A GREEK WORD"

This pronouncement came from an indignant reviewer responding to the suggestion that Greek definitions of rhetoric might be limited by cultural bias. It points to a central methodological paradox underlying cross-cultural studies. Reflective and responsible researchers have an immediate aversion to simply projecting one set of categories (theirs) onto another culture's practices, categories, explanations, and theories and then resting content with their results. But those interested in another culture must start somewhere, with some questions and basic organizing principles, at least as an interim way of securing a foothold of understanding in unfamiliar terrain.

Thus, for instance, in a 1988 National Endowment for the Humanities seminar on Asian rhetorics, participants delivered papers on *logos, pathos,* and *ethos* in Chinese rhetoric. There is nothing inherently wrong with such a step, if it is used provisionally, with awareness of the dangers of forcing a fit, of overlooking significant aspects of the material, of misinterpretation, and so on. Such a heuristic application of a foreign framework may allow the researcher to notice aspects of a phenomenon that she would not see otherwise, and she may even conclude that in some instances the foreign term or category is more illuminating than misleading. The point is simply that the usefulness, appropriateness, and fit of these terms should always be in question and should never be assumed, and that their application must always bear a burden of proof when applied outside their original cultural contexts.

The cross-cultural application of the term *rhetoric* presents special challenges, for several reasons. First, rhetoric is something of an "essentially contested term." Its definitions within the Western rhetorical tradition vary according to the historical period, the social and technological context, and the rhetorician's own intellectual and ethical commitments. Depending on which conception of rhetoric is taken as the defining lens, rhetoric in the other culture will be pictured differently.

For instance, let us take the definition of rhetoric attributed to Gorgias: "the ability to persuade with words judges in the law courts, senators in the Senate, assemblymen in the Assembly, and men in any other meeting which convenes for the public interest" (Plato, trans. 1952, p. 10). Turning to China, we might look for instances of deliberative rhetoric in which one speaker in a public setting orally addresses large groups of citizens, who then exercise their decision-making powers. But we won't find much—rhetorical acts of this sort are the exception rather than the rule. And if we look for a theory of rhetoric based on this paradigm, that is, for an equivalent of Aristotle's

*Rhetoric* in a fairly narrow sense, and we do not find one, we might be tempted to conclude that the Chinese did not have what George Kennedy (1980) refers to as "conceptualized rhetoric," that is, a theoretical development of rhetoric.

If we take this definition of rhetoric somewhat more loosely, as, say, "the ability to persuade with words politically powerful people on issues of the public interest," then much more appears. The dynastic histories are replete with records of debates, both oral and written, held at court over policy issues. From the Han dynasty (206 B.C.E. to 220 C.E.) on, court conferences, discussions, and debates were frequently convened as a way of letting the ruler see all sides of an issue and make an informed decision. In addition, members of the elite argued these controversies among themselves, through essays, letters, and other works that were intended to circulate broadly among the literati.

If rhetoric is seen as something closer to "persuasion in interpersonal contexts," then we might emphasize the wealth of examples of skillful speaking liberally scattered through the historical records and also collected in such works as *The Records of the Warring States* [*Zhanguo ce*] (see also Raphals, 1992, for a good overview of this strand of the Chinese rhetorical tradition). Those interested in the conceptual treatment of such communication could consult the relevant sections of *Han Feizi* (see Lu, 1993) or one of the translations of the *Master of Demon Valley* [*Guigu zi*] (Cleary, 1993), a text that provides a full-blown "conceptualization" (in Kennedy's sense) of such rhetorical suasion.

If rhetoric is considered more broadly, as "an organized study of discourse" (Liu, 1996b), then the horizons open up considerably. As Liu shows, over the centuries, Chinese literati produced a vast corpus of handbooks and more theoretical tracts that analyze the structures and strategies of the various genres of Chinese discourse, both the purely pragmatic and the more literary. In these works, they presented methods of generating discourse, developed critical vocabularies for evaluating particular specimens of discourse, and grounded their treatments of discourse in theories of language and expression.

If, for the sake of completing the argument, we define rhetoric as "symbolic inducement," then our study could arguably comprise much of traditional Chinese culture, to the extent that it is a self-consciously didactic culture in which not just spoken and written communication, but all symbol systems, from posture, behaviors, clothing, and ornamentation to music, art, and architecture, were to express and reinforce cultural values and significations.

There are advantages as well as drawbacks in applying any one particular definition of rhetoric cross-culturally. But for reasons of intellectual politics among 20th-century rhetoricians, there is a strong tendency to give pride of place to classical rhetorics, especially Greek rhetorics, and especially Aristotelian rhetoric. When rhetoric was revived as an area of study in the early decades of the 20th century, it was primarily classical texts and theories, and especially those of the Greeks, that were recovered first and made central—not Boethius, Cassiodorus, or Fenelon. Much ink is still spilled in attempts to claim Plato's *Gorgias* and *Phaedrus* for rhetoric, even though both are notably problematic texts for rhetoricians. And there has been a curious fascination with Aristotle's *Rhetoric:* curious in light of how little influence the work had throughout most of the European tradition when compared with that of Cicero. Thus, when Thomas Conley (1990) traced the Byzantine response to the *Rhetoric,* the burden was on him to explain why it did not have much impact, the presumption being that it should have.

The decision to trace the origins of the discipline to Greece has several attractions and advantages for late-20th-century rhetoricians. Greece and Rome offer contemporary rhetoricians the vision of a society in which rhetoric played a powerful and essential role in public decision making on vital issues. Given the 20th-century bias toward theory, the Greeks are more compelling than, say, the *ars dictaminis* or the *De Copia.* A lineage that springs from Plato and Aristotle gives rhetoric a certain philosophical cachet. Conversely, there is a squeamishness about claiming the seamy underside of rhetoric, the power to sway a crowd to laughter or tears or to throw dust in the eyes of the jury. Aristotle, with his conception of the audience as reasonable judges, allows rhetoric to be a respectable participant in recent conversations on ethical public decision making in democratic societies. Those with postmodern leanings, on the other hand, may champion the Sophists, the "other side" of Greek rhetoric.

This is a powerful and seductive, but highly partial and provincial, origin myth for the discipline of rhetoric, and it presents a danger to which Western and Western-trained rhetoricians (and I include myself in this group) are particularly susceptible. I hope the reader will be able to judge how deeply she is still influenced by such Hellenism by pondering her responses to the following paired passages, the first of each pair being an actual quotation, the second my slight revision of it.

1a. "As the momentum toward freedom increases around the world, masses of people will have to learn the ancient arts of communication first identified by Aristotle: how to deliberate policy, how to decide issues involving justice, and how to assure social stability." (Osborn, 1990, p. 3)

1b. "As the momentum toward freedom increases around the world, masses of people will have to learn the ancient arts of communication first identified by Confucius: how to deliberate policy, how to decide issues involving justice, and how to assure social stability."

2a. "Though rhetoric is colored by the traditions and conventions of the society in which it is applied, it is also a universal phenomenon which is conditioned by the basic workings of the human mind and heart and by the nature of all human society. Aristotle's objective in writing his *Rhetoric* was not to describe Greek rhetoric, but to describe this universal facet of human communication. The categories he identifies are intended to exhaust the possibilities, though the examples of them which he gives are drawn from the specific practice of a Greek city state. It is perfectly possible to utilize the categories of Aristotelian rhetoric to study speech in China, India, Africa, and elsewhere in the world, cultures much more different from the Greek than was that of Palestine at the time of the Roman empire." (Kennedy, 1982, p. 10)

2b. "Though rhetoric is colored by the traditions and conventions of the society in which it is applied, it is also a universal phenomenon which is conditioned by the basic workings of the human mind and heart and by the nature of all human society. Liu Xie's objective in writing his *Literary Mind and the Carving of Dragons* [*Wenxin diaolong*] was not to describe Chinese rhetoric, but to describe this universal facet of human communication. The categories he identifies are intended to exhaust the possibilities, though the examples of them which he gives are drawn from the specific practice of a Chinese elite. It is perfectly possible to utilize the categories of Liu Xie's rhetoric to study speech in Greece, India, Africa, and elsewhere in the world."

Why might lingering vestiges of Romantic Hellenism be a particular concern for those engaging in cross-cultural rhetorical studies? It is because such Romantic Hellenism is usually tied to Orientalism, the term coined by Edward Said to label what he sees as a characteristic Western stance toward Eastern cultures during the past two centuries. When the militarily and technologically dominant Western culture encountered these unfamiliar cultures, it took itself, usually an idealized version of itself, as the standard and projected its antithesis onto the other culture. From the Romantic era on, Orientalism is expressed in such familiar sets of opposites as male to female, light to dark, reason to emotion, change to stagnation, mind to body, content to form, freedom to servitude, individual to group, originality to conformity, and so on. As this list suggests, "the essence of Orientalism is the ineradicable distinction between Western superiority and Oriental inferiority" (Said, 1978, p. 42).

Orientalism of this stripe usually rests on highly questionable conceptions of how "we" Occidentals behave. Excellent examples of this phenomenon can be found in Carl Becker's 1986 article "Reasons for the Lack of Argumentation and Debate in the Far East." To give but one example, Becker proclaims that "in many situations, then, oriental language is used less to communicate than to commune, congratulate, emote, and to begin and end activities" (p. 82). One piece of supporting evidence for this generalization is that "[a] large part of the language activity of any oriental dinner or drinking party consists of the parroting of each others' sentiments in the same words; as the evening wears on, singing and chanting take the place of speech" (Becker, p. 82). Apparently Occidentals do not misuse language in these ways, even at cocktail parties, and in their everyday settings they refrain from employing language to "commune, congratulate, emote, and to begin and end activities."

Orientalism need not manifest itself so starkly to have pernicious effects. Starting from the assumption that the other is Other—is different, exotic, mysterious, and strange—the scholar may gravitate toward what seems most different, exotic, mysterious, and strange in the other culture. Thus, in studies of Chinese rhetoric, there is an inordinate amount of attention paid to Daoist (Taoist) rhetoric. Indeed, one of my initial motivations for learning Classical Chinese was to read the Daoist classic *The Way and the Power* [*Daode jing*] in its original language. Daoist texts are intriguing, Daoist ideas are an element of Chinese thought, and Daoism does deserve to be studied, but the amount of attention Daoism has received is extraordinarily disproportionate to the actual influence it has had on Chinese rhetorical practices and theories. Such assumptions of the exotic may also create expectations of what counts as "real" Chinese rhetoric; for instance, I was asked to rewrite a survey of Classical Chinese rhetoric because in my rendition "it wasn't different enough."

It is but one step further to an idealizing Orientalism that simply reverses the valuation of the binaries. Put somewhat crudely, if Western thought is masculine, linear, logical, objective, objectifying, and so on, and such masculine thought is bad, and if feminine is the opposite of masculine, and thus good, and if Chinese thought is non-Western, then Chinese thought is feminine and good. Thus, for example, as someone who works with Chinese materials, I was asked to participate in a panel on invitational rhetoric, on the assumption that Western rhetoric is not invitational, and so Chinese rhetoric would be. But in China, as in the West, invitational rhetoric is the exception. Speaking more generally, this recurring association of China with a valorized feminine hardly squares with the overtly patriarchal nature of the Chinese family, state, and culture.

I would like to touch briefly on one further manifestation of Orientalism, that being the justification of cross-cultural studies as a way to understand ourselves better, a justification I have also resorted to. Cross-cultural studies can indeed result in viewing ourselves differently, and this effect can lead to greater understanding of our culture. But if this is the motive behind the study, it becomes an intellectual version of the joke about the Hollywood producer who subjected a listener to a long monologue about himself, and then concluded, "But enough about me; let's talk about you. What do you think about me?" Endlessly interrogating other cultures to find out more about ourselves can be an unattractive kind of cultural narcissism.

## "WE DON'T ARGUE"

So it might seem that the logical alternative (in the logic of binaries, anyway) would be to listen to and accept what those who belong to a culture say about it. I have been told by Chinese people, many of them college students, such things as "we think differently," "we don't argue," "we're not logical," "we don't have rhetoric," "our language is written in pictures," and "our language is monosyllabic."

Taking such evidence at face value is to fall into the wherefore-art-thou-Romeo? syndrome, the fallacy of believing that people are necessarily reliable authorities on their own culture, literature, history, and language, simply by virtue of growing up in a particular place. Think of the misinformation available from Americans, including college students, on U.S. politics, English literature, or Western culture more generally. (An American student once qualified her analysis of American gender relations to me with the phrase "since the 1950s." When I asked her why she chose this time frame, she replied, "Because that's when television was invented, and that's where I get all my information.")

The view that Chinese people are all experts on their own culture is exacerbated by the misconception that speakers of Modern Chinese dialects such as Cantonese or Mandarin can thereby read Classical Chinese (the written language of the dominant elite culture for roughly two millennia). But if this were true, there would be no need for all the translations of Classical Chinese literature (*guwen*) into Modern Chinese (*baihua*), translations that are readily available in any Chinese-language bookstore.

For the average Modern Chinese reader, early Chinese texts present some additional challenges. Many of these texts were compiled by many hands, over time. There is no assurance that Confucius actually said a single thing attributed to him in the *Analects* [*Lunyu*]; he probably made some of the remarks recorded there, but scholars have agreed that he did not make others, such as the very famous "rectification of names" passage. Sometimes early texts were written in an anachronistic style, and dated retroactively (forged, if you will). For instance, the first few chapters of the *Book of Documents* [*Shang shu*] represent themselves as speeches of the Xia dynasty (from approximately 2200 B.C.E. to approximately 1750 B.C.E.). Whether these chapters bear any relationship to any speech actually given during that time is hard to tell, because there are no extant archaeological documents from the Xia dynasty. The earliest surviving continuous written records in China are divination records scratched into tortoise shells and ox scapulae, which date from the middle of the Shang dynasty (from approximately 1750 B.C.E. to approximately 1100 B.C.E.). A parallel problem arises with some Chinese Buddhist texts, such as the *Platform Sutra,* which were also reworked over centuries. The moral of the story is that it can be very dangerous to draw conclusions about these texts without consulting the appropriate scholarly apparatus.

Somewhat different problems of reliability and interpretation arise in the case of Chinese academics who are trained in the Classical Chinese language, philology, and bibliography. Chinese scholars, like all scholars, cannot but speak from a particular ideological perspective. This ideological orientation is glaringly obvious in the case of Chinese Marxist academic writing, but the nature of the bias is less obvious in the case of traditionally trained Chinese scholars (as well as the Western sinologists they trained), who tended to espouse neo-Confucianism. On the one hand, their ideological assumptions are more congenial to Western humanistic scholars than those of Marxist scholars and are thus less likely to be noticed as ideology; on the other hand, their bias dovetails nicely with the bias of much of the historical materials. Most of the surviving written materials are records of, by, and for the elite of Chinese society, the 5 to 10% of the population that was literate and could afford books. These materials concentrate on issues of concern to this well-off, educated, male elite: statecraft, ethics, ritual, and history, all filtered through the perspective of enacting and maintaining a Confucian society.

A neo-Confucian perspective often entails an idealized, homogenized view of Chinese culture and history. Chinese society is seen as always having been staunchly Confucian, despite the varied criticisms of Confucian thought during the Warring States era (481 to 220 B.C.E.), despite periods of widespread rejection of Confucianism such as occurred after the fall of the Han dynasty (221 C.E.), and despite the eclipsing of Confucianism by Buddhism during the Tang dynasty (618 to 906 C.E.) and, to a lesser extent, during the Song dynasty (960 to 1280 C.E.). There is a tendency to "read back" the importance of those texts that were eventually regarded as the Confucian classics. *Mengzi,* for instance, which eventually was sanctified as one of the "Four Books," represents but one of "the hundred different schools of thought" that arose during the Warring States period, and it was not declared a canonical work until the Song dynasty. Because the ideal Confucian state is harmonious, there is a tendency to disparage debate and argumentation, and thus to downplay the historical importance of such activities, or even to ignore them, despite the ample textual evidence to the contrary.

The neo-Confucian perspective continues to influence studies of Chinese rhetoric, even when these studies are done by mainland Chinese scholars.

Liu (1996b) assessed two "landmark" publications in the study of Chinese rhetoric during the 1980s, Zheng Dian and Tan Quanji's *Gu Hanyu xiucixue ziliao huibian* and Zeng Ziyu's *Zhongguo xiucixue shigao.* As Liu notes, each work is something of a mixed bag as far as conceptions of rhetoric go—but not mixed enough, in some ways. There is very little attention to institutionalizations or to actual instances of argumentation and debate in either work. Buddhism hardly appears, even though Buddhists engaged extensively in such rhetorical activities as preaching and religious disputation, and they also developed new genres such as *yulu* ("collected sayings") and *bianwen* (storytelling with illustrations).

## WHAT CAN BE DONE?

The first step, obviously, is to become aware of these various methodological issues, and the corresponding first caution is the obvious one: to maintain the critical spirit applied in other areas of academic work in cross-cultural rhetorical studies as well. There is no reason to abandon the trained skepticism that characterizes good scholarship, with its demands for sufficiency of evidence, appropriate credentialing of authorities, awareness of bias and underlying ideological commitments, and so on.

Sometimes this critical attitude involves nothing more than a basic reality check. To give but one example of how this might work, consider Becker's (1986) claims that the Chinese lacked a principle of noncontradiction (p. 83), had "no internal standards for determining when one set of arguments were [*sic*] better than another" (p. 84), and "had no standards for matching propositions with other propositions (coherence) or with other states of affairs in the world" ("correspondence tests of truth") (p. 79). How was it possible, then, for the Chinese bureaucracy to administer a far-flung empire, with its large armies, legal system, tax and labor requirements, irrigation systems, and public work projects, and to do so for century after century? Did they just get lucky? Perhaps so!—but at the very least, such discrepancies should send up a warning signal to the careful researcher.

It is also crucial to bear in mind that scholarship on China, especially early China, has advanced very rapidly in the past few decades. Archaeological discoveries; application of knowledge and methods from other fields, such as anthropology and linguistics; new perspectives, such as feminist analyses; and advances in textual scholarship have led to a much fuller understanding of Chinese culture. This makes it even more imperative for those investigating Chinese rhetoric to familiarize themselves with the most recent work in sinology. It is also essential to assess the reliability of recent translations and other book-length works by seeing how they are received in the field of

Chinese studies. This is easily done by reading the book reviews in the major sinological journals, and these journals are usually located in the East Asian reading room of major libraries. By this method one may discover, for instance, that Stephen Mitchell's recent translation of *The Way and the Power* [*Daode jing*] may leave something to be desired for some readers, because he "translated" this text without knowing any Classical Chinese, and arrived at his English-language version by dint of relying on other translations.

It is important to keep in mind that materials with which Western rhetoricians might wish to acquaint themselves may not be labeled, located, or organized as they might expect. Sometimes this is an effect of how Chinese terms are translated. The word *wen*, for instance, is often translated as "literature," but for some periods and for some theorists it referred more broadly to almost all genres of writing, both poetry and prose, and within prose included such genres as letters, reports or policy positions sent up through the bureaucracy, anecdotes and tales (*xiaoshuo*), and philosophical essays. There may be much to interest a rhetorician in a Chinese work with the word *wen* in its title.

As for the word *philosophy*, which is often used to label certain Chinese texts, this, too, can reflect more of the translators' biases than the nature of the texts themselves. Liu (1996a) argues cogently that it is more accurate to consider what are usually called Classical Chinese philosophical works to be intensely rhetorical productions, with a strong argumentative dimension. His position seems to be increasingly shared among sinologists; in a publisher's flyer for Carine Defoort's (1996) *The Pheasant Cap Master: A Rhetorical Reading*, the sinologist John S. Major praises her treatment by saying that "the focus here is not only on what the *He guan zi* [*The Pheasant Cap Master*] says, but how things are said, and how language is used in argumentation."

Liu's and Defoort's orientations to use and to function point to a more rewarding procedure than looking for term-to-term or structure-to-structure correspondences. To give a trivial example, it is sometimes claimed that Chinese lacks a word corresponding to the English *no*. However, if we ask instead about negation, we find there are several different verbal forms of negation in Chinese, depending on what type of statement is to be negated. Similarly, there may not be a term corresponding exactly to *ethos*, or even an Aristotelian conception of *ethos*, in the Chinese rhetorical tradition. However, there was great concern with development and expression of the moral self, especially in a communicative context.

Questions of use and function should also be kept in mind when it comes to the location of materials. Often materials bearing on Chinese rhetoric are arranged for the convenience of their original Chinese readership, rather than the contemporary Western academic. Thus one may come across an *ars dictaminis* in a handbook for officials or find instructions on how to lecture the populace into moral behavior in an imperial edict. A little open-mindedness, and some willingness to wander, may be greatly rewarded.

## REFERENCES

Becker, C. (1986). Reasons for the lack of argumentation and debate in the Far East. *International Journal of Intercultural Relations, 10,* 75-92.

Cleary, T. (1993). *Thunder in the sky: On the acquisition and exercise of power.* Boston: Shambala.

Conley, T. (1990). Aristotle's *Rhetoric* in Byzantium. *Rhetorica, 8*(1), 29-44.

Defoort, C. (1996). *The pheasant cap master: A rhetorical reading.* Albany: State University of New York Press.

Kennedy, G. (1980). *Classical rhetoric and its Christian and secular tradition from ancient to modern times.* Chapel Hill: University of North Carolina Press.

Kennedy, G. (1982). *New Testament interpretation through rhetorical criticism.* Chapel Hill: University of North Carolina Press.

Liu, Y. (1996a). Three issues in the argumentative conception of early Chinese discourse. *Philosophy East and West, 46*(1), 33-58.

Liu, Y. (1996b). To capture the essence of Chinese rhetoric: An anatomy of a paradigm in comparative rhetoric. *Rhetoric Review, 14*(2), 318-335.

Lu, X. (1993). The theory of persuasion in Han Fei Tzu and its impact on Chinese communication behaviors. *Howard Journal of Communication, 5,* 108-122.

Momigliano, A. (1975). *Alien wisdom: The limits of Hellenization.* New York: Cambridge University Press.

Osborn, M. (1990, January 17). A defense of our discipline. *Chronicle of Higher Education,* pp. B2-B3.

Plato. (1952). *Gorgias* (W. C. Helmhold, Trans.). New York: Bobbs-Merrill.

Raphals, L. (1992). *Knowing words: Wisdom and cunning in the classical traditions of China and Greece.* Ithaca, NY: Cornell University Press.

Said, E. (1978). *Orientalism.* New York: Pantheon.

# III

## RHETORIC IN INTERCULTURAL CONTEXTS

# 8

## George Bush Goes to Rio

*Implications for U.S. Participation in Global Environmental Governance*

TARLA RAI PETERSON • *Texas A&M University*

KATHI LYNN PAULEY • *Calvin College*

The United Nations Conference on Environment and Development (UNCED), held in Rio de Janeiro from June 3 to 14, 1992, symbolizes a growing concern with the relationship between human development and the natural world on which life depends. Although this concern is widespread, suggestions for future management of the environment diverge dramatically both within and between the world's nations. In this chapter, we first summarize the goals and accomplishments of this international conference, using media accounts of U.S. participation in the conference to explore perceptions of the role played by the United States. Second, we examine the speech George Bush delivered at Rio and the responses to it, arguing that Bush destroyed his bid for international leadership by his strategic choice to emphasize a conflicting, apparently selfish motive of promoting the U.S. economic agenda over global concerns. Finally, we discuss the possibilities offered by conceptualizations of nature extending beyond the market-economy approach exemplified by Bush.

### AGREEMENTS REACHED AT THE EARTH SUMMIT

The first principle of the *Rio Declaration on Environment and Development* (UNCED, 1992e) indicates sustainable development as the central tenet of the Earth Summit (UNCED): "Human beings are at the center of concerns for sustainable development. They are entitled to a healthy and productive life in harmony with nature" (p. 3). The meeting was successful in many ways. Although conflicts between North and South limited both the quantity and quality of agreements reached, the opposing factions did sign several accords.

Despite these successes, however, several participants were disappointed by the conference, as well as by U.S. performance there. Both participants and observers expressed dismay that the Bush administration had abdicated the United States's historical leadership in the area of environmental policy.

Five concrete accords came out of the Earth Summit: two conventions, also referred to as treaties, and three statements of intent. The conventions, which propose to limit emissions of greenhouse gases and to protect the diversity of the planet's plant and animal life, were voted on and signed by most nations attending the conference. The United States was the only industrialized nation that refused to sign the second convention. For the third accord, delegates accepted the *Rio Declaration on Environment and Development* (UNCED, 1992e), a nonbinding statement of the philosophy on which all Summit accords were based. As the above excerpt from the *Rio Declaration* suggests, human health is assumed to be complementary with environmental health. The fourth accord was a nonbinding statement of principles to guide forest conservation. Finally, *Agenda 21* (UNCED, 1992a), a comprehensive blueprint for international environmental policy, was finalized and accepted. Both conventions, as well as the *Rio Declaration,* were negotiated in separate committees and were concluded shortly before the Rio meeting began. Although no vote was taken on them, conference attendees had to work out details of the *Forest Principles* (UNCED, 1992c) and *Agenda 21* (UNCED, 1992a) at Rio.

## *Conventions*

One of the most controversial aspects of U.S. participation at UNCED was the Bush administration's behavior regarding the conventions. The United States alienated both traditional friends and foes during presummit negotiations of the climate treaty. The climate treaty, or *Framework Convention on Climate Change* (UNCED, 1992d), took 15 months to prepare and was adopted on May 9, 1992. It focuses largely on reducing energy demand and stabilizing carbon dioxide emissions. The major difficulty during negotiations for the climate treaty was reaching an agreement between the United States and the European Community on how to limit carbon dioxide and other heat-trapping gases emitted as a result of human activity. The Europeans insisted that carbon dioxide emissions be stabilized at 1990 levels by the year 2000, whereas the United States rejected the notion of targets and timetables. Bush, who had maintained considerable distance from specific environmental issues during his entire presidency, insisted that it was unrealistic and counterproductive to include timetables in the climate treaty. To persuade the United States to sign the binding treaty, disgruntled European nations agreed to delete all timetables and deadlines. However, not everyone was dissatisfied by the removal of target dates and timetables. When Donald Pearlman, who represented U.S. coal and utility interests, learned of the decision, he told the press, "Notwithstanding attempts by certain European countries to rewrite these paragraphs so as to create at least an impression of a requirement to return to 1990 levels by the year 2000, those efforts failed. . . . Obviously we're pleased" ("Compromise," 1992). Statements such as this alienated both developed and developing nations from the U.S. negotiating team.

Conflict followed the convention to Rio, where the oil-producing states of Kuwait, Saudi Arabia, United Arab Emirates, Iran, and Iraq refused to sign because of its emphasis on carbon dioxide emissions. Delegates from the Netherlands, Austria, and Switzerland, who had argued to retain deadlines, introduced a separate, nonbinding agreement that included timetables and deadlines that had been deleted from the original draft of the climate treaty. Although this did not become an official UNCED document, Germany led several other European nations in announcing that it would support the agreement. Washington, on the other hand, advised the three nations that to persist with such an initiative would damage their relations with the United States. For example, the Swiss environment minister received a memorandum from the U.S. State Department telling him that the resolution was "potentially embarrassing, unnecessary in light of the treaty, and detrimental to Swiss-American relations" (Robinson & Weisskopf, 1992a). The three nations expressed hostility toward U.S. pressure to drop the initiative, with the Austrian minister complaining that "they [the U.S. State Department] treated us like we are some kind of colony" (Robinson & Weisskopf, 1992a).

The second convention focused on protecting biodiversity. The *Convention on Biological Diversity* (UNCED, 1992b) took nearly 4 years to prepare, and it was adopted by its negotiating committee on May 22, 1992. It is intended to encourage national action to curb destruction of biological species and ecosystems. Contracting parties are required to adopt regulations that conserve their biological resources, to assume legal responsibility for environmental impacts of their private companies operating in other countries, to transfer technology on a preferential basis to other participants, and to compensate developing countries for extraction of genetic material from their environments. Industrialized countries agree to provide developing countries with financial assistance that will facilitate species conservation.

Bush refused to sign the treaty, claiming it was flawed because language included in it could harm the U.S. biotechnology industry and require the United States to provide unconditional financial aid to developing countries. He feared that the vagueness of the treaty regarding how living organisms can be exploited commercially and who shall retain the resulting patent rights would retard the U.S. biotechnology industry, fail to protect intellectual property, and reduce royalties. In a nationally televised news conference in the United States, Bush explained that he refused to sign this convention because he would "not sign a treaty that in my view throws too many Americans out of work" (Schneider, 1992a). Further, the White House Council on Competitiveness, headed by Vice President Dan Quayle, explicitly opposed the treaty. The U.S. biotechnology industry also lobbied extensively against it. For example, Richard Godown, director of the Industrial Biotechnology Association, explained on May 14 that the treaty would "hurt an industry that the U.S. dominates so that other countries may impede the U.S. industry's growth while developing their own industries using our technology" (Devroy, 1992). Unlike his response to the climate treaty, Bush did not suggest alterations in the biodiversity treaty.

In fact, when William Reilly, administrator for the U.S. Environmental Protection Agency (EPA), sent a confidential memorandum asking the White House to approve an amended version of the biodiversity treaty, a White House official leaked a copy to the *New York Times.* The memo indicated the Brazilian delegation's willingness to alter aspects of the treaty that were most bothersome to the Bush administration:

> As I indicated last night, Brazil has offered to try to "fix" the Biodiversity Convention so that the United States could sign it. . . . As I indicated last night, the U.S. refusal to sign the Biodiversity Convention is the major subject of press and delegate concern here. . . . The changes proposed, while not making everyone in the U.S. Government totally happy, would address the critical issues that have been identified. (Reilly, 1992a)

Reilly, who learned of the leak from a reporter, spent the next few days defending U.S. policy to both the press and fellow delegates. Following the leak, negative characterizations of the United States became more vocal. Jamsheed Marker, Pakistan's ambassador, explained that "the perception of the U.S. is not one of leadership, but that of blocking" (Weisskopf, 1992b). Ros Kelly, Australia's environment minister, suggested that, based on conferees' perceptions of U.S. policy, Bush "will not receive an enthusiastic reception . . . [when he] arrives" (Weisskopf, 1992b). A senior European negotiator said that the leaked memo "confirms what many people have suspected—that Bill Reilly is a fig leaf for a not very committed government" (Weisskopf, 1992b). German environment minister Klaus Topher said sadly, "I am afraid that conservatives in the United States are picking 'ecologism' as their new enemy" (Brooke, 1992c). The Bush administration's widely reported references to the Earth Summit as "a circus" did not allay Topher's concerns (Brooke, 1992f). In the end, the United States was the only industrialized country that did not sign the *Convention on Biological Diversity* at Rio.

## *Nonbinding Statements*

In addition to the conventions, three nonbinding statements were adopted by the UNCED participants. These statements, which did not entail a vote and did not require separate ratification by participating nations, provide a potential foundation for constructing future international agreements on environmental governance. When Bush arrived in Rio, he attempted to lead a drive to include a convention on forest principles in the agreements signed at the Earth Summit. Developing countries, however, traditionally have opposed international forest initiatives, which they see as an abridgment of their national sovereignty. Given the current gulf between the standard of living experienced in the United States and in most developing nations, Bush's refusal to consider the biodiversity treaty because it might handicap the U.S. biotechnology industry compounded existing suspicions toward his motives. Ting Wen Iian, a Malaysian diplomat, declared, "We are certainly not holding our forests in custody for those who have destroyed their own forests and now try to claim ours as part of the heritage of mankind" (Stevens, 1992c). This statement illustrates the perception of many developing nations that, because Bush was not willing to share economic and technological resources with developing countries, they were not interested in sharing local forest resources with the United States.

Klaus Topher, leader of the German delegation, finally brokered a compromise statement between the United States and developing countries on the forest issue. The resulting statement of principles calls for "global consensus on the management, conservation and sustainable development of all types of forests" (UNCED, 1992c). The statement designates forests as natural resources and recognizes that in developing countries, people depend on forest products for food, fiber, fuel, and shelter. It also acknowledges the global value of forests as sources of medicine, wildlife habitats, and carbon fixation. The statement further suggests that the principles outlined therein should serve as a guide for constructing binding international policies for forest conservation.

The summit also produced a statement of philosophy "recognizing the integral and interdependent nature of the Earth, our home" (UNCED, 1992e, p. 1). The statement encourages international cooperation in achieving "a higher quality of life for all people," because "eradicating poverty [is] an indispensable requirement for sustainable development" (p. 4). It encourages international cooperation to promote economic systems that more accurately assess the costs of environmental degradation, require polluters to bear the cost of pollution, and lead to sustainable development. The declaration encourages "developed countries [to] acknowledge the responsibility that they bear in the pursuit of sustainable development in view of the pressures their societies place on the global environment" (p. 5). They are encouraged to share financial and technological resources with developing regions. The declaration also mentions the importance of protecting resources for marginalized groups, including "indigenous people," "women," and "people under oppression" (p. 5).

Although the *Rio Declaration* (UNCED, 1992e) is not legally binding, it provides guidelines for negotiating binding international agreements regarding conservation and development in the future. However, even the broad, humanistic sentiments articulated in the declaration sparked conflict between the United States and developing countries. For example, when meeting with Kenya's negotiators in his office, Kamal Nath, India's Minister of Environment, said, "The United States told us they want to remove the phrase 'right to social and economic development'. . . . We must not budge from 'the right to social and economic development'" (Brooke, 1992c).

Finally, *Agenda 21* (UNCED, 1992a) is a detailed blueprint for future environmental action that covers all the major environmental issues discussed at the summit. This voluminous document elaborates strategies and programs to reverse environmental degradation and to promote sustainable development in all societies. It is made up of 4 sections that are divided into approximately 10 chapters each, resulting in a total of 40 chapters. The sections are titled "Social and Economic Dimensions," "Conservation and Management of Resources for Development," "Strengthening the Role of Major Groups," and "Means of Implementation."

The UNCED Preparatory Committee, which completed the draft of *Agenda 21* that was used in Rio, grouped programs around seven organizing themes:

1. revitalizing growth with sustainability (The Prospering World),
2. sustainable living (The Just World),
3. human settlements (The Habitable World),
4. efficient resource use (The Fertile World),
5. global and regional resources (The Shared World),
6. managing chemicals and waste (The Clean World),
7. participation and responsibility (The People's World).

The section titled "Social and Economic Dimensions" addresses the first two themes. "Conservation and Management of Resources for Development" addresses the third, fourth, fifth, and sixth themes. The section titled "Strengthening the Role of Major Groups" addresses the seventh theme. The final section details "Means of Implementation," such as science, technology, and legal mechanisms.

## EVALUATIONS OF THE EARTH SUMMIT

Evaluations of the Earth Summit and of the role played by the United States are mixed. The process and protocol were carefully designed. Each problem was subdivided into smaller components to create more manageable units, and the conference was preceded by an extensive prenegotiation phase. Although direct participation by scientists was minimal, the conference relied on extensive preliminary scientific groundwork to produce initial drafts of conventions and of nonbinding statements. Finally, the protocol resulting from the conference was designed to be dynamic. All conventions were written so they could be adapted to new scientific information with minimal changes to their basic structure (Robinson, 1992).

Maurice Strong, a Canadian businessman who made his fortune in the oil industry and who is now involved in ecotourism, was director of the Rio Summit. At the conclusion of the summit, he was "disappointed we don't have targets and timetables," for the climate treaty. Without them, "we have to push like hell to make sure implementation takes place" (Brooke, 1992b). He told wealthy nations that "no one place on the planet can remain an island of affluence in a sea of misery. . . . We're either going to save the whole world, or no one will be saved" (Weisskopf & Preston, 1992). Strong was disappointed that pledges for increased aid to developing countries (which primarily came from Germany, Japan, and France) did not bring the total close to the $125 billion a year he had asked for.

Direct participation from the private sector also was problematic. Although extensive preliminary scientific research was available to negotiators involved in preliminary meetings, independent scientists were not directly involved in negotiations. Instead of emphasizing a need to proceed based on the best available scientific evidence, Bush repeatedly emphasized the potential harm any actions posed to the fragile U.S. economy. Rather than working from the assumption that science is inherently uncertain, the existence of several differing estimates of the potential environmental damage caused by human activities was used to avoid decisive action. Nongovernmental environmental organizations participated in the summit to the degree that they were allowed. Such groups were excluded from much of the deliberations, however, and much of their energy was diverted by the "alternative" summit held concurrently with the UNCED. Finally, critical industries, particularly companies centered in the United States, expressed hostility toward the entire proceeding. Organizers had hoped that Strong's professional affiliation with the energy industry would induce cooperation from that sector. Representatives of both the biotechnology and energy industries, however, were widely quoted as being opposed to the proposed conventions.

By the time the summit concluded, the United States had isolated itself completely. Attempts to pressure Austria, the Netherlands, and Switzerland to drop their timetable for implementation of the climate treaty resulted in accusations that the United States was "shooting sparrows with a cannon" (Robinson & Weisskopf, 1992a). Britain, France, and Japan joined forces in an unsuccessful attempt to persuade Bush to sign the biodiversity treaty (Stevens, 1992a). Although he did not respond directly to Britain, Bush lashed out at Germany and Japan, accusing them of "Bush-bashing" and character- izing their pledge to increase aid to developing nations as a "guilt-induced effort to be politically correct" (Devroy, 1992). The Japanese responded sim- ply that they "have never engaged in Bush-bashing" (Weisskopf, 1992a). The German response was more heated:

> Guilty about what? The war? The Nazis? The last 500 years? If it's wealth we should be guilty for, the Americans are the richest of all of us. But we are the ones who feel the responsibility to help others. (Weisskopf, 1992a)

Exchanges such as these dismayed Australian Minister of the Arts, Sports, and the Environment Ros Kelly, who claimed that the United States was "abdicating their leadership role." She added that the United States is "the biggest economic power in the world; they should take a leadership role at this conference and they're not doing it. It seems a great shame" (Robinson & Weisskopf, 1992b).

Many delegates claimed that the conference would have been more pro- ductive if the United States had adopted a more cooperative stance. Events such as the White House leakage of Reilly's confidential memo, as well as senior administrators' references to the summit as "a circus," led to an im- pression that the U.S. delegation in Rio was paralyzed by cynical political maneuvering (Brooke, 1992f). The United States was characterized as a "vil- lain" (Brooke, 1992g) that was "dragging its feet" (Stevens, 1992c), was "blocking the summit's progress" (Weisskopf, 1992b), and had "abandoned its role as the world's most environmentally concerned country" (Schneider, 1992b). Environmentalists at the summit put the United States at the top of their list of "worst" nations (Brooke, 1992d). Another article notes that "the United States, a pioneer of environmental protection, has emerged as a prin- ciple [*sic*] obstacle to key agreements on global warming and financial assis- tance, ceding leadership to less cautious governments in Europe and Japan" (Weisskopf & Preston, 1992). The U.S. leadership that had been so signifi- cant in negotiating previous international environmental agreements was no- ticeably absent from Rio.

On the other hand, Richard E. Benekick, the former State Department of- ficial who led the U.S. negotiating team for the international ozone-layer treaty during 1986 and 1987, claimed that "the history books will refer back to this day as a landmark in a process that will save the planet from deterio- ration." He said that the summit "should not be judged by the immediate results, but by the process it sets in motion" (Stevens, 1992b). Michael Zammit-Cutajar, the executive secretary of the UNCED negotiating committee, was optimistic about the future of the climate convention. Although individual signatories still needed to ratify both treaties in appropriate national forums, Zammit-Cutajar was confident that, despite the U.S. refusal to set target dates, "the treaty [will] be in force within two years" (Stevens, 1992d). Gregg Easterbrook (1992) claimed that negative evaluations of U.S. behavior at the Rio Summit were inaccurate and overblown. He wrote that the press was so busy covering Bush's blunders at the summit that it ignored significant ecological progress occurring in the United States. Easterbrook also suggested that Reilly wielded more power than was indicated in press accounts describing him as a mere pawn before the White House Council on Competitiveness.

A third perspective, represented by Baruch Boxer (1992/1993), who has served as a consultant to the United Nations Environmental Program and the White House Council on Environmental Quality, is that conferences such as the Rio Summit "are not the way to preserve the environment" (p. 42). Boxer claimed that those who blame the Bush administration for the conference's frustrating conclusion are mistaken. He argued that public forums such as the UNCED are inappropriate for reconciling the fundamental conflicts between rich and poor nations. Although Boxer did not claim that these fundamental conflicts would dissolve by themselves, he believed that resources would be better spent on "finding workable, short-run technical and policy solutions" than on attempting to resolve differences in perspective (p. 43). According to Boxer, because comprehensive global agreements are doomed to failure, the Rio Summit did more harm than good by raising unwarranted expectations and encouraging antagonism between conferees.

## GEORGE BUSH AS THE "LONE RANGER"

As president of a nation that had participated fully in international environmental forums over the past decades, Bush was in a position to further invigorate world opinion in support of environmentally sound development policies. In examining political discourse, rhetorical critics often assess how presidential discourse has galvanized the U.S. public. For example, Branham and Pearce (1985) reconstruct Lincoln's "Gettysburg Address" as a healing memorial for one of the most tragic battles of the Civil War. Duffy and Ryan (1987) claim that Kennedy's inaugural address captured the sentiment of citizenship and commitment in the United States at the beginning of the 1960s. Ritter and Henry (1992) demonstrate that Reagan's speeches both responded to and strengthened the United States's need for hope during the 1980s. These and other studies of successful presidential rhetoric indicate that such rhetoric serves as a unifying symbol within U.S. culture.

The office of the U.S. presidency, however, does not guarantee rhetorical success, even within the United States. Studies of failed presidential appeals reveal that presidents are susceptible to difficulties involving a bad fit between the rhetorical situation and the discourse used. For example, Zarefsky (1986) argues that President Johnson's War on Poverty failed largely because public policy could not produce the fully restructured society that the president envisioned. Hahn (1984) attributes President Carter's failure as a public speaker to Carter's inability to understand that his constituents wanted more affluence, rather than suggestions for how to live with less. His propositions for resource conservation failed to energize the people because he misinterpreted the nation's desires.

President George Bush's attempt to assert U.S. dominance in the realm of international environmental governance falls into the category of failed presidential rhetoric. When he spoke before the delegates assembled at UNCED on June 12, 1992, Bush attempted to reassert an imperialist agenda that conflicted with the rhetorical tone established by other conference attendees. Bush's speech was delivered within a rhetorical situation created by his negative characterization of environmental regulation in the United States, his comments about the Earth Summit's relative insignificance, related statements made by White House staffers and other insiders, and his increasingly urgent campaign for reelection. Perhaps these contingencies combined to induce his definition of the environment as an economic resource best managed by U.S.-guided market forces.

## Bush's Address at UNCED

Statements prior to the Earth Summit set the tone Bush would carry throughout his speech. On May 12, Bush announced his decision to attend the Earth Summit, declaring that the United States "has been a leader for environment matters." Bush's response to reporters' queries about whether he would attend the entire conference did not enhance his credibility as a world leader, however: "Well, no. I couldn't possibly do that," he answered. "We have an election on in the United States this year" (Bush, 1992, p. 845). When discussing his upcoming visit to Rio, Bush proclaimed, "When we go to Rio, the U.S. will go proudly as the world's leader, not just in environmental research, but in environment action" (Bedard, 1992). The day before he delivered his address, Bush threw down the gauntlet, announcing, "I will stand up for American interest and the interests of a cleaner environment. And if the United States has to be the only nation to stand against the biodiversity treaty as now drawn so be it" (Bush, 1992, p. 1035). Given statements such as these, perhaps the speech's emphasis on solitary leadership was inevitable,

despite its clash with the emphasis on cooperation stressed by the conference organizer and by other attendees.

Bush faced an antagonistic audience when he stepped up to speak before
the Earth Summit delegates. His brief address offered an opportunity to ame-
liorate hostility between the United States and other conference attendees.
However, instead of presenting a conciliatory message, Bush delivered a
highly confrontational speech (Bush, 1992, pp. 1043-1044). He immediately
followed his perfunctory greeting to conference organizers and delegates
with a claim that the "pessimism" of those who warn of the potential disas-
ters posed by nuclear war and by unlimited growth "is unfounded." He then
presented a list of equally "unfounded" perceptions regarding environmental governance, including many of the central concerns expressed by Earth
Summit organizers. He provided the U.S. corrective for each inaccurate assumption and then listed U.S. plans for future development. He concluded
by telling delegates that, although their attendance at Rio was commendable,
it was trivial. Instead, undertaking individual actions modeled on the U.S.
plans he had listed would be far more significant. Throughout the speech, he
emphasized the United States's role as a world leader.

The first major section of Bush's speech lists, then corrects, five
misperceptions. Each begins with the phrase, "There are those who say . . ."
and then proceeds to correct the error. Both intuitive sense and speech-act
research indicate that agreements are preferred over disagreements. In addition, direct disagreement, especially when used unnecessarily, creates the
appearance that the disagreeing party holds authority over other participants
(Peterson, 1988b). Bush therefore began his speech by creating a
rhetorical situation within which his opponents must admit their willing subordination to the United States if they recast their current perspectives according to the corrective he offered.

After correcting the rest of the world's thinking, Bush listed six U.S. goals
for Rio (Bush, 1992, pp. 1043-1044). Six times he repeated, "We come to
Rio . . ." and then pointed out how the United States had outperformed other
nations in environmental conservation. Bush responded to "those who say
that cooperation between developed and developing countries is impossible"
by suggesting that they "come to Latin America" to see how wrong they
were (Bush, 1992, pp. 1043). Those who assumed that environmental protection should be directed by the state, rather than by the market, were directed to the pollution of central and eastern Europe. Those who feared that
"the interests of the status quo" (p. 1043) would retard change were referred
to Brazil's policy for managing its rain forests. Those who questioned the
compatibility of "economic growth and environmental protection" (p. 1043)
were referred to the United States as an exemplar of successful integration
between economic growth and environmental protection measures. Finally,

those who thought that world leaders did "not care about the earth" (p. 1043) were told to look at the attendance at the Rio Conference.

Bush led into his second section by "inviting [his] colleagues to join in a prompt start on the [climate change] convention's implementation" (Bush, 1992, pp. 1043-1044). These colleagues, however, were still smarting from Bush's insistence that they delete all implementation timetables from that convention. Bush then outlined U.S. proposals for forest conservation, technology cooperation, and aid to developing nations. Finally, he explained that he had "come to Rio prepared to continue America's unparalleled efforts to preserve species and habitat" and that he was "proud of what [the United States has] accomplished" (p. 1044). Both prior to and during the speech, Bush indicated that the United States was more committed to the issue of forest conservation than to any other issue dealt with at the conference. Bush's plan to conserve the world's remaining forests ran into difficulty, however, because developing nations hold most of this resource. Their representatives were not eager to accept direction from the man who had refused to sign the biodiversity treaty because it might limit foreign ownership rights. They saw that refusal as an attempt to block, rather than to facilitate, the spread of science and technology.

Throughout the speech, Bush emphasized his role as the leader of the nation whose "record on environmental protection is second to none" (Bush, 1992, p. 1044). He attempted to reconstruct his refusal to sign the biodiversity treaty as an example of this leadership, explaining, "It is never easy to stand alone on principle, but sometimes leadership requires that you do. And now is such a time" (p. 1044). He followed this explanation with references to the proud "record on American leadership" (which he promised to "extend") and to his "continuing commitment to leadership" (p. 1044). However, at Rio, Bush was a leader with few followers.

### Responses to the Address

Conference responses to Bush's plea for a forest treaty were mixed, with support from most western European nations and opposition from several southern nations. Although William Reilly, who inherited the task of persuading others to support the U.S. initiative, echoed the themes Bush had presented, he adopted a less confrontational tone. He began his formal statement to the conference by explaining that because the delegates were "meeting in the nation that is home to the largest and richest forests on earth, it is fitting that we here give to conservation of forests our highest priority" (Reilly, 1992b, p. 236). He then explained the U.S. initiative that Bush had presented 2 days earlier and invited all countries "to join [the United States] in this initiative" (p. 237). Representatives of developed countries responded positively to the forest initiative and ignored the rest of Bush's address. For example, German Chancellor Helmut Kohl said that, because forests were important to "[him] personally [he welcomed] the initiative of President George Bush" (Kohl, 1992, p. 230). Australian Minister for Environment Ros Kelly said that Australia would "support the development of a non-binding statement of forest principles" (Kelly, 1992, p. 226).

Developing countries, however, were less enthusiastic. Malaysian Prime Minister Mahathir Mohamad tied the biodiversity convention to the forest conservation initiative in his conference address:

> The poor countries have been told to preserve their forests and other genetic resources on the off-chance that at some future date something is discovered which might prove useful to humanity. . . . But now we are told that the rich will not agree to compensate the poor for their sacrifices. The rich argue that the diversity of genes stored and safeguarded by the poor are of no value until the rich, through their superior Intelligence, release the potential. . . . The North demands a forest convention. Obviously the North wants to have a direct say in the management of forests in the poor South at next to no cost to themselves. The pittance they offer is much less than the loss of earnings by the poor countries and yet it is made out as a generous concession. (Mohamad, 1992, p. 232)

His speech was a veiled reaction to the United States's refusal to sign the biodiversity convention while pressuring those nations that stood to benefit from it into preserving their natural resources for the benefit of all humanity. If Bush were unwilling to grant nations holding most of the world's forests a share of the profits accruing from industrial development of products discovered in their forests, he should not expect them to willingly share their forests with economically privileged nations such as the United States.

Others rebuked Bush more politely. After explaining "why the European community would have preferred the Convention on climate change to establish more precise commitments and objectives," the Commission of the European Community's statement pointed out that it likewise "regards the Convention on biodiversity as being too timid" (1992, p. 238). The Commission then highlights the point at which Europe parts company with the United States:

> But the Community has decided nonetheless to sign them [conventions] both, for there is no denying their importance . . . I am very pleased . . . by the initiative of Chancellor Kohl in inviting all the signatory states of the convention on climate change to take part in the first follow-up conference to be organized in Germany. (p. 238)

A similar invitation extended by George Bush, the man who insisted on removing the "precise commitments and objectives" from the treaty, was ignored. Although UNCED Secretary-General Maurice Strong mentioned the need for "continuing progress towards an effective regime for conservation and sustainable development of the world's forests" (Strong, 1992, p. 244), this recommendation was simply one item in a long list of concerns, including decertification, war, trade barriers, and so forth (pp. 243-244).

Informal responses to Bush's performance at Rio amplified the negative tone. Brooke (1992a) reported that, "in contrast to other Western leaders speaking here today, Mr. Bush did not make public any major financial initiatives . . . Chancellor Helmut Kohl of Germany, a nation widely seen to have assumed a major leadership role here, promised to increase Germany's aid for development of poor countries to 0.7 percent of its gross national product." Later, both Japan and France announced specific increases in aid, heightening "the isolation of President Bush from environmental policies advocated by the other six major industrialized nations" (Brooke, 1992e). The day after Bush delivered his address, Tommy Koh, chairman of the conference's main working session, muttered, "This will teach the United Nations not to hold a conference in an American election year" (Stevens, 1992b). Michael Oppenheimer, senior scientist for the Environmental Defense Fund, added, "You can't be treated as a world leader on any issue without being a player on the environment" (Stevens, 1992b). Lewis (1992) wrote that "the Bush administration appeared divided and paralyzed" at Rio.

Bush had suggested that his position stemmed from his ethical responsibilities to U.S. citizens. Indeed, he was heavily lobbied by several industries that feared negative economic consequences would result from both the climate change and the biodiversity conventions. Biotechnology interest groups, including the Association of Biotechnology Companies, the Industrial Biotechnology Association, the Pharmaceutical Manufacturers' Association, and the American Intellectual Property Law Association lobbied the Bush administration to oppose the biodiversity treaty. However, even within those industries, reactions were mixed. For example, the president and chief executive of Genetech Inc. wrote a letter commending Bush for his refusal to sign the biodiversity treaty. However, a group of scientists employed by Genetech disagreed. They composed a letter of dissent, stating that the treaty was important for scientific advancement and that although it might raise difficulties for some biotechnology companies, its long-term business impact would be favorable. The letter of dissent was sent through electronic mail, reaching at least 2,000 additional employees before management halted its circulation (Lehrman, 1992). An article in the *Wall Street Journal* argued that "because of the stand taken by Bush by not signing the Biodiversity Treaty, other countries are likely to retaliate by sharply restricting U.S. access to key raw materials: the genetic and biochemical resources used in agriculture, medicine, and industry" (Reid, 1992). Frye (1992, p. 344) pointed out that, given the solitary position of the United States on this issue, the global market might pressure U.S. biotechnology firms to fall in line with the rest of the world. Developing nations probably would prefer to sell their genetic stock to firms that agree to pay royalties, rather than to U.S. firms. French (1992) added that developing countries would cooperate more willingly with those nations that provide them with needed economic resources. Thus, even among those sources upon which Bush relied for support, responses were mixed.

## A Failed Bid for Leadership

Bush expressed the United States's desire to lead global efforts to achieve environmentally sustainable development when he spoke before the delegates of the UNCED. However, he attenuated any leadership potential by emphasizing an apparently selfish agenda of promoting the U.S. economy and his reelection to the U.S. presidency. By explaining his refusal to sign the biodiversity treaty as protection for the U.S. biotechnology industry, Bush contradicted the claim that he could fairly mediate issues in the era of global environmental governance. He emphasized past U.S. leadership and his own bid for reelection to such a degree that he dismissed or denigrated issues important to other participants.

Rio also was a domestic disaster for Bush. Faced with a challenger to his bid for reelection who was steadily gaining ground with labor, Bush was under severe pressure in the upcoming presidential election. The lagging U.S. economy contributed to the fear that the timetables included in the climate change treaty might produce environmental regulations that could eliminate U.S. jobs. He also would have alienated important political supporters had he signed the biodiversity convention. A second explanation for Bush's stance toward UNCED may stem from the fact that throughout his presidency Bush had endured criticism for neglecting domestic affairs in favor of international issues. This could explain the Bush administration's decision to downplay UNCED, even considering the possibility of ignoring it altogether.

Environmental governance may not be the most propitious international issue for a U.S. president to ignore, however. It is an issue about which the public has an abundance of information and one to which the public is regularly exposed. The significance of the relationship between humans and the natural environment has retained a profound place in U.S. tradition since pre-Revolutionary War times (Peterson, 1986, 1988a). Further, environmental conservation appears to have retained strong bipartisan support in the United States.

Responses to Dunlap, Gallup, and Gallup's *The Health of the Planet* (1993), which was timed to coincide with the UNCED, suggest that Bush may have made a tactical error. When asked to choose whether environmental concerns should be emphasized over economic concerns, or whether economic concerns should be emphasized over environmental concerns, 58% of U.S. respondents preferred emphasizing environmental concerns, 26% chose to emphasize economic concerns, and 8% said that both should receive equal emphasis (Dunlap et al., 1993, p. 78). Furthermore, 65% said they were willing to pay more for products that protected the environment, 24% said they were not, and 11% were unsure. Conventional wisdom says that, although people may respond favorably to questions about the environment, that response does not translate into action. However, within the past year, 57% of the respondents had purchased products that were less harmful to the environment, even though they were more expensive than an equivalent product that was more damaging to the environment (p. 86). This purchasing behavior gains additional significance when one considers that purchasing the "green product" required consumers to change a past purchasing habit. In short, environmental governance is one international issue that U.S. citizens seem to embrace.

When George Bush went to Rio, he failed to fulfill the leadership role he prescribed for himself, and in so doing, he ultimately limited both opportunities for U.S. participation in global environmental governance and his own election campaign. Even if U.S. public opinion had fit more closely with Bush's actions, his performance shows the fallacy of converting a national mandate into international policy. Bush White House staffers constructed a mandate from their supporters' beliefs and from what they thought the American people believed, and then they extrapolated this mandate to the world. By privileging a single perspective toward the natural world over all others, Bush could only fail to fulfill the globally representative duties he prescribed for himself.

## THE NATURE OF NATURE

We can move beyond strategic explanations of the failed U.S. attempt to impart leadership at Rio by exploring Bush's definition of nature as a commodity for trade. Bush repeatedly stressed the centrality of "economic growth," both before and during his visit to Rio. According to Bush, those who worried about the "limits to growth" have been proven wrong. "Today," he claimed, "we realize that [economic] growth is the engine of change and the friend of the environment" (Bush, 1992, p. 1043). In Bush's account, nature easily reduces to economic terms, becoming no more than a source of production and consumption. Peterson and Peterson (1993) maintain that economic valuation of natural resources unnecessarily constricts environmental policy options. The economic account also encourages technological hubris, wherein people forget that their material existence is grounded in nature. Kenneth Burke (1984) argues that such an attitude, or technological psychosis, contributes to a cycle wherein society devotes ever-increasing resources to producing technologies that undo the damage done by previously developed technologies. This increasingly frenetic activity derives from a concomitant expectation that, if humans continue their technological progress, they can transcend their own mortality by achieving absolute control over nature. Although Burke endorses neither the desirability nor the practicality of this goal, he claims it provides the patterns we use to measure the appropriateness of all decisions. Given this construction of the relationship of humans to nature, Bush's refusal to sign the biodiversity convention, thereby creating a potential trade barrier, was nearly inevitable. As a trade agreement, the biodiversity convention smacks of protectionism. Given recent moves to streamline the global marketplace, an agreement that limits the importation of biological commodities from southern to northern nations is no more reasonable than an agreement that limits the importation of automobile components in the same direction.

### Nature as Commodity

Bush is not unique in his commodification of nature. In fact, during negotiation of the *Convention on Biological Diversity* (UNCED, 1992b), the issue of compliance to the market provisions of the General Agreement on Tariffs and Trade (GATT) and of the North American Free Trade Agreement (NAFTA) and the issue of the degree to which the convention would facilitate implementation of those agreements upstaged concerns with biological diversity. Martin Khor Kok-Peng, who emerged as a key nongovernmental organization lobbyist, asserted that the Earth Summit was "no longer a forum on the environment, on greenhouse gas, or on scientific data, but rather a conference about conference" (Cooper, 1992). In defining the environment as a commodity, Bush simply joined the ranks of "corporate environmentalism," which offers "technological solutions to narrowly defined ecological problems, seeks a form of sustainable development that somehow seems to imply no real social change, and generally avoids more troublesome political perspectives" (Athanasiou, 1992, p. 69). Despite their vilification of Bush, other industrialized nations profited handsomely from his strategic choice not to appropriate the language and ideas of the traditional environmental movement. The director of the United States-based Institute for Food and Development Policy commented, "Japan and Europe were really happy [with Bush's statements]. They didn't even have to do anything to look good. They just had to have the good sense to shut up" (Athanasiou, 1992, p. 62). Bush's refusal to sign the *Convention on Biological Diversity,* for example, diverted attention from real problems connected with biodiversity.

*Biodiversity* is a contested term in its own right. Although the general public tends to think about biodiversity in terms of the potential extinction of panda bears and seals, northern governments and multinational corporations have been primarily concerned with the far more economically significant area of agricultural crop seeds. In recent years, industrialized nations have stockpiled wide varieties of seeds in "gene banks," mostly in the United States and Europe. These seeds provide critical material researchers can use to expand the narrow genetic base of the modern, high-yield plant varieties produced by the Green Revolution ("Intellectual Property Rights," 1991). In addition, ethnobotanist Darrell Posey (1992) writes that $54 billion is already grossed annually for pharmaceuticals resulting from what might be called "indigenous research," though less than 0.0001% of that amount has ever been returned to the discovering communities. Although the biodiversity convention allows existing genetic collections to be treated as the intellectual property of the North, it also grants southern nations such rights for materials that are collected within their boundaries in the future. This means that intellectual property rights for new genetic discoveries made in the South will belong to the South, rather than to the corporations that are becoming increasingly dependent on them for industrial agriculture production. Although transnational corporations can maintain some of their past advantage by adapting operations to the economic and political policies of southern nations, the convention does give southern governments additional negotiating power. The Bush administration preferred to retain the current system, which directly cedes royalty rights to discovering corporations, rather than to the countries in which materials are found or to the indigenous people, who often lead corporate scientists to materials.

One of the most fundamental problems with reducing nature to an economic commodity is that it refines the cultural imperialism illustrated by genetic research. The world of GATT and NAFTA gives new power to Schiller's (1976) vision of a "world system within which there is a single market" (p. 5). Viewing the environment as nothing more than a bundle of marketable commodities blinds us to broader human development issues, for there are no terms for their description.

It has become increasingly clear that imperialistic development programs based on traditional export-intensive models of modernization have led to social decay and ecological degradation. Conventional aid programs accompanying the Green Revolution often increase poverty within subsistence economies. In Sikandernagar, for example, international aid has further impoverished subsistence producers by reducing their access to cropland and forest resources. Policies encouraging the transfer of commonly held land to private ownership force subsistence producers to go farther to collect fuel and fodder for their families. Women who had supplemented these resources with money earned by hiring themselves out for part-time labor also have to work longer for less money because they now must compete with tractors. The cultural impoverishment associated with traditional development programs extends beyond economic devastation. For example, Shakuntala (1993) discovered that oral women in India know that "people cannot live without (or by destroying) nature" (p. 334). Her subjects understood clearly that when people cut live trees rather than using their dead branches and other debris, not only are natural resources depleted, but "the temporal conditions of nature have been acutely disrupted" (p. 337). Their understanding was embedded in traditional acknowledgment of a complementary and reciprocal "relationship of humans to nature" (p. 338). This sense of connectedness, which cannot be described adequately in economic terms, gradually is disappearing from Indian culture.

The need to broaden our analysis of environment and development beyond market economics does not mean that poverty is not grounded in economics. Mies and Shiva (1993) warn us to "beware of simply up-ending the dualistic structure by discounting the economy altogether" (p. 11). Athanasiou (1992) writes that the United Nations Development Program's 1992 report demonstrates that the global polarization of wealth doubled between 1960 and 1989. In 1989, the poorest fifth of the world's population received 1.4% of the world's total income, whereas the richest fifth of the world's population received 82.7%. Despite this disparity, however, Schiller (1976) cautions that "economic determinism overlooks many consequences of the [colonization] process it seeks to analyze. Though the economic imperative initiates the cultural envelopment, the impact extends far beyond" the economic sector (p. 8). Although most of those living on 1.4% of the world's total income live in the southern hemisphere, the difference in perspective between northern and southern definitions of the relationship between humans and the natural systems in which they are grounded goes beyond market-economy issues. Athanasiou (1992) argues that poor people who live in the South "are less susceptible to the odd and assiduously cultivated illusion that environmental protection is either possible or desirable without fundamental social changes" (p. 76). Those changes must include the political and legal structures that have encouraged southern nations to pillage their own environments. Although the collaboration of some groups within dominated nations complicates efforts to halt environmental degradation, their status remains that of collaborator, rather than initiator. Athanasiou points out that Malaysia, for example, is the home base of logging companies that clear-cut their native forests even more voraciously than do the Japanese. The Malaysian government, he adds, has made a "mission of mystifying both social repression and environmental destruction as the costs of development" (p. 82). Malaysian Prime Minister Mahathir's opposition to the North's desire to have "a say in the management of [Malaysian] forests while we have no say on their carbon dioxide emissions" (Athanasiou, 1992, p. 82), however, seems reasonable.

Martin Khor Kok-Peng (1992) adds that environmentally sensitive "solutions [to development problems] cannot be attained through technological means alone, but will principally involv[e] fundamental changes in economy, development models, lifestyles, distribution of resources and income, and international political relations" (pp. 44-45). The decision to allow existing markets to control development ensures that the financial goals of technology-producing countries will be met. Given that development aid centers around technologies designed in and for the hyperdeveloped nations, the failure of this aid to improve living conditions for most of those in the South should surprise no one. First, there is no reason to assume that the technologies of advanced capitalism are appropriate for a developing nation. Even if an appropriate infrastructure existed, these technologies only enable the recipients to replicate outmoded structures from the donor nation, for the development of technology depends entirely on its encouragement from powerful decision makers within the donor society. Scientific research itself is shaped by an international market, wherein topics of importance are determined by the needs of countries such as the United States, Germany, and Japan. Accordingly, certain areas are regarded as worthy of attention and receive generous financial support. Other lines of research, no matter how potentially exciting scientifically, remain undeveloped. Filipino Walden Bello noted, for example, that the North set an agenda for the UNCED in which ecological issues of great concern in the South, such as widespread lack of access to fresh water, desertification, and the international toxics trade, were not featured. He described UNCED as "a conference about environmental problems as they are seen in the North. It should have been called the 'UN Conference on Environment as Seen by the North'" (Athanasiou, 1992, p. 75). Given the increasingly centralized control over science, the technologies that result from applying new discoveries rarely represent, and are sometimes incompatible with, the urgent needs of most of the world's poorest people.

### Life Beyond the Market

There are alternatives to the market-based interpretation of the relationship between humans and their environment. Shiva (1993) draws a distinction between "poverty as subsistence" and "poverty as deprivation" (p. 72). The modernistic paradigm of development views people who remain closely connected with nature as somehow deficient. However, living in houses built with natural material, wearing garments of natural fiber, and eating home-grown and home-produced materials in order to protect global marketplaces, they convert subsistence to deprivation. An alternative approach replaces the global market with holistic understanding of human life and its relationship with other life forms. Shiva points out that destruction of biodiversity exacerbates malnutrition and deficiency disease in subsistence economies. "For example, *bathua* has been declared a 'weed' to be eliminated by herbicides" (Shiva, p. 81). Families are thus deprived of an important nutrition source, and their environment is saturated with chemicals. As Shakuntala (1993) demonstrates, subsistence does not necessarily imply a low quality of life.

Shakuntala (1993) maintains that the limited amount of biomass energy available in urban areas of India has its maximum impact on the female slum population. In many parts of India, women who spend 14 to 16 hours working every day "may have literally reached their 'carrying capacities'" (p. 332). She argues that reconstituting knowledge of the natural environment to include nonmarket aspects is "necessary in the face of the environmental disaster that India is experiencing" (p. 338). Similar conditions exist throughout large portions of the world today, where the poor live in abject misery, which both fuels and is fueled by degradation of their natural environment. Shakuntala asserts that conditions such as those endured in India "require an examination and introduction of new forms of knowledge (and management) that might reestablish the connection between orality and ecology" (p. 338). This reevaluation of humankind's relationship to nature may require an "epistemological revision" that includes a "reinvented orality" (p. 337). Such revision need not, and probably should not, entail a return to preliteracy, wherein we seek to understand, rather than to control, natural processes.

The realization that human activity can destroy life on earth throws into question many of the assumptions of industrial society and the technological enterprise. If nothing else, the hostility between North and South at the Earth Summit indicates that the market-based environment, which was articulated most clearly by Bush and espoused by most other conference attendees from northern nations, has proven inadequate to political questions of power and justice. Perhaps global social governance can become a tool for reducing the disproportionate impacts of environmental degradation on different groups of people, rather than remaining a means for further enriching the world's transnational corporations. Understanding the limitations of a market-based conceptualization of nature encourages us to reevaluate the very categories of nature and society. Admittedly, the attempts to define an alternative have produced no clear answers to date. However, the very emergence of the term "sustainable development" as a semiofficial notion indicates growing awareness that the old model is not sufficient.

## REFERENCES

Athanasiou, T. (1992). After the summit. *Socialist Review, 22*(4), 57-92.

Bedard, P. (1992, June 2). Bush proposes plan for planet. *Washington, D.C., Times,* p. A1.

Boxer, B. (1992/1993). Getting beyond Rio. *Issues in Science and Technology, 9*(2), 42-48.

Branham, R. J., & Pearce, W. B. (1985). Between text and con text: Toward a rhetoric of contextual reconstruction. *Quarterly Journal of Speech, 71,* 19-36.

Brooke, J. (1992a, June 13). Bush attempts to mend fences. *New York Times,* p. A10.

Brooke, J. (1992b, June 15). Chief closes summit with an appeal for action. *New York Times,* p. A8.

Brooke, J. (1992c, June 12). Delegates from 4 nations warm to a high-profile role: Global powerbroker. *New York Times,* p. A10.

Brooke, J. (1992d, June 10). Earth Summit races clock to resolve differences on forest treaty. *New York Times,* p. A8.

Brooke, J. (1992e, June 14). Japan promises lead role in battle against pollution. *New York Times,* p. A8.

Brooke, J. (1992f, June 12). U.S. delegation in Rio strained and divided over policy. *New York Times,* p. A10.

Brooke, J. (1992g, June 2). U.S. has a starring role in Rio summit as villain. *New York Times,* p. A10.

Burke, K. (1984). *Permanence and change.* Berkeley: University of California Press.

Bush, G. H. (1992). *The weekly compilation of presidential documents, 28.* Washington, DC: Office of the Federal Register.

Commission of the European Community. (1992). Extracts from statements: Plenary and summit segment. *Environmental Policy and Law, 22*(4), 237-238.

Compromise reached on emissions. (1992, May 9). *Washington Post,* p. A8.

Cooper, M. (1992, June 16). Blame it on Rio. *Village Voice,* pp. 27-29.

Devroy, A. (1992, June 10). White House scorns summit foes. *Washington Post,* p. A1.

Duffy, B. K., & Ryan, H. R. (1987). *American orators of the twentieth century: Critical studies and sources.* New York: Greenwood Press.

Dunlap, R. E., Gallup, G. H., & Gallup, A. M. (1993). *Health of the planet: A George H. Gallup memorial survey.* Princeton, NJ: George H. Gallup International Institute.

Easterbrook, G. (1992, July 6). Green Cassandras. *New Republic,* 23-25.

French, H. F. (1992). *After the earth summit: The future of environmental governance.* Washington, DC: Worldwatch Institute.

Frye, R. S. (1992). Uncle Sam at UNCED. *Environmental Policy and Law, 22*(4), 340-346.

Hahn, D. F. (1984). The rhetoric of Jimmy Carter, 1976-1980. *Presidential Studies Quarterly, 14,* 266-285.

Intellectual property rights: The politics of ownership [Special issue]. (1991). *Cultural Survival Quarterly, 15*(3), 1-79.

Kelly, R. (1992). Extracts from statements: Plenary and summit segment. *Environmental Policy and Law, 22*(4), 226.

Kohl, H. (1992). Extracts from statements: Plenary and summit segment. *Environmental Policy and Law, 22*(4), 230.

Kok-Peng, M. K. (1992). *The future of north-south relations: Conflict or cooperation.* Penange, Malaysia: Third World Network.

Lehrman, S. (1992, July). Genetech's stance on biodiversity riles staff. *Nature, 367,* 97.

Lewis, P. (1992, June 15). Storm in Rio: Morning after. *New York Times,* pp. A1, A8.

Mies, M., & Shiva, V. (Eds.). (1993). *Ecofeminism.* London: Zed Books.

Mohamad, M. (1992). Extracts from statements: Plenary and summit segment. *Environmental Policy and Law, 22*(4), 233.

Peterson, M. J., & Peterson, T. R. (1993). A rhetorical critique of "non-market" economic valuation for natural resources. *Environmental Values, 2,* 47-65.

Peterson, T. R. (1986). The will to conservation: A Burkeian analysis of Dust Bowl rhetoric and American farming motives. *Southern Speech Communication Journal, 52,* 1-21.

Peterson, T. R. (1988a). The meek shall inherit the mountains: A dramatistic criticism of Grand Teton National Park's interpretive program. *Central States Speech Journal, 39,* 121-133.

Peterson, T. R. (1988b). The rhetorical construction of institutional authority in a Senate subcommittee hearing on wilderness legislation. *Western Journal of Speech Communication, 52,* 259-276.

Posey, D. (1992). Protecting biocultural diversity. In S. Lerner (Ed.), *Beyond the Earth Summit: Conversations with advocates of sustainable development* (pp. 136-142). Bolinas, CA: Commonweal.

Reid, W. V. (1992, October 8). Bush biodiversity policy risks dangerous side effects. *Wall Street Journal,* p. A15.

Reilly, W. K. (1992a, June 5). Excerpts from Rio Memo: A plea for the environment. *New York Times,* p. A6.

Reilly, W. K. (1992b). Extracts from statements: Plenary and summit segment. *Environmental Policy and Law, 22*(4), 236-237.

Ritter, K., & Henry, D. (1992). *Ronald Reagan: The great communicator.* New York: Greenwood Press.

Robinson, E., & Weisskopf, M. (1992a, June 9). Europe may stand united on emission. *Washington Post,* p. A20.

Robinson, E., & Weisskopf, M. (1992b, June 6). "No" leaves U.S. isolated at summit. *Washington Post,* p. A1.

Robinson, N. A. (Ed.). (1992). *Agenda 21 and the UNCED proceedings.* New York: Oceana.

Schiller, H. I. (1976). *Communication and cultural domination.* White Plains, NY: International Arts and Sciences Press.

Schneider, K. (1992a, June 6). President defends U.S. envoy in Rio. *New York Times,* p. A6.

Schneider, K. (1992b, June 5). White House snubs U.S. envoy's plea to sign Rio treaty. *New York Times,* pp. A1, A6.

Shakuntala, R. (1993). Nature and oral women in India: Reconstituting social knowledge. *Howard Journal of Communications, 4,* 329-341.

Shiva, V. (1993). The impoverishment of the environment: Women and children last. In M. Mies & V. Shiva (Eds.), *Ecofeminism* (pp. 70-90). London: Zed Books.

Stevens, W. K. (1992a, June 9). Bush plan to save forests is blocked by poor countries. *New York Times,* pp. A1, A8.

Stevens, W. K. (1992b, June 14). Lessons of Rio. A new prominence and an effective blandness. *New York Times,* p. L10.

Stevens, W. K. (1992c, June 7). U.S. trying to buff its image, defends the forests. *New York Times,* p. A20.

Stevens, W. K. (1992d, June 13). With climate treaty signed, all say they'll do more. *New York Times,* pp. A1, A4.

Strong, M. (1992). Extracts from statements: Plenary and summit segment. *Environmental Policy and Law, 22*(4), 242-244.

United Nations Conference on Environment and Development. (1992a). *Agenda 21: Adoption of agreements on environment and development.* Rio de Janeiro, Brazil: Author.

United Nations Conference on Environment and Development. (1992b). *Convention on biological diversity.* Rio de Janeiro, Brazil: Author.

United Nations Conference on Environment and Development. (1992c). *Forest principles.* Rio de Janeiro, Brazil: Author.

United Nations Conference on Environment and Development. (1992d). *Framework convention on climate change.* Rio de Janeiro, Brazil: Author.

United Nations Conference on Environment and Development. (1992e). *Rio declaration on environment and development.* Rio de Janeiro, Brazil: Author.

Weisskopf, M. (1992a, June 11). Behind the curve in Rio. *Washington Post,* p. A1.

Weisskopf, M. (1992b, June 8). Outsider EPA chief being tested. *Washington Post,* p. A1.

Weisskopf, M., & Preston, J. (1992, June 3). U.N. earth summit opens with calls to save planet. *Washington Post,* p. A20.

Zarefsky, D. (1986). *President Johnson's War on Poverty.* Tuscaloosa: University of Alabama Press.

# 9

# Rhetoric and Intercultural Friendship Formation

ELIZABETH GAREIS • *Baruch College/City University of New York*

When U.S. American friendship patterns are examined intraculturally, the following picture emerges. The term *friend* has a broad category width and applies to many different kinds of relationships; to narrow it down, research usually focuses on close or best friendship (Pogrebin, 1987). American friendship is not formalized; that is, it is usually not marked by social rituals, public ceremonies, behavioral norms, and obligations (Matthews, 1986; Pogrebin, 1987; Rubin, 1985). Instead, it is defined by the values of similarity, affection, support, trust, honesty, and loyalty (Bell, 1981; Blieszner & Adams, 1992; Fehr, 1996; Matthews, 1986; Pogrebin, 1987; Rawlins, 1992; Rubin, 1985). Friendships among females are said to be more intimate, self-revealing, and nurturing, whereas friendships among males are more group-oriented, marked by activities rather than intimate talk, and defined by roles rather than holistically (Bell, 1981; Mitchell, 1986; Rubin, 1985). Individuals range in their need for close friendships: Some people have a steady number of close friends throughout life—keeping, dissolving, and replenishing friendships as they move away or experience turning points in life. Others grow old having had only one or two very close friends, and still others are content without close friendships altogether (Matthews, 1986).

Although this internal picture provides insights, it offers only a one-sided perspective. It also ignores rhetorical considerations that must be made in the process of friendship formation. For a more well-rounded examination, interculturally oriented texts furnish relativity and thus illuminate the subject matter further. Most of these intercultural publications are geared toward interested parties in academe, business, or the travel industry and include handbooks for foreign students, their advisers, business personnel, immigrants, and tourists (e.g., Althen, 1995; Lanier, 1996; Stewart & Bennett, 1991). Among the variety of topics covered in these publications, there are always sections on personal relations or friendship that reiterate, almost verbatim, the same message: Americans are friendly and warm during initial contact, but close friendships either are rare or, if they do happen, are usually less intense and more short-lived than in other cultures.

Some publications elaborate on this blanket statement by adding details or examples of difficulties foreign sojourners experience in the formation of friendships with Americans. Of all the problems mentioned, the biggest one seems to be that initial displays of friendliness on the part of the Americans or gestures such as invitations to an American's home are often misinterpreted as signaling the desire for a close friendship, and many foreigners feel betrayed when this perceived promise is not fulfilled. A similar situation of disappointment arises when friendships are actually formed but then quickly fade as the American party moves or undergoes other life changes. It comes as no surprise that frustrated foreigners often conclude that American relationships are superficial in nature (Althen, 1988). The following statement from a foreign student from India illustrates these feelings:

> "Let's not think of years and years ahead, let's just think of here and now. . . . We're in school for two, three years together—fine we're friends. But then when you leave, who cares really if we do meet again." They just find a new friend. The Americans are very nice . . . friendly, but this friendliness, which is so easily seen, can at times smack of a certain superficiality, which I'm not saying is wrong—because I guess if it works for them, it works for them—but to me, I'm coming from a way that is more old-fashioned, that's still steeped in ways that have been going on for thousands of years. It can be a bit unsettling at first to know that when someone smiles or when someone says that they're your friend, that doesn't have the same meaning. And even though you've been warned about it and you know what to expect, when it actually happens to you, it can be a slight shock. (Gareis, 1995, p. 101)

In an attempt to aid the foreign visitors' understanding of American friendship patterns, intercultural publications often supply rationales for common points of contention. Du Bois (1956), for example, explains that U.S. friendships are widespread and trusting but lacking in a sense of obligation and permanence. She cautions Americans against entering relationships with persons from high-obligation and high-duration cultures, because it is in such relationships that American openness and friendliness are often ethnocentrically interpreted as promises of closer involvement, and a sense of disappointment and failure ensues on the part of the foreigners when this promise does not become realized. From another angle, Du Bois warns that the proverbial American friendliness might "appear to foreigners as a tactless intrusion into cherished areas reserved for close relationships" (p. 62) and is, therefore, doubly problematic. Du Bois also notes that the role of interpersonal relations in general needs to be taken into account. In the United

States, for example, the emphasis is more on material well-being than relationships, placing a lower value on interpersonal relations in general than in some other cultures.

Stewart and Bennett (1991) explain that the widespread nature and compartmentalization of American friendship (into friends at work, friends at school, tennis friends, etc.) may be a function of the wish to be popular. They purport that popularity and friendship are "matters of social success and not the conditions for establishing deep relationships" (p. 108). Foreign sojourners also often note that Americans avoid commitment when it comes to assisting others, which in turn makes many sojourners uncomfortable asking for help. Stewart and Bennett's explanation for this perceived unavailability or inconvenience is that Americans in need of help, support, or solace frequently search for professional help rather than making demands on friends.

The frequently mentioned lack of commitment and obligation may also be based on the American ideal of independence and self-reliance. Thus, when asked about values, Americans rank freedom first, well ahead of friendship (according to *The Connecticut Mutual Life Report on American Values in the '80s,* cited in Pogrebin, 1987). This, in all likelihood, is rare in the rest of the world and is probably one of the causes for clashes with people from other cultures who do want to get closer (Althen, 1988). In many countries, value is placed on relationships instead of on the individualistic pursuits of autonomy and success, and friendships are considered permanent, carrying with them obligations and responsibilities. The relative paucity of these traits in American friendship leads to descriptions of American life as a "grand tour of handshakes," "a hall into which people step for a minute on their way somewhere else," and "a mass of bits performed by half-known actors" (Brown, 1986, p. 14). In a contrasting culture, such as India, on the other hand, once a person has found a nourishing relationship, he or she "wants to grow a garden around it," and "each relationship thus becomes a play with many scenes" in an atmosphere of "unmovable permanence" (Brown, 1986, p. 14). Or, as a student from India at a U.S. university observes:

> I see them [Americans] with each other; even though they're very close, there's a certain kind of shield that comes in the way, which I don't see with my friends back home. . . . I think people in the States are a bit self-conscious when it comes to showing their warmth and love to each other. There's a feeling that sentimentality shouldn't be there, it shouldn't be too sappy, you shouldn't cling. I sense that even when you're in love with somebody, it's not the same as being in love back in India. It's just the feeling that something's being there in the way. It's like, "we want to be in love, we want to be very close friends, but I still have my own goals, my own aims, and I don't have to be reached. And if you are there with me, in love with me, in a way you have to compete with those goals I want to reach." (Gareis, 1995, pp. 100-101)

The comparatively low level of involvement and perceived short duration of American friendships can be explained not only by the values of independence and self-reliance but also by American mobility patterns. Having grown up in families that might have changed their residence every few years, many Americans have either not had sufficient practice in forming close friendships or have developed self-protective habits of keeping relationships casual in order not to get hurt by repeated separations (Bell, 1981). When frequent moving is also accompanied by turnings in adult life, chances for friendships' surviving become slim. American historic mobility patterns do not match the ideals of commitment, responsibility, obligation, and permanence espoused in other cultures; the result is that Americans have learned to develop instant intimacy but also to let go quickly and with ease (Rubin, 1985).

Presupposing this status quo and the absence of formal rules for establishing and maintaining friendships (Argyle & Henderson, 1984), the question is how intercultural friendships do get formed. Intercultural friendship is a complex entity that is influenced by many factors, including cultural similarity, commonalities in values as well as interests, proximity, and intercultural adjustment (Gareis, 1995). One of the most prominent variables influencing friendship formation across cultures, however, is communication. Besides questions of general communicative competence, topics of particular importance are communication issues and strategies that hinder or aid the formation of close interpersonal relationships.

This chapter argues that sojourners in the United States should be aware of these rhetorical aspects of friendship formation and select the most appropriate course of action in their search for American friends. I will be drawing from student narratives that I have collected in the course of research on foreign students and their levels of contact with host nationals as well as from reflections of English as a second language (ESL) teachers on their own and their students' experiences with intercultural friendship. The chapter thus explores the issue from the perspective of both sojourners in the United States and native speakers with frequent intercultural contact.

Section 1 overviews communication issues arising from intercultural differences. Questions of friendship terminology, the initiation of contact, and the early maintenance stage of friendship are explored. Section 2 describes rhetorical strategies that influence friendship formation, highlighting negative as well as positive influences. Section 3 provides specific suggestions for sojourners in the United States who seek friendships with Americans. The chapter concludes with a reference to the intangible aspects of friendship and the still unresearched areas of interpersonal attraction.

## COMMUNICATION ISSUES

### *Terminology*

A factor at the base of many misunderstandings in intercultural friendship formation is the absence of linguistic forms to clearly delineate different kinds of relationships. Thus, the term *friend* in English is used to describe a variety of relationships, ranging from short-term, superficial relationships to those that are long-standing and deeply committed (Matthews, 1986). For the exacting language user, terms such as *acquaintance, casual friend, close friend,* and *best friend* offer the promise of differentiation; however, even they have no clear demarcation, as is illustrated by Merriam-Webster's equivocal definition of *acquaintance* as "a person whom one knows but who is not a particularly close friend" (*Merriam-Webster's,* 1998, p. 10). To understand this definition, one would of course first have to know what a close friend is. Yet, the term *close friend,* as well as the terms *casual, good, true, real,* or *best friend,* is used with highly subjective variations and is largely unexplored in the research literature. This lack of definitive criteria makes it very difficult to differentiate among the terminology and to determine the existence of degrees of friendship. It is under this premise that Rubin (1985) states:

> Without institutional form, without a clearly defined set of norms for behavior or an agreed-upon set of reciprocal rights and obligation, without even a language that makes distinctions between the different kinds of relationships to which we apply the word, there can be no widely shared agreement about what is a friend. Thus it is that one person will claim as a friend someone who doesn't reciprocate; that another who has been called a good friend says, when I ask him about his relationship, "Oh, yeah, John, we worked together a year or so ago. Haven't seen him since." (p. 8)

Despite the lack of established definitions, most studies focus on the description of what seems to correlate with best and close friendships, disregarding more casual relationships. One criterion for differentiation lies in numbers. Thus, when asked how many casual friends they have, people respond with numbers as high as 30 to 50 (Matthews, 1986). Close friendships, on the other hand, are fairly consistently limited to numbers between 3 and 7 (Pogrebin, 1987), and best friendships should by definition refer to only 1 person. To draw a more descriptive line between these three dimensions, we might use Du Bois's (1974) definition of exclusive, close, and casual friendships. Thus, exclusive friendships are marked by a dyadic character, inclusive intimacy (i.e., confidences and responsibilities), and assumed permanence; close friendships occur in multiple dyads with selective intimacy and hoped-for durability; and casual friendships are polydyadic, with incidental intimacy and an unstressed attitude toward durability.

Native speakers of English are aware of these differentiations and know that the word *friend* encompasses a wide range of meanings. Nonnative speakers, however, are often confused about the semantic width of the term and mistakenly assume that it connotes the generally narrower meaning of the equivalent term in their own languages. This semantic confusion is at times heightened by the linguistic similarity of the terms. One of the most elemental observations concerning American and German friendship patterns, for instance, is the etymological kinship between the English word *friend* and the German equivalent *Freund.* Unlike the English term, however, the German word has a much narrower category width and refers exclusively to close friends. This difference, as small as it may seem, becomes a major stumbling block for many sojourners, causing much confusion and limitless debates.

In a study of foreign students' friendships with Americans, for example, many German respondents complained that American friendships are shallow and short-lived (Gareis, 1995). One respondent found it preposterous that Americans are friends "as soon as you talk more than 10 sentences" and explained that it takes much more time and effort to become someone's *Freund* in a German context (Gareis, 1995, p. 79). Negative judgments based on semantic confusion are unnecessary and do not have to cloud sojourners' perceptions of the host culture. Sojourners and host nationals should strive for a clarification of terminology during early intercultural contact in order to preclude faulty interpretations and allow for a focus on more concrete communication issues related to intercultural friendship formation.

### Friendship Initiation

Having contact with conationals is beneficial to sojourners in a new culture. Vital information is exchanged, adjustment facilitated, and the worst of culture shock made more endurable (Oberg, 1979). Some sojourners, however, never really leave the secure conational community and venture out to form close friendships with Americans. This seclusion may be the result of peer pressure from a conational community that discourages full adaptation (Paige, 1983; Tjioe, 1972). It may also be due to the sojourners' strong identification with their home culture (Ting-Toomey, 1989), negative attitudes related to low levels of intercultural sensitivity (Bennett, 1986), or a predominantly task-oriented reason for the sojourn, as, for example, when an academic degree or work assignment is the sole objective, and the sojourner plans to return home upon its completion (Roland, 1986). Commenting on the "cliquishness" of his conationals, an Indian student suggests yet another reason, namely a "fear of cultural differences, . . . not being able to communicate, . . . being ridiculed, not doing something right, just being different"

(Gareis, 1995, p. 104). The fate of social isolation is sealed when unfavorable attitudes, prejudice, and discrimination against foreign-looking individuals on the part of the host-country nationals create additional barriers and adverse intergroup relations (Schaffer & Dowling, 1966; Ting-Toomey, 1989). A student from Taiwan, for example, reports that she gave up on contacts with Americans, because people on the phone were often rude to her when they did not immediately understand what she was trying to say. She concluded, "It's easy for me to give up; I rather call people I know" (Gareis, 1995, p. 116).

For newcomers who want to make friends with Americans, experienced sojourners often suggest strategies that include being outgoing and pursuing activities. Two foreign students, from India and Germany, respectively, elaborate on this approach.

> Everybody in a sense is going about their own life. . . . People here are not going to get out of their way to come and get to know you, but they are rather open about getting to know you if you go out and try to be friends. (Gareis, 1995, p. 104)

The German student adds:

> I would say start with activities, like join a club or do something that you are interested in . . . and you'll find somebody who has the same interests. It's a lot easier to approach Americans that way—do things together first, and then you might get to talk and find out that you are similar in other respects. I think, usually here you don't start out talking; you start out doing things together, and then you might talk. (Gareis, 1995, p. 82)

But even if sojourners are interested in contact with host nationals and do take initiative, certain communication issues usually arise on the road from contact initiation to close friendship. Reflected in these issues are rhetorical requirements that come into play during the interchanges common to early stages of friendship. The following section lists these interchanges and delineates specific points where rhetoric is to be found and expectations between interactants have to be coordinated to ensure the continuation of the friendship formation process.

### Greetings

Establishing contact interculturally is not as easy as in intracultural contexts. In the pursuit of intercultural friendship, cultural and linguistic differences often cause misunderstanding. Problems start at the greeting level. The English *How are you,* for example, is formulaic and does not call for an actual description of one's well-being. In other cultures, however, similar questions are true inquiries, soliciting honest and detailed responses. This discrepancy can lead to awkward encounters with newcomers who are not aware that *How are you* is simply a greeting, not a request for information. An Austrian student, for example, remembers that a few weeks after his arrival in the United States he saw an American acquaintance in town who asked *How are you* as she approached. The Austrian started to give a detailed account of how he felt, expecting her to stop and listen. In the meantime, however, the American had passed him, oblivious to his response. She had expected a short greeting in return to hers and did not even hear the lengthy answer to her question. The Austrian student soon learned to respond appropriately but continues to consider the exchange pattern superficial and strained, preferring instead an honest account and a shared experience with a possible therapeutic outcome (Brown, 1986; Roland, 1986).

Rhetoric related to greetings may seem unproblematic at first glance. However, it is often the first obstacle perceived by recently arrived sojourners. Especially at the beginning of a nonnative speaker's stay in the United States, this obstacle can deter him or her from further contact with Americans and cause unnecessary stereotyping of U.S. culture in general.

### Self-Disclosure

Another cultural difference concerns the strategies with which interactants reduce uncertainty in initial contact. Whereas members of group-oriented, collectivistic cultures, such as Chinese culture, reduce uncertainty by sharing group-based information, members of individualistic cultures, such as the United States, seek out person-based information (Gudykunst & Nishida, 1986). The reliance on groups in collectivistic cultures has another interesting side effect. Thus, Gudykunst, Ting-Toomey, and Nishida (1996) report that Chinese people find it difficult to interact with strangers and often prefer that intermediaries initiate contact, which may be difficult when sojourning in a foreign culture. Studies also suggest that to get a relationship off the ground, reciprocity in self-disclosure is important (Scollon & Scollon, 1995). In group-oriented cultures, however, personal information is not only disclosed differently (i.e., implicitly rather than through direct statements), but also, such disclosure is not as common among out-group members (Gudykunst, Ting-Toomey, & Nishida, 1996). Sojourners from collectivistic cultures therefore seem at a disadvantage when it comes to initiating friendship in the United States.

The problem many Asian students experience is compounded when a loss of face is feared or occurs. A student from Taiwan, for example, describes how an unfortunate meeting with her adviser at the beginning of her stay in the United States discouraged her from pursuing close contacts with Americans. During the first meeting with her adviser, he pointed out that her English was very poor and recommended that she not take a full load of classes.

He also refused to sign a recommendation she needed to get a lease for an apartment in which she was interested, explaining, "I never sign these contracts for any student." During her first quarter here, this adviser, who was also her major professor and who she says is "very funny" with American students but serious with her, also told her "you make me crazy" in front of the whole class when she committed an error. The student concedes that she is sensitive and that this advisor might not have meant any harm; nevertheless, she felt treated as less intelligent than she is, not respected in her personality, and like an outsider. She says, "It really hurt my heart." The loss of face this adviser caused cast a "big shadow" over the $2^1/2$ years of her sojourn, reducing her motivation to make American friends in the process:

> Maybe I have a narrow mind to make a friendship with Americans because the beginning when I came here, I cannot set a very good relationship between my adviser, so this is the reason . . . because in beginning I failed, and now sometimes I feel no necessary because sometime I don't trust them. (Gareis, 1995, p. 118)

The student also concedes, however, that because of the common language and cultural background, it is easier to make friends and talk with fellow Chinese. ("I'm lazy to make a friend with the different language people I guess.") Likewise, she has looked for friends only among her classmates but finds it difficult to connect with them. "I don't have a chance. Everybody just in class . . . and when the class over, everybody just say 'bye-bye.' Seldom to have a chance to make a close" (Gareis, 1995, p. 117).

Differences in self-disclosure practices and related issues of face are powerful factors influencing friendship formation. How sojourners and native speakers negotiate expectations related to self-disclosure and face frequently determines the future of the relationship.

## Invitations

Invitations are another point of contention that often causes friction at the initial stages of intercultural friendship. Another student from Taiwan, for example, has had such disappointing experiences with Americans that she has lost trust and keeps her distance at the beginning of a relationship. Thus, she recounts many occurrences where Americans promised or suggested something (e.g., a weekend invitation to someone's family) but never followed up on it and never apologized either. The student details one situation where she was matched with a family in a community friend program who just wanted knowledge and information ("I don't know your culture at all, tell me more, tell me more"), but who were not interested in friendship. They told her about a lot of interesting places but never took her there. She believes that they signed up for the community friend program just to look good in their church. "They think they're Christians, and Christians should offer help. They are liars. When you see them laugh or smile, you can tell it's not genuine" (Gareis, 1995, p. 116).

Scollon and Scollon (1995) provide an interesting observation that may explain at least some of the invitation problems so often mentioned by foreign sojourners. They point out that important points in conversations among Western speakers of English are placed near the beginning of the interaction. Important points in Asian discourse, however, are made near the end. Invitations at the end of a conversation are therefore of little major significance to Western interactants but are taken far more seriously by Asian counterparts.

Naturally, the wording with which invitations are extended also plays a role. Many sojourners are not aware that vague statements such as *Let's get together some time* may function more as a pleasantry and formulaic closing than a true invitation. Likewise, the farewell *See you later* is often misunderstood by nonnative speakers. Stories abound in which a foreign student took the utterance literally and showed up at the doorstep of the surprised American who had uttered the phrase earlier in the day.

Even if invitations are sincere and a get-together takes place, problems often ensue. Apparently, an invitation to someone's home in many cultures means that a friendship has begun and that more contact and closer involvement will follow. Similar to actions such as calling someone by their first name or giving someone a brief hug, invitations to someone's home, however, hold little promise of closeness in the United States (Lewin, 1948). Sojourners are often unaware of this difference and feel betrayed when expectations are not fulfilled. This feeling of betrayal is based on their misinterpretation of signs and the mistaken belief that a threshold to extended involvement and close friendship has been crossed. Unfortunately, this misinterpretation leads many sojourners to conclude that American friendships are shallow and superficial, although from an American perspective the encounter was based on friendliness and not yet actual friendship. This and related misunderstandings can be avoided if sojourners and native speakers are aware of rhetorical and cultural differences and learn to align expectations with respect to invitations.

### Topic Selection

When initial contact is established and the potential friends get together for activities and conversation, topic selection becomes an issue. Students from Germany, for example, often mention that Germans prefer interaction featuring analysis, criticism, and seriousness of content and form, whereas Americans generally communicate on a lighter plain. An American friend of a German student explains that she does not like the intensity and seriousness of

European conversations: "You just sit, look into each other's eyes, and discuss problems." The German student, however, counters that "it's just the way of talking that makes it sound like a problem" and that her friend, like many Americans, just wants to joke and be entertained primarily (Gareis, 1995, p. 80). In general, she observes:

> I noticed that a lot of times when I met Americans, and they asked me to go out for lunch or to stay with them even, you couldn't get that close to them. . . . They ignore or they just don't touch some areas you would like to talk about. . . . And even if you start talking about it, it's just on the surface, it's not going to the real problem. It's stuck at a certain point, and they just don't open themselves. (Gareis, 1995, p. 79)

When this barrier is reached, Americans "have special phrases or patterns they say, and then you just notice they've switched the topic." Marlene feels that not just Germans but "Europeans in general are more open to analyze their own faults, their own problems, their own thoughts. They have more patience to sit down and talk about it." Americans "are not used to hard criticism . . . always polite, polite, polite . . . even if you don't want to hurt them, if you just want to help them . . . they're not able to handle it." In summary, Americans just "don't go into the depth" (Gareis, 1995, p. 79).

Another German student puts it this way:

> Germans spend more time talking together than anything else; the emphasis is more on understanding what's going on with each other's life. . . . Many Americans just don't want to spend a whole evening sitting there and talking together; they want to go out or they want to do something. (Gareis, 1995, p. 82)

Yet another German student says that he treasures complete honesty in friendship, to the point of being blunt.

> I sometimes mention things in a rather blunt way, as they put it here—that might be because of my Berlin background. If I dislike something or somebody, I say so, and I don't try to cover it up; I say it very straightforward. (Gareis, 1995, p. 87)

Matching his preferences, he describes his best friend in Germany as follows.

> We really have the most in common. He's the most liberal I can think of, and he's my best critic—he never minds criticizing me, and I never mind criticizing him—and he's the only male person I can show affection to, to a certain extent. . . . And between the two of us there is really no limitation whatsoever about what we can talk about. (Gareis, 1995, p. 89)

In contrast, a close friend from an American perspective, according to this student, is "somebody you can have a good time with . . . somebody you can share emotions with also, but not necessarily all the time your problems." Thus, Americans have a tendency to "pretend everything's okay"; they lack "seriousness" and try to be "constantly funny" (Gareis, 1995, pp. 87-88).

Interestingly, although foreign students often declare that they share more personal information with their friends than Americans do, discussing family matters among friends seems taboo in many of the same cultures. A student from Taiwan, for example, explains that she would rather deal with family matters within the family rather than with "outside people" (Gareis, 1995, p. 112).

Asking about each other's families, on the other hand, is an important ritual in many cultures. A Taiwanese student, for example, states that "general Americans will not ask a person about his [her] family. . . . But in my culture, when we meet a new friend, we will ask about his [her] family" (Gareis, 1995, p. 122). Another student feels very comfortable with one American friend because he is very considerate (e.g., regularly asks her about her family) and does not push her ("He lets you decide what you really want, just gives a little help"; Gareis, 1995, p. 115).

Whereas German nationals seem to be more direct than Americans—especially when discussing problems or criticizing their friends—sojourners from many Asian countries tend to be less verbal and expressive. A student from Taiwan explains that Asians are more intuitive concerning interpersonal relations. Thus, "you just know what the friends need. We don't need them to ask first, we just do for them. Maybe we do secretly, they don't know we try to help them. . . . But in the U.S. I must speak out" (Gareis, 1995, p. 112). Similarly, another Taiwanese student mentions that "Americans always speak up, but sometimes Chinese, they don't speak up. Maybe out of 10%, they speak up 8%, leave 2% to guess what you're thinking" (Gareis, 1995, p. 121).

Concerning topic selection and levels of directness, many rhetorical decisions have to be made. Interactants from contrasting cultures usually recognize the differences but often find it difficult to appreciate and adjust to the opposing rhetorical style.

### Commonalities

Considering findings on dissimilarities between cultures, one could be tempted to assume that commonalities are difficult to find in intercultural contact. However, recent research has shown that attitudinal similarity in friendship formation is a much stronger variable than cultural similarity and even language competence (Kim, 1991). In general, pronounced and developed persuasions (opinions, attitudes, and values) and strong interests override other considerations and open the door for meaningful and relatively uncomplicated interaction (Hammer, 1989; Lee & Boster, 1991; Paige, 1983).

It may therefore seem that, given a similarity in persuasions and interest, initiating friendship may not be as difficult as expected. Persuasions and strong interests, however, are more a construct of Western, individualistic cultures than collectivistic cultures of the East. In Chinese society as well as neighboring cultures, for example, the postulates of Confucianism have implications that may complicate friendship formation in individualistic contexts. Thus, it is said that the focus on group harmony and role requirements prevalent in collectivistic cultures generate as side effects a rigidity in personality, stifled creativity, a lack of cognitive complexity, an inhibited verbal and ideational flow, and a perceived incapacity to influence events (Ho, 1986; Hoosain, 1986; Liu, 1986; Yang, 1986). Although these traits have positive effects on the emotional stability of the individual and on the stability of family and society, they also impede the development of persuasions and strong personal interests. Sojourners from collectivistic cultures may therefore be at a disadvantage when it comes to forming friendships in the United States where creativity, opinions, and assertiveness are valued and where the absence thereof is not attractive to many Americans. In an attempt to bridge the gap, a student from India suggests that intercultural curiosity should be added to the factors that influence friendship formation:

> They showed an interest in me . . . they just wanted to know. That in itself is kind of rare, because kids over here don't really care. They don't care what happens here in the States or around the world. . . . There's a total lack of interest. But when you meet somebody who has no idea but who would like to learn, and they want to share things, and they see the same things in you, that is when you click. (Gareis, 1995, p. 98)

When intercultural curiosity is present in both sojourner and native speaker, communication is greatly facilitated and obstacles are diminished. However, if this curiosity is not mutual or not fully developed, differences in the rhetoric of persuasions and interests can cause frustration and can result in the premature termination of the relationship.

## Gender and Discourse

In addition to philosophical orientations, intercultural friendship formation is influenced by differences in gender-related discourse. In India, for example, intimacy levels between heterosexual men are markedly different from those in the United States. Even though women and men are traditionally more separated than in the United States and are not allowed to intermingle as much (Lannoy, 1971), levels of self-disclosure and nurturance are similar in both sexes (Berman, Murphy-Berman, & Pachauri, 1988). Thus, Indian men are as free as women to form intimate friendships with revelation of deep feelings, failures, and worries and to show their affection physically by holding hands, for example (Berman, Murphy-Berman, & Pachauri, 1988; Brown, 1986; Roland, 1986). Berman, Murphy-Berman, and Pachauri comment on the phenomenon:

> At first this seems surprising. One thinks of the United States as a "liberated," androgynous society in which roles for males and females are increasingly merging and becoming less and less distinct. On the other hand, one thinks of India as a place where sex roles are very traditional and highly differentiated. The answer to this puzzle may be found . . . in the role that males are allowed to play in each society. Because Indian males are allowed a full gamut of emotional expression, they can provide all functions and activities of friendship to each other, unlike their U.S. counterparts who cannot provide some of the functions (e.g., problem sharing) or engage in some of the activities (e.g., private conversations). (p. 69-70)

A student from India explains that "back in India, whether you're a man or woman, you always want to feel or touch people. . . . You can't do that over here, you can't touch men over here" (Gareis, 1995, p. 101). He mentions an occurrence when he sat next to a male American friend and in conversation put his hand on this friend's knee. For him it was merely a coincidental gesture without sexual connotations; his American friend, however, was rather surprised, if not taken aback. The greater show of affection among heterosexual men is not limited to India. Many cultures allow physical contact—a fact that frequently leads to misunderstandings when new sojourners arrive in the United States unaware of the differences.

With respect to women, researchers note that women in some cultures are not meant to have friends but get their support from kin and neighbors instead (Du Bois, 1974). In addition, Asian women have often traditionally been educated not to open conversations and initiate contact (Tjioe, 1972). Differences between the sexes and their interactions in same- and cross-sex relationships are vast even within one culture. The amount of negotiation it takes to coordinate expectations is multiplied in intercultural contact. Issues such as communication between heterosexual men and friendship strategies of women often have rhetorical significance and need to be resolved if the relationship is to proceed.

### *Language Proficiency*

Even if interactants come to a cultural understanding, language difficulties can greatly inhibit friendship formation. A Chinese student, for example, states that "it's much easier to talk to a friend from the same culture. . . . You don't need to explain so much and lose the fun part. On the deep level it's hard to explain cross-culturally." Related to this factor, she observes that

"Americans are not patient" with Asians, who often speak at a slow speed, and that Asians "are not very aggressive" in standing up for themselves and insisting on being heard. Thus, she advises foreign students, "If you need to say something, just go ahead and say, no matter how bad your English is . . . you need courage. Don't be scared. Some people might not be interested in you, but some people, they may want to be friends with you. . . . Try" (Gareis, 1995, p. 114).

The student is not alone with her observation about impatient Americans. Sojourners often remark that Americans should show more sensitivity by adjusting their rate of speech and vocabulary selection, increasing their listening skills, and avoiding paternalisms (such as baby talk or higher volume during communication difficulties) (Strom, 1988). To give a counterexample, a German student describes American friends who were patient with him at the beginning of his stay in the United States:

> The most important thing is that they showed me they are willing to sit down—especially at the beginning when you weren't as fluent and when you had many more problems not just with the language but also with the environment, with the culture—they could make some time to teach you something. They were willing to help you out. (Gareis, 1995, p. 84)

He feels that Americans who are open for intercultural friendships tend to "treat you in an equal manner; it's not like they are superior just because they have this language advantage or they know more about America" (Gareis, 1995, p. 84).

### Cultural Knowledge

With the lack of specific cultural knowledge about the United States (e.g., details about past political events, old TV shows, childhood and teenage practices), foreigners often find it difficult to participate fully in conversations. According to a German student, some Americans are able to adjust to this lack of knowledge on the part of the nonnative speaker and help bridge the gap. These interculturally sensitive Americans "come down to your level so that one can communicate on the same base." The student states that if an American somehow tries "to tell these things [specific cultural knowledge] in such a manner that he [she] invokes an interest in you, and you can respond to it by telling about your experience, then it's much easier to start and become friends." Americans with such a patient predisposition are "willing to listen . . . even if it doesn't make much sense or if it takes a long time to express certain things" (Gareis, 1995, p. 84).

Cultural knowledge is also important for understanding humor. Much of humor (in movies and jokes and on TV) is based on cultural knowledge or current events that are unfamiliar to new sojourners. Yet a sense of humor plays an important part in communication and is attractive in the process of friendship formation. Unfortunately, humor is not easy to understand across cultures, even when it is not based on cultural or current information. A Taiwanese student, for example, recounts asking an American friend whether she could borrow a certain trinket for a class presentation. Knowing her as an honest and dependable person, he jokingly said no, pretending that she had taken and not returned many things in his house. The student, however, did not understand the irony, got very upset, and unbeknownst to the friend "cried for many days" until the matter was clarified (Gareis, 1995, p. 126).

### Communication in Established Friendships

The nature of rhetorical requirements shifts when relationships move from the initiation to the maintenance stage. It appears that once friendships are formed, differences in culture become secondary. Gudykunst, Nishida, and Chua (1987) explain this phenomenon by delineating four stages of social penetration: orientation, exploratory affective exchange, affective exchange, and stable exchange. Close friendship occurs during the affective and stable exchange stages. Whereas cultural and sociological data play a role during initial contact and often introduce problematic intercultural complexities, cultural dissimilarities have little impact once people move to the friendship stage. In this stage, intra- as well as intercultural interactions have a person-alistic focus, that is, each person is treated uniquely, predictions are based on psychological data, and cultural stereotypes are broken down (Gudykunst, 1985).

Further supporting the notion that cultural factors may retreat into the background in established intercultural friendships, Argyle and Henderson (1984), in a study involving subjects from four locales (Great Britain, Italy, Hong Kong, and Japan), found a set of friendship rules that were endorsed across cultures. The rules include sharing news of success, showing emotional support, volunteering help in time of need, striving to make the other person happy while in each other's company, trusting and confiding in each other, and standing up for the other person in their absence.

In established friendships, personal differences between the interactants are therefore more significant than cultural differences. Some of these personal differences may be based on preferences for interaction patterns. Mitchell (1986), for example, found four prevalent friendship types among adult friendships. The first type is labeled expressive-confirming, which encompasses friendships that focus on conversation rather than activity and that are usually maintained through separation and change. The second cluster is called active-affirming and is characterized by activity and external affirmation of skills, behavior, and progress. The third type is named possessive-ambivalent; individuals with this disposition tend to find separation or changes difficult and show a high level of jealousy. The last pattern is termed competitive-accepting, and friendships in this cluster are marked by both shared activities and conversation and by a high level of conflict resolution. Thus, it is possible that interactants from different cultural backgrounds may have similar communication and interaction styles and therefore constitute promising matches across cultural lines.

Similar to preferences for friendship types, needs for independence and intimacy may deviate from intracultural tendencies but correspond across cultures. Contradicting the stereotypical picture of dissatisfied sojourners in the United States, for example, most international respondents in a study by Gareis (1995) reported contentment with their American friends. Some of the respondents were satisfied because they as well as their friends had high intimacy needs and spent much time sharing thoughts and feelings; others were satisfied because they as well as their friends had low needs for intimacy and were quite content doing sports and other activities together without much self-revelation and emotional nurturance.

Even though established friendships are more personalistic, however, cultural differences may still enter the picture and cause at least some confusion. A student from India, for example, explains that his home culture differs from the United States in that friends in India socialize in groups, spend time together on a daily basis, and may call or visit each other at any time. He elaborates on the differences but also mentions some drawbacks of friendship in India:

> I think people have more time for friends because the way of life is not as fast-paced. . . . You can do things with your friends. . . . You're expected in a way to be more than surface friends. Friendship over there, I mean really true, deep friendship is for your whole life. It's not something you can keep three or five years and then say 'Okay, that's it; I'm ready to get out.' It's like, you choose your circle of friends, but then you expect that they be true to you and you in turn faithful to them. It can be a bit too intense sometimes—that's the other side of the coin, I guess. . . . You can feel a sense of suffocation. There sometimes doesn't exist the choice of having your own space as we have over here . . . that's one point which I don't really care so much for. You have to tell your friend what you've been doing, who you've been seeing, especially if they're part of the same circle. . . . It's like you have to do things with the same people all the time . . . whereas over here, you can have your gang but at the same time you can have friends of your own, and you don't always have to be together. (Gareis, 1995, p. 99)

Needless to say, the friendship pattern this student describes is not easily translated into U.S. contexts. In fact, a person exhibiting the listed characteristics would in all likelihood be evaluated negatively as a "clinging vine" who fears rejection, lacks independence, and is therefore not desirable as a friend (Ambrester & Strause, 1984).

In line with this student's comment on the relatively short duration of some American friendships, the U.S. researcher Brown (1986, p. 12) explains that some friendships are terminated with the drying up of a single common interest. He states that many friendships in the United States are a "series of times together into which topics are stuffed, and when the topic has fallen flat or the available topics have been exhausted, the relationship becomes boring" and is often discarded.

## STRATEGIES INFLUENCING FRIENDSHIP FORMATION

In an intracultural study by Miell and Duck (1986), college students reported that they would be more likely to pursue a friendship with someone who was easy to talk to (in addition to being available, similar, trustworthy, and easygoing). A survey of 30 ESL teachers furnishes similar results (Gareis, 1997). Sharing their observations concerning language ability and intercultural friendship formation, the teachers report that Americans often shy away from the extra effort it takes to communicate with a nonnative speaker. Pronunciation is singled out by several respondents as the greatest obstacle. One teacher explains,

> Americans will put up with listening to a sentence with grammar errors if the pronunciation of the words is clear—but few of our students are easy to understand. Americans are just not patient enough to be sympathetic interlocutors. (Gareis, 1997)

Other respondents add that a lack of fluency and vocabulary gets "tiring after a while" and that one can see why native speakers give up when "it becomes so much work to communicate" (Gareis, 1997).

With respect to their own intercultural friendships, the teachers have different experiences. Many comment on friendships with students and remark that such friendships are complicated because roles become confused and overlap. Many of the teachers have been approached by students who "wanted free English lessons" and were using the teachers to improve their English. One teacher describes his experience.

> They [nonnative speakers] would say, "I want to be your friend; let's speak in English/please teach me English." The pragmatic force in this utterance was very clear: They were more interested in my English than in me. We would call them "English hounds." (Gareis, 1997)

Another teacher adds that she has met "many students who want to make American friends [but] you get the feeling they are just targeting people because of their nationality," not because they have much in common.

For other teachers, the problem is not so much the instrumental nature of some students' pursuit of friendship but the problem of having to adjust their communication patterns to the needs of nonnative speakers. They are willing to do so in the classroom, but they desire a repose in their leisure time. As one teacher puts it:

> In my own close friendships, language ability is very important. I have very little time for friendships, very few friends, and I want to have long-term friendships, not many many short or long-distance friendships. Because I'm careful to speak clearly when I'm teaching, I like to slip into slang, cultural associations, informalities when I'm not. I like to relax with friends, and gaps in understanding are not relaxing. (Gareis, 1997)

Most respondents, however, were satisfied with a less accomplished degree of proficiency and did not consider native-like fluency and accuracy necessary for successful intercultural friendships. Presupposing a certain level of communicative ability, respondents detail specific strategies employed by nonnative speakers that hinder or aid friendship formation with Americans.

### *Obstacles to Friendship Formation*

One of the biggest obstacles to friendship formation, according to the teachers surveyed, is that sojourners are often too demanding on the time and attention of the native speaker. Drawing from their own experiences, teachers report that sojourners who approach them with a desire for friendship often "demand too much of my time too soon," are "too intense," "tend to be overwhelming," and are "too clingy." Some respondents also remark that, at times, near strangers ask them for "friendship." One teacher describes his reaction:

> Probably . . . anytime someone says they want to be friends, before a basis of friendship has been established, it implies the other person is obligated regardless. I would probably respond by offering a nebulous suggestion to meet sometime and then firmly avoid the person. (Gareis, 1997)

Many teachers also report that the content of conversations, if unsatisfactory or inappropriate, can cause a loss of interest. One respondent, for example, complains that some sojourners

> want daily contact. . . . [They] may have nothing new to say but want to phone and chat anyway. My U.S. friends tend to call less often when they need to discuss a particular problem, ask a favor, catch up with what's new or feel lonely. (Gareis, 1997)

Another informant points out that phone conversations are also problematic, because misunderstandings occur more frequently than in face-to-face interaction. Limited to one channel of communication, interactants cannot use facial expressions, gestures, or graphic means to express themselves. Interlocutors are often not versed in verbal clarification (including isolating causes for miscommunication, careful articulation, paraphrasing) and can therefore become frustrated with the comprehension difficulties that ensue.

Other teachers remark that nonnative speakers in the United States frequently ask too many questions (of both linguistic and personalistic content) and share too little, making interchanges one-sided. One respondent stresses that it is very important to "have an ongoing conversation" during the initial stages of friendship formation; another teacher suggests that, to do so, foreign interlocutors should

> go with the flow of the conversation and not try to question everything they don't understand. They also have to participate in the conversation and not make it like pulling teeth for the person carrying the brunt of the conversation. (Gareis, 1997)

One technique employed by native speakers to make conversations engaging and to share themselves is telling stories. Nonnative speakers, however, are often not familiar with effective storytelling techniques and thus lose out on an important part of interaction (McCarthy, 1991).

When involved in a conversation, sojourners should also be careful to avoid taboo topics. Some teachers mention that they are often asked improper questions. One informant, for example, reports that "Asian students . . . have a tendency to grill a new acquaintance mercilessly about everything from their weight to how much money they make." Another teacher adds that

> something really important is knowing what not to say. Like, "You are fatter than the last time I saw you" or "What's wrong with you? You look tired" or "Why don't you have children?" or maybe "Why did you get divorced?" Especially at the beginning of friendship. (Gareis, 1997)

Some teachers have similar feelings about criticism of the United States by nonnative speakers and the glorification of their home cultures. One teacher explains, "I've met students who have failed at forming a friendly relationship with me because they've over-criticized my culture! I get tired of listening to how violent and unfriendly and greedy Americans all are." Another teacher adds, "My friends from other cultures are bent on showing me that their culture is better, and it gets exhausting to let them know that their culture is fine without belaboring the point. Or trying to defend the United States" (Gareis, 1997).

Informants also mentioned that a nonnative speaker's failure to find the right balance between formality and informality or between directness and indirectness can be a turnoff in the initial stages of intercultural friendship formation. One teacher asserts that some sojourners "overdo formality or informality." Other teachers mention that nonnative speakers are either too polite or impolite. One informant elaborates:

> I think failing to use polite forms of language, especially when expressing something negative, could hinder friendship. As a teacher, sometimes I hear "give me my homework" or "you should teach this." Personally, I don't like to hear command language, even when I understand the person intends politeness. (Gareis, 1997)

Analyzing the question of politeness, some teachers single out incorrect modal use as the main cause. One respondent, for example, theorizes that the "lack of correct modal use . . . may make the initial encounters too direct or indirect (depending on the culture and the level of grammatical control and vocabulary knowledge)" (Gareis, 1997). Another teacher asserts that "the use of modals . . . can make [nonnative speakers] appear too bossy or too weak"; she warns that some "forms of communication [like incorrect modal use] send the average American's defense mechanism into orbit" and advises that "modals like *must* [for example] should be used sparingly" (Gareis, 1997).

In addition to conversation content, issues of conversation management are important. Teachers list knowledge of conversation openers, small talk, and closings as often absent in nonnative speakers' discourse. Foreign interlocutors in search of American friendship also need to know how to maintain conversations with as much naturalness as possible. One teacher mentions that the long pauses common in some nonnative speech patterns are distracting and make the speaker appear unenthusiastic. Another teacher recounts an example for a similar image problem related to listening skills:

> One student once told me about a communication problem she discovered. She didn't have the American habit of giving constant reinforcement to the other speaker with *Umhmms* and *reallys* etc. She just listened silently. The American got a little bit irritated and asked "Are you listening?" (Gareis, 1997)

Other teachers list clarification and turn-taking strategies as conversation elements often missing in nonnative discourse. In addition, knowledge of language functions related to expressing emotions (e.g., expressing joy or compassion, accepting compliments) are mentioned as important ingredients of interpersonal contact that are too often lacking in the repertoire of foreign sojourners.

Last, but not least, respondents comment that idioms, slang, colloquialisms, and humor can be obstacles in the development of intercultural relationships. As language teachers, they are aware of difficult vocabulary items or cultural information that may be unfamiliar to nonnative speakers of certain proficiency levels. Most teachers adjust their language accordingly when they communicate with people from other cultures and do so willingly. Americans without experience in language teaching or intercultural communication, however, are not as acquiescent and find it difficult to interact with nonnative speakers. One of the respondents provides this example:

> I asked my husband this question. He is not an ESL teacher. He finds it difficult that his international friends and coworkers don't understand slang and colloquialisms. I hadn't thought about this since I'm so accustomed to avoiding them with students. But this can be a big hindrance to the communication of humor, which is an important way that my husband communicates. (Gareis, 1997)

### Strategies Aiding Friendship Formation

To counterbalance the list of communication factors that hinder intercultural friendship formation, teachers also point out strategies that aid nonnative speakers in the process (Gareis, 1997). The ability to initiate contact is at the top of the list. Successful sojourners are not only willing "to make mistakes" but also willing "to risk rejection and just try to strike up conversations." They do not wait for Americans to come to them but "take the initiative, suggesting activities, involving others, reaching out. In doing so, they sometimes appear to be forsaking their own culture, not spending much time with compatriots." They also show "willingness to try to fit in a bit—not always insist their culture is better—to at least try to see the American point of view and do some thing the 'American' way."

In line with research findings on positivity in interpersonal communication in the United States (Canary & Stafford, 1994), one teacher gives the following advice: "Be positive. Show enthusiasm for something you are doing. Do not walk away from a conversation with an acceptable candidate for friendship without trying to arrange an activity or future conversation with the person" (Gareis, 1997). Similarly, another teacher encourages nonnative speakers to smile and "be friendly and completely unconcerned about how others react. . . . As long as [the sojourner] can exude warmth, cheerfulness, and interest without care as to whether individuals return that friendliness or not, [he or she] is successful" (Gareis, 1997).

In addition, "flexible attitudes" and an "open mind" toward the culture are mentioned as elements aiding intercultural friendship formation. One teacher also asserts that cultural knowledge and sensitivity may override linguistic prowess. As an example, she mentions the controversial differentiation between friendliness and friendship in the United States:

> I think cultural sensitivity is much more important than linguistic skills (though both are of course necessary). Students are too easily misled into thinking that

because Americans are generally friendly, relaxed, and helpful when meeting someone, they want to be friends—and instantly. This isn't true; in general, Americans make a clear distinction (and separation!) between being friendly and being friends. Students take a long time to pick up on this. (Gareis, 1997)

## IMPLICATIONS

When taking into account the communication issues raised by foreign students in the United States as well as by ESL teachers, a number of rhetorical strategies emerge as helpful for intercultural friendship formation. The following suggestions are advanced to aid nonnative speakers in search of American friends.

- Be aware that the term *friend* has different levels of meaning in American English and that friendliness alone does not denote friendship.
- Don't wait for Americans to approach you. Initiate contact by suggesting activities, involving others, and reaching out.
- Don't walk away from a promising first encounter without trying to make plans.
- Be willing to risk rejection. Project a positive, cheerful, and warm image.
- Don't ask whether you can be someone's friend early in a relationship. Let the relationship develop naturally.
- Seek friendship with people for their personal merits, not because of their nationality or because they can help you improve your English.
- Be aware of different perceptions of time and intensity in interpersonal relationships. Avoid being too demanding of the American's time and attention.
- Learn to understand and use functions of American English related to interpersonal communication: greetings, conversation openers and closings, small talk, expressing emotions, accepting compliments, and so forth. Specifically learn which expressions are of a formulaic nature and should not be taken literally (e.g., *See you later, Let's get together sometime*).
- Familiarize yourself with conversation-management strategies, specifically how to take turns, how to pause effectively, and how to give reinforcements.
- Try to make conversations smooth and reciprocal. Don't ask too many questions; instead, participate actively, reciprocate self-disclosure, and share your own experiences and opinions.
- Learn how to tell stories effectively in order to engage your conversation partners.
- Be aware of the appropriate level of politeness and directness. Learn to use modals correctly, especially when expressing something negative or when uttering a request.
- Avoid being too formal or too informal. Avoid taboo topics (such as questions about someone's weight, salary, or marital status).
- Develop effective strategies for conversing on the phone. Don't call too frequently if there is nothing new to share.

- Learn strategies for verbal clarification of misunderstandings (e.g., determining causes for miscommunication, repeating with better enunciation, paraphrasing).
- Don't criticize U.S. culture too often or glorify your home culture. Keep an open mind and flexible attitudes toward the host culture.
- Don't compare your home culture to U.S. culture unless there is a clear interest on the part of your conversation partner.
- Learn about U.S. culture so that you may understand cultural references and nonverbal cues in interacting with native speakers. Specifically, familiarize yourself with differences in space requirements and touching behavior.
- Strive for good pronunciation and fluency.
- Strive for a workable vocabulary. Familiarize yourself with idioms, slang expressions, and colloquialisms.
- Learn about U.S. humor and the background information necessary to understand it (including current events, pop culture, common stereotypes).
- Be confident and willing to risk mistakes.

## CONCLUSION

Intercultural friendship is a little-researched field of communication studies. Many factors influencing the formation of close relationships across cultures are not yet clearly delineated. As some informants in the teacher survey suggest, cultural sensitivity and personality, for example, may be variables outweighing language proficiency in the successful formation of intercultural friendships. Another factor, and perhaps the least tangible of all, is what we may term *chemistry,* defined as a "strong mutual attraction, attachment, or sympathy" (*Merriam-Webster's,* p. 196); the usage example given is "matching personalities or some other special chemistry or vibes to make the relationship click" (p. 231). Probably because of its vague and nonphysical nature, the concept has received only minimal attention in the research literature. Thus, only two references with a more or less cursory mention of the subject could be found. In a phenomenological paper, Dziegielewska (1988) sketches friendship as an "invisible bond" (p. 67) and notes that "what draws us into the relationship that deserves the name friendship . . . [is] an interest in the essential person of the other" (p. 59). A more explicit analysis of the concept in its broadest psychical sense is provided by Chang and Holt (1991) in their description of the Buddhist concept of *yuan,* or secondary causation. In Buddhist philosophy, "any relationship has its roots in uncounted numbers of lifetimes and is situated in a complex web of interdependent causative factors that are outside the control, or even the comprehension of the human mind" (p. 34). Thus, when two individuals meet, their karmic selves, built up through these lifetimes, meet, and it is *yuan* that will determine who will be involved with whom, to what degree, in what kind of relationship, and how long. Having *yuan* with another person means that the conditions are right for the meeting. Out of many contacts, only a few have *yuan.* When there is a lot of *yuan,* the relationship will last for a long time, but even the smallest such encounters are important and might have been prepared for thousands of years. *Yuan,* of course, cannot be forced; one must wait until conditions are right. By the same token, however, two individuals will meet if they are destined to, even if thousands of miles apart. If correct, this Buddhist concept, as well as the similar American notion of chemistry, is thus ultimately responsible for whether a relationship will come to fruition or not. Consequently, even if all other factors are favorable, the final decisive force behind friendship formation lies with the presence or absence of this last intangible factor.

As the intangibility of the last factor, chemistry, shows, it is necessary to remember that a logical and comprehensive compilation of knowledge does not suffice to explain friendship or any other complex concept involving whole beings and their intricate connections and interdependencies (Dziegielewska, 1988). Not only do individuals belong to multiple discourse systems through ethnic, generational, gender, and other group or personal differences (Scollon & Scollon, 1995), some of the factors influencing friendship formation also remain indefinable.

## REFERENCES

Althen, G. (1988). *American ways: A guide for foreigners in the United States.* Yarmouth, ME: Intercultural Press.

Althen, G. (1995). *The handbook of foreign student advising.* Yarmouth, ME: Intercultural Press.

Ambrester, M. L., & Strause, G. H. (1984). *A rhetoric of interpersonal communication.* Prospect Heights, IL: Waveland Press.

Argyle, M., & Henderson, M. (1984). The rules of friendship. *Journal of Social and Personal Relationships, 1,* 211-237.

Bell, R. R. (1981). *Worlds of friendship.* Beverly Hills, CA: Sage.

Bennett, M. J. (1986). A developmental approach to training for intercultural sensitivity. *International Journal of Intercultural Relations, 10,* 179-196.

Berman, J. J., Murphy-Berman, V., & Pachauri, A. (1988). Sex differences in friendship patterns in India and in the United States. *Basic and Applied Social Psychology, 9,* 61-71.

Blieszner, R., & Adams, R. G. (1992). *Adult friendship.* Newbury Park, CA: Sage.

Brown, R. H. (1986). Self and polity in India and the United States. In R. H. Brown & G. V. Coelho (Eds.), *Studies in third world societies: Vol. 38. Tradition and transformation: Asian Indians in America* (pp. 1-25). Williamsburg, VA: Department of Anthropology, College of William and Mary.

Canary, D. J., & Stafford, L. (1994). Maintaining relationships through strategic and routine interaction. In D. J. Canary & L. Stafford (Eds.), *Communication and relational maintenance* (pp. 3-22). San Diego, CA: Academic Press.

Chang, H. C., & Holt, G. R. (1991). The concept of yuan and Chinese interpersonal relationships. In S. Ting-Toomey & F. Korzenny (Eds.), *Cross-cultural interpersonal communication* (pp. 28-57). Newbury Park, CA: Sage.

Du Bois, C. (1956). *Foreign students and higher education in the United States.* Washington, DC: American Council on Education.

Du Bois, C. (1974). The gratuitous act: An introduction to the comparative study of friendship patterns. In E. Leyton (Ed.), *The compact: Selected dimensions of friendship* (pp. 15-32). Toronto, Canada: University of Toronto Press.

Dziegielewska, J. (1988). The intercultural dimension of friendship: A study in the phenomenology of communication. *Dissertation Abstracts International, 50,* 301A. (University Microfilms No. 8909316)

Fehr, B. (1996). *Friendship processes.* Thousand Oaks, CA: Sage.

Gareis, E. (1995). *Intercultural friendship: A qualitative study.* Lanham, MD: University Press of America.

Gareis, E. (1997). [Intercultural friendship: Observations and experiences of teachers of English as a second language]. Unpublished raw data.

Gudykunst, W. B. (1985). An exploratory comparison of close intracultural and intercultural friendships. *Communication Quarterly, 33,* 270-283.

Gudykunst, W. B., & Nishida, T. (1986). Attributional confidence in low- and high-context cultures. *Human Communication Research, 12,* 525-549.

Gudykunst, W. B., Nishida, T., & Chua, E. (1987). Perceptions of social penetration in Japanese-North American dyads. *International Journal of Intercultural Relations, 11,* 171-189.

Gudykunst, W. B., Ting-Toomey, S., & Nishida, T. (Eds.). (1996). *Communication in personal relationships across cultures.* Thousand Oaks, CA: Sage.

Hammer, M. R. (1989). Intercultural communication competence. In M. K. Asante & W. B. Gudykunst (Eds.), *Handbook of international and intercultural communication* (pp. 247-260). Newbury Park, CA: Sage.

Ho, D. Y. F. (1986). Chinese patterns of socialization: A critical review. In M. H. Bond (Ed.), *The psychology of the Chinese people* (pp. 1-37). Hong Kong: Oxford University Press.

Hoosain, R. (1986). Perceptual processes of the Chinese. In M. H. Bond (Ed.), *The psychology of the Chinese people* (pp. 38-72). Hong Kong: Oxford University Press.

Kim, H. J. (1991). Influence of language and similarity on initial intercultural attraction. In S. Ting-Toomey & F. Korzenny (Eds.), *Cross-cultural interpersonal communication* (pp. 213-229). Newbury Park, CA: Sage.

Lanier, A. R. (1996). *Living in the U.S.A.* (5th ed.). Yarmouth, ME: Intercultural Press.

Lannoy, R. (1971). *The speaking tree: A study of Indian culture and society.* New York: Oxford University Press.

Lee, H. O., & Boster, F. J. (1991). Social information for uncertainty reduction during initial interactions. In S. Ting-Toomey & F. Korzenny (Eds.), *Cross-cultural interpersonal communication* (pp. 189-212). Newbury Park, CA: Sage.

Lewin, K. (1948). Some social-psychological differences between the United States and Germany. In K. Lewin (Ed.), *Resolving social conflict* (pp. 3-33). New York: Harper.

Liu, I. M. (1986). Chinese cognition. In M. H. Bond (Ed.), *The psychology of the Chinese people* (pp. 73-105). Hong Kong: Oxford University Press.

Matthews, S. H. (1986). *Friendships through the life course: Oral biographies in old age.* Beverly Hills, CA: Sage.

McCarthy, M. (1991). *Discourse analysis for language teachers.* New York: Cambridge University Press.

*Merriam-Webster's collegiate dictionary* (10th ed.). (1998). Springfield, MA: Merriam-Webster.

Miell, D., & Duck, S. (1986). Strategies in developing friendships. In V. J. Derlega & B. A. Winstead (Eds.), *Friendship and social interaction* (pp. 129-143). New York: Springer-Verlag.

Mitchell, C. (1986). Adult friendship patterns: The implications of autonomy, connection and gender. *Dissertation Abstracts International, 47,* 382B. (University Microfilms No. 8606859)

Oberg, K. (1979). Culture shock and the problem of adjustment in new cultural environments. In E. C. Smith & L. F. Luce (Eds.), *Toward internationalism: Readings in cross-cultural communication* (pp. 43-45). Rowley, MA: Newbury House.

Paige, R. M. (1983). Cultures in contact: On intercultural relations among American and foreign students in the United States university context. In D. Landis & R. W. Brislin (Eds.), *Handbook of intercultural training: Vol. 3* (pp. 102-129). New York: Pergamon Press.

Pogrebin, L. C. (1987). *Among friends.* New York: McGraw-Hill.

Rawlins, W. K. (1992). *Friendship matters: Communication, dialectics, and the life course.* New York: de Gruyter.

Roland, A. (1986). The Indian self: Reflections in the mirror of American life. In R. H. Brown & G. V. Coelho (Eds.), *Studies in third world societies: Vol. 38. Tradition and transformation: Asian Indians in America* (pp. 43-52). Williamsburg, VA: Department of Anthropology, College of William and Mary.

Rubin, L. B. (1985). *Just friends: The role of friendship in our lives.* New York: Harper & Row.

Schaffer, R. H., & Dowling, L. R. (1966). *Foreign student friends.* (Cooperative Research Project No. 5-0806). Bloomington: Indiana University. (ERIC Document Reproduction Service No. ED 010 008)

Scollon, R., & Scollon, S. W. (1995). *Intercultural communication: A discourse approach.* Cambridge, MA: Blackwell.

Stewart, E. C., & Bennett, M. J. (1991). *American cultural patterns: A cross-cultural perspective.* Yarmouth, ME: Intercultural Press.

Strom, W. O. (1988). Cross-cultural friendships on the university campus: Testing the functional and identity validation models (Doctoral dissertation, University of Iowa, 1988). *Dissertation Abstracts International, 49,* 3204A.

Ting-Toomey, S. (1989). Identity and interpersonal bonding. In M. K. Asante & W. B. Gudykunst (Eds.), *Handbook of international and intercultural communication* (pp. 351-373). Newbury Park, CA: Sage.

Tjioe, L. E. (1972). *Asiaten über Deutsche: Kulturkonflikte ostasiatischer Studentinnen in der Bundesrepublik* [Asians about Germans: Cultural conflicts of female East Asian students in the Federal Republic of Germany]. Frankfurt am Main, Germany: Thesen Verlag.

Yang, K. S. (1986). Chinese personality and its change. In M. H. Bond (Ed.), *The psychology of the Chinese people* (pp. 106-170). Hong Kong: Oxford University Press.

# 10

# Water-Related Figurative Language in the Rhetoric of Mencius

RINGO MA • *State University of New York, Fredonia*

The status of Confucianism as the orthodox philosophy in China can be traced back about 2,000 years (Fairbank & Reischauer, 1973). Confucianism has also entered three other cultural areas since its rise in China: Japan, Korea, and Vietnam (Tu, Hejtmanek, & Wachman, 1992, p. 109). Despite the iconoclastic attack on Confucianism during the May Fourth Movement beginning in 1919 and in the Communist ideology, a revival of Confucianism was reported in China recently (Ching, 1994; Tu et al., 1992, pp. 102-103).

Some scholars attribute the dominance of the Confucian doctrine in ancient China to the advocacy of Mencius (e.g., Oliver, 1971, p. 161; Pye, 1984; Suzuki, 1914, p. 64). According to Pye,

> Possibly the fate of Confucianism was determined by Mencius, a later disciple also from the state of Lu, who lived from 373 to 288 B.C. and devoted his life to spreading the thoughts of his master. He too wandered from state to state, preaching good government, seeking to advise rulers, and helping to establish the legitimacy of Confucian doctrines. (p. 40)

The heavy influence of Confucianism on communication in East Asia has been addressed in previous research (e.g., Bond & Hwang, 1986; Chang & Holt, 1991; Lee & Campbell, 1994; Yum, 1988). However, the rhetoric of Mencius, which seems to have had a direct impact on the dissemination of Confucianism, has been investigated in only a few publications (e.g., Oliver, 1969, 1971). The purpose of this study is to analyze both the rhetoric of Mencius from a selected perspective and the social reality that his rhetoric attempted to construct. First, the water-related figurative language in the rhetoric of Mencius is identified. Second, the social reality that his discourse attempted to construct in the Chinese culture is discussed.

## CHINESE RHETORIC

Chinese rhetoric has been compared with its Western counterpart in previous research (e.g., Garrett, 1991, 1993a, 1993b; Garrett & Xiao, 1994; Lu, 1994; Oliver, 1961, 1969, 1971; Xiao, 1995, 1996). Xiao (1995) claims that at the end of the nineteenth century, rhetoric in some Western books was so culture bound that a Chinese translator had to "rhetorically" adapt some original arguments to his Chinese audience. Similarly, Tan Sitong had to search for "a meaningful way of mediating the Chinese and Western modes of experiences" in his book *A Study of Humanity,* which was written in 1896-1897 and has been referred to as the first Chinese "manifesto of egalitarianism" (Xiao, 1996, pp. 38-39). Garrett's (1991) examination of the rhetorical tradition in China yields that "the most powerful form of persuasion . . . was for persuaders to embody their beliefs in their own lives and persons" (p. 196). She also notes that, in ancient China, persuasion was usually targeted at one individual, usually the ruler (Garrett, 1991, 1993a). In dealing with this one-person audience, "the situational, psychological, and interpersonal factors often had much more bearing on success than the logical validity of the inferences" (Garrett, 1991, p. 299). This consideration in Classical Chinese rhetoric is also reported in Lu's (1994) study on the theory of persuasion developed by Han Fei Zi (Han Fei Tzu) in the third century before the common era.

## MENCIUS AND CONFUCIANISM

The hybridization of Confucianism, Taoism, and Buddhism constitutes the mainstream Chinese philosophy. Whereas Buddhism was imported from India, Confucianism and Taoism were deeply rooted in China. McAleavy (1967) contends that these can be viewed as three religions of China (p. 15). However, there is no superpower introduced in the original text of either Confucianism or Taoism. The Chinese version of Buddhism is not so exclusive as many religions in the West, so most Buddhists in China can worship their ancestors as well as the Buddha. None of the three explicitly prohibits people from affiliating with the other two religions. It also has been argued that Confucianism is more compatible with other traditions than most other religions are: "Confucianism is not a religion limited to a particular culture, race, or nationality. It is a dynamic force that flows, has different currents, and has the capacity to interact with other traditions in a pluralistic context" (Tu et al., 1992, p. 10).

The three religions, according to Chan (1953), "have been mutually penetrated, interrelated, and partially identified" and "have become 'three roads to the same destination,' as the Chinese people are fond of saying" (pp. 180-181).

Both Confucianism and Taoism promote social harmony, yet by different means. Taoism, according to Oliver (1961), sponsors a rhetoric emphasizing *wu-wei* (the avoidance of action), *wu-hsin* (negation of mind), and *te* (the principle of spontaneous functioning).[1] Confucianism, on the other hand, has prescribed moral codes for both individuals and governments. Confucian virtues include, but are not limited to, *jen,* or benevolence; *yi,* or righteousness; *hsin,* or faithfulness; and *li,* or propriety. *Jen* and *yi* have also been translated as, respectively, "humanity" and "justice" by Dobson (1963). Confucius urged people to adhere to the highest standards for five key role relationships—between ruler and subject, neighbor and neighbor, father and son, husband and wife, and brother and brother. Oliver (1971) states, "The central theme of Confucianism was that ethical conduct creates conditions that result in just and harmonious human relations" (p. 124). Yum (1988) further argues, "As a philosophy of humanism and social relations, Confucianism has left a strong impact on interpersonal relationships and on communication patterns [in East Asia]" (p. 374).

Mencius, the latinized form of the name *Meng Tzu,* was a prominent disciple of Confucius in the period of Warring States (403 to 222 B.C.), which, according to Garrett (1993a), "witnessed nearly-continuous and brutal warfare between many city-states struggling for hegemony, or less ambitiously, for survival" (p. 22). Garrett (1993a) also notes that "there was an especially intense and self-conscious interest in persuasion, argumentation, and social influence" because of the social and political instability of this period (p. 22). Chai and Chai (1961) write that the period of Warring States was "an age of feverish intellectual activity in which many schools of thought developed in a fantastic heterodoxy that . . . threatened to undermine orthodox Confucianism" (p. 50). The situation "provided the stimulus for Mencius' brilliant lifelong defense of Confucianism" (p. 50). Chai and Chai (1973), however, ascribe the successful development of Confucianism by Mencius largely to his idealistic approach:

> Before the end of the Chou Dynasty [1122? to 255 B.C.], several divisions of thought developed within the Confucian school . . . Mencius and Hsun Tzu, both great champions of the Confucian school, gave widely different versions of what Confucius taught, which ultimately led to the formation of two rival camps, the idealistic and the realistic. . . . The teachings of Mencius were akin to the whole rationale of Confucian thought, his temperament and philosophy being idealistic; while the major tenets of Hsun Tzu were obviously at odds with the Confucian orthodoxy, his temperament and philosophy being realistic. (p. 48)

During the period of Warring States, Mencius traveled to many states, including Liang, Yen, and Chi, trying to convince feudal lords as well as others to accept a key concept of Confucian political philosophy, "benevolent government." To meet challenges in a chaotic era, Mencius, in his dialogues with others, applied different rhetorical skills to promote the concept. For example, his use of analogies and examples has been discussed in previous studies (e.g., Lau, 1970, pp. 235-263; Oliver, 1971, p. 169; Richards, 1932, pp. 44-47). His argumentative style has also been noted. One of his disciples, Kung Tu, asked, "Master, the people beyond our school all speak of you as being fond of disputing. I venture to ask whether it be so." Mencius replied, "Indeed, I am not fond of disputing, but I am compelled to do it" (Legge, 1895, p. 279).[2] When comparing Mencius with Confucius, Legge holds that Mencius adopted a more "vehement" style in expressing his views (p. 47).

## WATER-RELATED FIGURATIVE LANGUAGE

The discourse of Mencius was recorded in the book that bears his name, the *Meng Tzu* (*The Works of Mencius*). The *Meng Tzu,* as one of the *Four Books* in traditional Confucian education in China, is believed to be the writing of Mencius himself and his disciples (e.g., Chai & Chai, 1973, p. 50; Fung, 1948, p. 68). A significant number of figures of speech (similes and metaphors) can be found in the *Meng Tzu.* A notable cluster among these figures of speech includes water-related imagery, such as "inundation," "rain," and the general term "water." These images were frequently used in association with power or superpower.

Ivie (1987) argues that "metaphor is at the base of rhetorical invention" (p. 166). Through clustering similar metaphors, the speaker's "system of metaphorical concepts" can be identified (p. 167). Foss (1989) indicates that metaphor is not just a decorative use of language; rather, it also "constructs a particular reality for us according to the terminology we choose for the description of reality" (p. 189). She also notes that by organizing reality in particular ways, our selected metaphors, which contain implicit assumptions, points of view, and evaluations, "prescribe how we are to act" (p. 189). Therefore, "metaphor does not simply provide support to an argument; the structure of the metaphor itself argues" (p. 190).

Although a complete investigation of the thought of Mencius and its differences from other Chinese philosophers is beyond the scope of this study, an examination of his water-related figures of speech should provide a good example and some insight into his rhetorical practice. The approach adopted in this paper thus includes an analysis of water-related figures of speech identified in the *Meng Tzu* based on Ivie's perspective on the use of metaphors.

Persuasion, as Burke (1950) notes, is an "identification" process (p. 21). Identification involves shared sensation, concepts, images, ideas, attitudes, and so forth among communicators (p. 21). Common experience or perception enables communicators to become "consubstantial" (p. 21). Water-related figurative language in the discourse of Mencius can first be viewed from this "identification" approach.

The choice of water-related figurative language by Mencius could be traced back to a shared legendary history. In China, the history before the Shang dynasty (1751 to 1111 B.C.) is treated as legendary because of the lack of written evidence. However, many legendary events are widely accepted. According to the legendary history, people suffered heavy casualties from inundation before the reputed founder of the Hsia dynasty, Yu, reduced the water to order (Fu, 1979, p. 11). As Mencius mentions in one of his dialogues, "In the time of Yao, when the world had not yet been perfectly reduced to order, the vast water, flowing out of their channels, made a universal inundation" (Legge, 1895, p. 250). On a different occasion, he mentions the same occurrence again: "In the time of Yao, the waters, flowing out of their channels, inundated the Middle Kingdom [the literal translation of China]" (Legge, p. 279).

Although stories of inundation or flood exist almost everywhere within the history of humanity, the one that Mencius remarked on was obviously a major one, in which the whole "universe" or "Middle Kingdom" sank into water. Not only could the flood inflict extreme tragedy on people, but it would also register as an irresistible superpower for them and their descendants. Mencius also notes, "It is said in the Book of History, 'The water in their wild course warned me.' Those 'waters in their wild course' were the waters of the great inundation" (Legge, p. 279). Despite the vagueness of the quotation, the inundation was a significant event in ancient China.

As noted by Cherwitz and Hikins (1983), people trying to communicate ideas can neither subjectively create nor objectively present the reality around them, and social interaction is just an exchange of different perceptions among them. In other words, people communicate based on their perceived reality. The "real" reality has little to do with people unless it becomes perceived. Similarly, whether the history of inundation was "real" was no longer important once it had become perceived by the general public. After the superpower of water was commonly perceived, *water* became a much more powerful word than it had been before.

An important theme in the dialogues between Mencius and others is that morality, including benevolence and righteousness, is the essential element of all truth. This perspective projected the following specific theme in the political context: "The benevolent has no enemy" (Legge, 1895, p. 136). Because of the special meaning that water had for his contemporaries, a skillful connection between the law of water and his law of morality could equate the two and make the former widely accepted. On one occasion,

Mencius mentioned the law of water directly: "Yu's regulation of the water was according to the laws of water . . ." (Legge, p. 443).

On other occasions, the law of water was implied and connected to the law of morality. For example, Mencius wrote,

> Now among the shepherds of men throughout the nation, there is not one who does not find pleasure in killing men. If there were one who did not find pleasure in killing men, all the people in the nation would look towards him with outstretched necks. Such being indeed the case, the people would flock to him, as water flows downwards with a rush, which no one can repress. (Legge, 1895, p. 137)

Other examples of water include, "The people turn to a benevolent rule as water flows downwards" (p. 300), "The tendency of man's nature to good is like the tendency of water to flow downwards" (p. 396), and "Benevolence subdues its opposite just as water subdues fire" (p. 420).

Differences among waters were also likened to differences among various people. In the following example, a person whose reputation was beyond his or her merits was compared to the water without spring:

> Suppose that the water has no spring—In the seventh and eighth months when the rain falls abundantly, the channels in the fields are all filled, but their being dried up again may be expected in a short time. So a superior man is ashamed of a reputation beyond his merits. (Legge, 1895, p. 325)

Furthermore, a moral leader, according to Mencius, is as captivating as the rain in a time of drought: "The people looked to him, as we look in a time of great drought to the clouds and rainbows. . . . His progress was like the falling of opportune rain, and the people were delighted" (Legge, 1895, p. 171). This statement was repeated a second time on a different occasion (Legge, p. 273). The water mentioned here explicitly represented power in a positive direction.

Ivie (1984) notes that the interplay of metaphor and logic constituted a major symbolic resource in Ronald Reagan's rhetorical efforts. According to Ivie (1984), Reagan used the metaphor of savagery and a set of decivilizing vehicles both to establish assumptions about Soviet conduct and to lead to his discussion of major issues of foreign affairs. Martin and Martin (1984) reveal implied arguments and rhetorical reinforcers as being two factors leading to the success of Barbara Jordan's speech given at a national women's conference. Implicitly expressed arguments and the schematic repetition of some words (rhetorical reinforcers), as argued by Martin and Martin, enabled Jordan to create shared perceptions and reassurances in her audience. Implied arguments in connection with repeated water-related figures of speech are also found in the discourse of Mencius. For example, take the "opportune rain"; the following logical sequence lay behind the statement:

1. The falling of opportune rain will be greatly appreciated by the people.
2. The (benevolent) deed of a leader is like the falling of opportune rain.
3. Therefore, the (benevolent) deed of a leader will be greatly appreciated by the people.

Through the shared meaning of water, Mencius used "opportune rain" to create a shared meaning of morality. The common experience served to bridge other gaps in perceptions. The figures of speech as reinforcers had deepened the conception of the statements and the referents that they sponsored. In other words, when water was interconnected with his proposal for action or his claim of truth, the latter became easily recognized and remembered.

Water-related figurative language has also elevated the main theme in the rhetoric of Mencius—"The benevolent has no enemy." By using figurative language, the ethical standards that he was advocating were raised in the auditor's mind to a level as significant as water. The real purpose, however, was to make his ethical standards transcend these figures of speech. These figures of speech provided a path for his auditor to appreciate his main theme, which was not to be replaced by water. To Mencius, although water is powerful, benevolence and righteousness are even more encompassing. One possessing these virtues would be able to solve any problem, including a disaster caused by water. The benevolent founder of the Hsia dynasty, Yu, for example, successfully reduced the water to order. Mencius describes the event as follows:

> Yu separated the nine streams, cleared the courses of the Tsi and Ta, and led them all to the sea. He opened a vent also for the Zu and Han, and regulated the course of the Hwai and Sze, so that they all flowed into the Chiang. When this was done, it became possible for the people of the Middle Kingdom to cultivate the ground and get food for themselves. (Legge, 1895, pp. 250-251)

That the virtues of a leader can gain dominance over the power of water was also mentioned in a dialogue Mencius had with the King Hsuan of Chi:

> Now the ruler of Yen was tyrannizing over his people, and your Majesty went and punished him. The people supposed that you were going to deliver them out of the water and the fire, and brought baskets of rice and vessels of congee, to meet your Majesty's host. (Legge, 1895, pp. 170-171)

Flood made people desert their homes. Tyranny forced people to betray their political leaders. Nevertheless, people could not always do what they wished to do, especially when they faced a powerful flood or tyrant. Only a benevolent leader could modify the exigency for them. The statement "to deliver them out of the water and the fire" implied that the benevolent leader could overcome the huge power of tyranny as well as the power of water. Instead of being resisted as an enemy, the benevolent leader would be treated as a leader of a relief team and sincerely welcomed. The power of water, in this situation, surrendered its first place to the power of morality.

According to Ivie (1984), the transcendence of the main theme over figures of speech can be a key to deciding whether the use of figures of speech by the rhetor is effective. Ronald Reagan's use of the metaphor of savagery in his speeches answered questions about the issue of foreign affairs (Ivie, 1984, pp. 39-50). The metaphor of savagery was, as Ivie (1984) states, not the final goal of Reagan's speeches. Through the use of theme metaphors, Reagan skillfully guided the audience to his main theme—how to maintain a strong America and face the Soviet threat. However, there is a major difference between Reagan's transcendence over the metaphor of savagery and that of Mencius over water-related figures of speech. The metaphor of savagery used in the former suggested a concept that the auditor had yet to identify, whereas water-related similes and metaphors in the latter were based on a common experience with water. In this sense, water-related similes and metaphors adopted by Mencius were more effective in transcending a main theme than was the metaphor of savagery for Reagan.

## WATER-RELATED FIGURATIVE LANGUAGE AND POLITICAL COMMUNICATION IN CHINA

As previously mentioned, whereas Confucianism has become the orthodox philosophy in China, for a long period of time the rhetoric of Mencius was an integral part of this philosophy. Most of his rhetoric was presented in a political context, so its influence on political thought in China has been persistent. For example, his water-related figurative language tends to guide the thinking of many Chinese on political affairs. The political thoughts derived from his water-related figurative language that have been predominant in China can be summarized as follows.

It is widely recognized that Mencius argued for the moral qualities of a leader and for the people's right to revolution in the case of an unethical sovereign (e.g., Legge, 1895, p. 167). Tu, Hejtmanek, and Wachman (1992) notes that Mencius, as a cultural elite in the Confucian tradition, "felt that he represented the conscience of society, and therefore the populace as a whole, whereas he saw the leader of the state as basically representing something like a private interest of a small group" (p. 132). Tu has also attributed the long history in China of student demonstrations to this cultural tradition (p. 132). The doctrine of Mencius is often transmitted through the sharing of his water-related figurative language. For example, it is commonly accepted that people would flock to a ruler who has no pleasure in killing, just as "water flows downwards with a rush, which no one can repress" (Legge, p. 137) and that the benevolent leader should punish the tyrannizing ruler in order to deliver people "out of the water and the fire" (Legge, pp. 170-171). Whereas Confucius underscored mutual obligations involved in the five key role relationships, Mencius championed the valuing of ordinary people in a traditional monarchy. Mencius stated, "The people are the most important element in a nation; the spirits of the land and grain are the next; the sovereign is the lightest" (Legge, p. 483). His doctrine was thus not popular among some rulers in China and Japan (Chiao, 1980, p. 6). The founding emperor of the Ming dynasty (A.D. 1328 to 1398), for example, was reported to express discontent and disrespect toward the *Meng Tzu* (Chiao, 1980, p. 6).

Regardless of whether the political thoughts advocated by Mencius through his water-related figurative language were appreciated by his one-person audience (the ruler), these thoughts, according to Fung (1948), "have exercised a tremendous influence in Chinese history, even as late as the revolution of 1911, which led to the establishment of the Chinese Republic" (p. 74). His water-related figurative language has, in a sense, served as a vision shared among Chinese people, from which predictions are made regarding the destiny of a political system. Both the Communist government in mainland China and the Nationalist government in Taiwan incorporated the water-related figurative language in their political slogans before the 1970s. Each expected to defeat the other in order to deliver their fellow Chinese "out of the water and the fire." Although the meaning for water per se has not been created consistently in the rhetoric of Mencius, water consistently symbolizes a major source of power. A benevolent leader is either represented by this power or able to overcome this power.

## CONCLUDING REMARKS

Water-related figurative language was an important component in the rhetoric of Mencius, one that unveils the main theme of his political philosophy. The choice of water was due to the unique social and historical milieu in which his rhetoric was performed. From a rhetorical point of view, his figurative language was used effectively in supporting the main theme—"The benevolent has no enemy." Because water was perceived to be powerful, the connection of benevolence to water enhanced or even enforced the acceptance of benevolence as being powerful. It also promoted the retention of the message in the auditor. The real purpose of the adoption of figurative language was to communicate the main theme and to make the transcendence of the main theme over the figurative language inevitable. Through such transcendence, a benevolent leader was believed to be able to solve problems caused by any superpower, including water.

Jamieson (1980) maintains that understanding recurrent patterns observable in the surface language is important in explicating one's rhetoric

(p. 51). Through clustering the water-related figurative language used by Mencius, his rhetoric on "benevolent government" and the impact of his rhetoric on Chinese communication become more manifest.

## NOTES

1. The Wade-Giles system of romanization is used to transliterate special Chinese terms and idioms in this paper.

2. Although the ideas introduced in this paper are based on the original Chinese version of the *Meng Tzu* (*The Works of Mencius*), the English translation by James Legge (1895) was adopted for references and quotations.

## REFERENCES

Bond, M. H., & Hwang, K.-K. (1986). The social psychology of Chinese people. In M. H. Bond (Ed.), *The psychology of the Chinese people* (pp. 213-266). Hong Kong: Oxford University Press.

Burke, K. (1950). *A rhetoric of motives.* New York: Prentice Hall.

Chai, C., & Chai, W. (1961). *The story of Chinese philosophy.* Westport, CT: Greenwood Press.

Chai, C., & Chai, W. (1973). *Confucianism.* Woodbury, NY: Barron's.

Chan, W. (1953). *Religious trends in modern China.* New York: Columbia University Press.

Chang, H. -C., & Holt, G. R. (1991). More than relationship: Chinese interaction and the principle of *kuan-hsi. Communication Quarterly, 39,* 251-271.

Cherwitz, R. A., & Hikins, J. W. (1983). Rhetorical perspectivism. *Quarterly Journal of Speech, 69,* 249-266.

Chiao, S. (1980). *Meng Tzu te chih hui* [The wisdom of Mencius]. Taipei, Taiwan: Kuo Chia.

Ching, F. (1994, November 10). Confucius, the new saviour: China, in shift, says sage holds key to West's problems too. *Far Eastern Economic Review,* 37.

Dobson, W. A. C. H. (1963). *Mencius: A new translation arranged and annotated for the general reader.* Toronto, Canada: University of Toronto Press.

Fairbank, J. K., & Reischauer, E. O. (1973). *China: Tradition and transformation.* New York: Houghton Mifflin.

Foss, S. K. (1989). *Rhetorical criticism: Exploration & practice.* Prospect Heights, IL: Waveland Press.

Fu, L. C. (1979). *Chung kuo tung shih* [The general history of China]. Taipei, Taiwan: Ta Chung Kuo.

Fung, Y. -L. (1948). *A short history of Chinese philosophy.* New York: Free Press.

Garrett, M. (1991). Asian challenge. In S. K. Foss, K. A. Foss, & R. Trapp (Eds.), *Contemporary perspectives on rhetoric* (2nd ed.) (pp. 295-314). Prospect Heights, IL: Waveland Press.

Garrett, M. (1993a). *Pathos* reconsidered from the perspective of classical Chinese rhetorical theories. *Quarterly Journal of Speech, 79,* 19-39.

Garrett, M. (1993b). Wit, power, and oppositional groups: A case study of "Pure Talk." *Quarterly Journal of Speech, 79,* 303-318.

Garrett, M., & Xiao, X. (1994). The rhetorical situation revisited. *Rhetorical Society Quarterly, 23,* 30-40.

Ivie, R. L. (1984). Speaking "common sense" about the Soviet threat: Reagan's rhetorical stance. *Western Journal of Speech Communication, 48,* 39-50.

Ivie, R. L. (1987). Metaphor and the rhetorical invention of cold war "idealists." *Communication Monographs, 54,* 165-182.

Jamieson, K. H. (1980). The metaphoric cluster in the rhetoric of Pope Paul VI and Edmund G. Brown, Jr. *Quarterly Journal of Speech, 66,* 51-72.

Lau, D. C. (1970). *Mencius: Translated with an introduction.* Baltimore: Penguin.

Lee, S. -C., & Campbell, K. K. (1994). Korean President Roh Tae-woo's 1988 inaugural address: Campaigning for investiture. *Quarterly Journal of Speech, 80,* 37-52.

Legge, J. (1895). *The Chinese classics: Vol. 2. The works of Mencius.* Oxford, U.K.: Clarendon.

Lu, X. (1994). The theory of persuasion in Han Fei Tzu and its impact on Chinese communication behaviors. *Howard Journal of Communications, 5,* 108-122.

Martin, D. R., & Martin, V. G. (1984). Barbara Jordan's symbolic use of language in the keynote address to the National Women's Conference. *Southern Speech Communication Journal, 49,* 319-330.

McAleavy, H. (1967). *The modern history of China.* New York: Praeger.

Oliver, R. T. (1961). The rhetorical implication of Taoism. *Quarterly Journal of Speech, 47,* 27-35.

Oliver, R. T. (1969). The rhetorical tradition in China: Confucius and Mencius. *Today's Speech, 17,* 3-8.

Oliver, R. T. (1971). *Communication and culture in ancient India and China.* Syracuse, NY: Syracuse University Press.

Pye, L. W. (1984). *China: An introduction* (3rd ed.). Boston: Little, Brown.

Richards, I. A. (1932). *Mencius on the mind: Experiments in multiple definition.* London: Kegan Paul.

Suzuki, D. T. (1914). *A brief history of early Chinese philosophy.* London: Probsthain.

Tu, W., Hejtmanek, M., & Wachman, A. (Eds.). (1992). *The Confucian world observed: A contemporary discussion of Confucian humanism in East Asia.* Honolulu, HI: The East-West Center.

Xiao, X. (1995). China encounters Darwinism: A case of intercultural rhetoric. *Quarterly Journal of Speech, 81,* 83-99.

Xiao, X. (1996). From the hierarchical *ren* to egalitarianism: A case of cross-cultural rhetorical mediation. *Quarterly Journal of Speech, 82,* 38-54.

Yum, J. O. (1988). The impact of Confucianism on interpersonal relationships and communication patterns in East Asia. *Communication Monographs, 55,* 374-388.

# 11

## The Cultural Perspective of a Public Health Facility for Oklahoma American Indians

### *Architectural Change as Rhetoric*

LYNDA DEE DIXON • *Bowling Green State University*

PAUL M. SHAVER • *Sabine Telecommunications Services, Inc.*

This study examines the rhetoric of architectural changes in a federal public health facility for American Indians[1] in Oklahoma. The architecture in 1984 is compared to the changes made in 1991, with discussion about these changes and their significance. These architectural modifications of the physical space in which the operations of the organization took place are postulated to be indicative of the organizational cultural perspective, which is argumentative. The argumentative communicative process contains the following elements: (a) architectural design (including fixed and semifixed space), (b) constraints on interpersonal communication, (c) documentary communication directed at clients, and (d) the ways in which clients are physically funneled through the organization.

### ARCHITECTURAL RHETORIC

Many studies have suggested that the physical environments of interaction have profound effects on the interactions. Early studies demonstrated the effects of colors and space specific to certain cultures (Hall, 1973; Key, 1973). Organizations and their members have been shown to be affected by both the fixed space—architectural surroundings—and the semifixed space—

AUTHORS' NOTE: *An earlier version of this paper was presented at the Western States Communication Association Conference, Boise, Idaho, in April, 1992, under the title "Signs in the Organization: Architectural Changes as Organizational Rhetoric in a Public Health Facility."*

furniture (Bantz, 1993; Weisman, 1992). Arguably, organizations and their members are often unaware of the rhetorical effects of statements made by developmental, processual physical changes in organizations. In health settings, such potential influences are particularly important, because they affect health outcomes for patients.

The study of language—verbal and nonverbal—from rhetorical theory (Burke, 1966) and semiotics (Eco, 1990) supports the notion that the perspectives of organizations and their clients will emerge through a close analysis. In a previous study, we have examined the signs (e.g., professionally printed and informally written) posted in federally funded American Indian health settings (Shaver & Dixon, 1998). The analysis revealed the central dilemmas created by the signs' primarily unconscious purposive arguments. The organization perceived that their limited resources of time, medicines, and space needed to be defended. The organization's posted signs further addressed these "sites of conflicts" (Shaver & Dixon Shaver, 1992, p. 2) and revealed that the organization's ways-of-doing were under attack from the patients. The posted signs had the cumulative effect of revealing the organization's resistance to patients' needs: more appointment times, medicines that were not approved for use in federal health facilities, and a response to the problem of limited patient waiting areas. The Indian ways-of-doing were incompatible with the organization's need to formalize and limit the use of spaces in the building to official business rather than to the Indians' needs to feed children, take care of social relationships, and be comfortable during long waits.

Examining language as printed signs, naturally occurring discourse, or architectural change is seen as indicative of perceived social realities, because language is the primary mechanism for creating and maintaining social realities. Thus, the operational perspective of a group or organization can be revealed by analysis of its discourse (Billig, 1987; Billig et al., 1988; Burke, 1966; Eco, 1990; Solomon, 1988). In addition, because active use of language is often a result of the necessity (especially within formal organizations) for a reinforcement or elaboration of existing organizational commitments, the production of language outputs within an organization can be seen as indicative of the pressure being felt at key points of stress within organizational processes (Hummel, 1994). Researchers have demonstrated that human thought and social discourse are made up of oppositions or dilemmatic elements that are both explicit and implicit, rather than reflecting schemata or templates that provide consistent perspectives within cocultural contexts such as organizations. For Billig et al. (1988) and for Cherwitz and Hikins (1986), the examination of dilemmatic themes is a methodology that brings to light unresolved issues and problems within ongoing social processes. These dilemmas are revealed by the sites of conflict.

This study suggests that when members of an organizational unit "speak" through dramatic and explicit architectural modifications of the physical spaces within which important organizational activities occur, such communication is indicative of perspectives implicit in the language culture of the organization. Furthermore, output of nonroutine organizational discourse can be seen as potentially indicative of a felt need to rhetorically reinforce, reframe, or redefine a social reality significant for the organizational process. In semiotic terms, such a response may be seen in terms of the dominant or central language culture reacting to a competing argumentative initiative from a subordinate or peripheral semiotic (Lotman, 1990). Burke (1966) has pointed out that such reactive rhetorical elaboration can often move purposefully toward "rotten perfection" (p. 16).

The ethnographic data presented in this paper indicate that this tendency toward overelaboration of perspectival commitments can so reveal the fundamental dilemma of an organizational process that such overelaboration becomes problematic for the organization and its clients.

## A FEDERALLY FUNDED CLINIC FOR
## AMERICAN INDIANS, 1984

In this analysis of a federally funded clinic for American Indians in the state of Oklahoma, the first author used the health care facility for 3 years as a naive participant (June 1984 through December 1987) and for 3 years as an informed participant-observer (January 1988 through May 1991). Data include field notes, informal discussions with clinic staff, and social intercourse with other patients at the facility. The visits were periodic and irregular, with no more than 3 months between visits during the 6 years.

### The Site

The clinic is located in a town of 30,000 in central Oklahoma. The clinic is part of a federal bureaucracy under the Department of Public Health that is the primary health care delivery system for American Indians' health (Dixon Glenn, 1990/1991; Indian Health Service, 1990). The clinic, with an attached hospital, is one of 10 clinics and 7 hospitals that treated 228,663 American Indians in Oklahoma in 1988 (Indian Health Service, 1990). The 1990 U.S. Census reports an Oklahoma population of over 150,000 tribally affiliated Indians. This clinic and the attached hospital have the diagnostic and treatment capacity of many standard hospitals, including optical, audiology, pharmacy, and dental clinics. At the time, the main clinic and hospital had to send patients to a local private hospital for mammography and other highly specialized diagnostic equipment.

## The Patients

The patients at this clinic are all members of one of the over 250 federally recognized American Indian nations[2] (Brandon, 1961). The primary population is Chickasaw,[3] because this town contains the tribal headquarters for the Chickasaw Nation. Other nations served include Creek, Seminole, Cherokee, Choctaw, Comanche, Apache, Osage, and Kiowa. Unlike other minorities, Indians must document their racial status through guidelines set up with each tribe and the federal government. All of these guidelines depend on paperwork and documentation of birth, death, and marriage. Children of Indians must have their own documentation as soon after birth as possible. Their parents' documentation does not automatically provide the children with a right to medical care. The interference of the federal government in declaring who is an Indian is addressed in Pratt (1998) and Dixon Shaver (1998). Attempts to limit the ancient and sacred right of Indian nations to determine its own members is part of governmental cultural genocide policies contributing to loss of tribal sovereignty (Deloria & Lytle, 1983). The complicated process of obtaining one's Certificate of Degree of Indian Blood (CDIB)—a tribal membership card with many restrictions and rules—and the clinic-specific card that allows Indians to use one of the various clinics or hospitals further alienates American Indians from the organization that is supposed to be helping them.

## The Organization

National policy controls the clinic and contributes to the sameness of the clinics' cultures across the United States (Dixon Glenn, 1990/1991). Although individual tribes may contract to manage in part the local clinics and hospitals, the organization remains a federal facility with rules, methods of operations, and organizational rhetoric of the controlling federal bureaucracy. The descriptive results of this study compare the changes at the Indian Clinic in 1984 and 1991 regarding the following: (a) the physical structure and furniture, (b) constraints on interpersonal communication, (c) the documentary communication directed at clients, and (d) the ways in which clients are funneled through the organization.

## Architectural Design, 1984

The clinic, built in 1980, was reflective of the brief architectural flirtation with high-technical design in public buildings of that period. The exterior is formed beige concrete panels with a flat roof. The asymmetrical front of the building had a suggestion of a canopy or covering; however, the open covering did not provide protection from the wind, rain, or snow in inclement weather. Style, not patient protection from the elements, appears to have been the influence for this architectural decision.

The front entrance had two sets of double-glass doors, which were not accessible through electronic controls for individuals unable to push the doors and which were difficult to open for people in wheelchairs. The area between the two sets of doors was 8 feet by 15 feet, with beige vinyl tiled flooring. The bronze plaque commemorating the dedication of the building, with the name of the White national political figure from Oklahoma for whom the building was named, was prominent on the right-hand side. The left side had a crowded, heavily filled bulletin board with current notices of public and private events, business cards, medical information, and other general information.

The ceilings were high and open, with maroon-, blue-, and white-painted steel struts and cables. Skylights were intended to increase the illumination. However, the ceiling and drop-lighting orb fixtures, which were white with blue accents, were inadequate for reading by waiting patients. The staff also had to add additional lamps for sufficient illumination for paperwork. The effect was very open and "contemporary," a neutral building that could be found in any city and in any state.

The commercial carpet in 1984 was designed with geometrical designs placed asymmetrically. The largest area was gray; maroon was the next most common color, and some small areas had blue carpet, which bore the marks of high traffic.

After leaving the area between the double-glass doors, the patients walked into a large open area 55 feet long and 40 feet wide. This area served as the waiting room for walk-in clinic patients, appointment patients, dental patients, patients waiting for their prescriptions, patients waiting for blood tests, and so forth. The furniture, upholstered with maroon cloth, was a series of free-standing couches that were slump-backed, making reclining necessary and upright posture impossible. No dividers were between the couches. People had to use their own sense of self-space and belongings in order to protect their territory or to avoid invading the personal space of others. Low square wooden tables were infrequently placed and piled with the requisite out-of-date magazines and medical brochures.

Moving from the front entrance to the immediate left, one would see the dental clinic, but patients were not allowed to wait inside and were sent to the general waiting area. Ten feet farther down the left wall was the medical records desk. This desk was triangular (6 feet per side), with a Plexiglas-enclosed area with two openings that were 18 inches by 24 inches. Only one opening was used—the farthest from the front doors. In the early part of 1984, the glass areas were open, but by the end of 1984, butcher paper had been taped to cover all areas except the opening through which the patients spoke.

At the end of the room, another 10 feet down the wall, on the left side but slightly toward the center, was a triangular (6 feet per side) medical appointment desk. This desk also was changed during 1984. In the early part of 1984, there was no Plexiglas. The first change was to add Plexiglas; the second change, a few months later, was to cover the Plexiglas with butcher paper, just as the medical records desk had done. This desk also had two openings that were 18 inches by 24 inches. (The dental, audiology, pharmacy, and optical offices had their own separate receptionists and rules.)

If patients were to go from the front entrance to their right, they would see a small, elongated room that was the snack bar. This was the only legitimate source of food for the hospital and the clinic. Its hours were from 8:00 a.m. to 3:30 p.m. The snack bar provided doughnuts, premade sandwiches, soft drinks, various chips, and candy. The counter was bordered by three small tables with four chairs at each table. No traditional hospital cafeteria was available. Food and drink were not allowed in any area except for this small space or outside.

Perpendicular to the snack bar was a long hall that led to the administrative offices. Patients were generally not sent to these offices unless there was a referral to be made by the contract health officer to send the patient to a private or state hospital for tests. This office was limited to a certain number of referrals by budgetary limitations, and the answer to patients after a doctor had suggested a referral was often, "The budget will not allow for your mammogram at this time. Come back in six months, and we will try again." By this "try again," the officer meant that a new doctor's appointment must be made, another referral might be written, and the patient would once again go to the contract referral officer for a decision.

Continuing on the right side of the large room after the snack bar, patients would see the pharmacy door. The pharmacy staff was accessed by knocking on a locked door and handing one's file through a half door to a staff person. Patients then stayed in the open waiting area and waited to be called by name when their prescriptions were ready.

Continuing past the pharmacy door, the patients had a view, through floor-to-ceiling glass, of a large courtyard in the center of the clinic and hospital. Patients had easy access through single doors to the benched outdoor area that was also the smoking area for patients and staff. This 30-foot expanse of glass wall ended with a long corridor that led to the audiology clinic, optical clinic, and laboratories.

One of the noticeable areas was the women's restroom. Although a confederate reported on the men's restroom, the first author's observations were that the restroom was small, with fewer stalls than were needed for the size of the facility. With the heavier traffic, the bathrooms were poorly kept, with supplies missing. With the circular effect of heavy use, poor condition, and inadequate supplies, vandalism to the bathroom, in the form of stopped-up toilets, trash on the floor, and heavy graffiti, was prominent.

### Constraints on Interpersonal Communication, 1984

In 1984, a large television was in the waiting area that was closest to the front entrance. The television was turned on in the morning and turned off in the evening by custodians. Over a period of 6 years, no patients were observed changing the channel or volume. Further, each of the three clinics—walk-in, gynecology-obstetrics, and pediatrics—had a television in the waiting area. Patients were subjected to whatever channel had previously been selected. The incongruent display of soap opera romances and noisy game shows was played out in front of American Indians of all ages who were forced to watch the preset channels. Although conversation occurred, it was negatively affected by the roar of the television. People would sometimes wander into hallways to try to have times of visiting, but patient and staff traffic made conversation equally difficult.

In 1984, the no-food-or-drink rule was rarely enforced. This rule was particularly hard because of the inevitably long waiting time to be seen at the clinic by the health care providers. People, especially those with young children and elders, needed to provide food and drink for themselves and for their children or elders. The organization's argument against food and drink was that people were abusing the carpet and furniture with food and drink. Further, people who brought in food and drink from the outside were hurting the business of the snack bar, an outside contracted service held by Whites. Conflict continued over the issue, but patients were still observed eating and drinking in noneating and nondrinking areas in 1984.

### Documentary Communication Directed at Clients, 1984

Surrounding each waiting area, at the medical records desk, in the main reception area, and in each hallway, signs instructed the patients on the behavior necessary for clients of the clinic. The characteristics of the signs and their content were important to understand the climate of the clinic and the rhetoric of the organization (Shaver & Dixon, 1998). The professionally produced, permanent signs were, with the exception of those regarding the food and drink issue, procedural. They were instructional in content, neutral in tone, and formally worded. Sanctions against patients for missing appointments, being late for appointments, or being disruptive or rude to the staff were listed, using bullets for emphasis. The sanction for missing three appointments was that the person was denied use of the clinic for 1 year. The sanction for being more than 15 minutes late was that the person would not be seen and would have to make a new appointment. The sanction for being disruptive or rude was that the security guard would be called and the person would be removed from the premises and would then be refused the services of the clinic for 1 year.

The handwritten signs on copy paper were also threatening but more emotional in tone, using *you* or *patients* to start sentences. Exclamation marks were used, as well as underlining and capital letters, for emphasis. These signs related to conduct, such as control of children or warnings about patients not asking how long it would be until one would see the doctor.

Both permanent and handwritten signs included the following topics: where to eat and drink; smoking areas (smoking was allowed in certain areas until 1987); information about clinic times—days and hours, as well as the times specific clinics were available; telephone numbers for appointments; listings of days during which one could make appointments for specialized care that was offered infrequently; messages about how to get certain information; and so forth.

## *Ways in Which Clients Were Funneled, 1984*

Patients were told by signs, by word of mouth, and by staff to go first to medical records. The line for records was usually one of the longest, regardless of the time of day. The building opened at 7:00 a.m., but the clinic (e.g., records, appointment desk, pharmacy, medical clinics, etc.) did not open until 8:00 a.m., and it closed at 5:00 p.m. Often at 7:00 a.m., the medical records desk would have a rush of people forming a line so that they could get an early start on receiving health care. This line was one of the constant barriers to the process of obtaining health care.

Because the glass had been covered and the opening was small, the patients had to lean down to ask for their records or state their business. People with problems hearing or individuals in wheelchairs often had particular trouble in hearing and being heard. The business to be conducted at the medical records desk included (a) receiving instructions on the necessity of receiving a tribal membership card and a CDIB, (b) instructions on applying for a local clinic card, with the admonition that the card used at Tahlequah was not valid at this clinic, (c) straightening out confusion or problems with records due to marriage, death, and birth changes, and (d) asking for and receiving one's medical record to begin the health care process. Interaction and business between Indian patients and staff was complex and difficult.

At the medical records window, patients produced their cards, stepped to the side while the next person was helped, and waited again until their names were called. No chairs were right at the desk. If patients stepped a few feet away to the maroon couches, they couldn't hear their names being called. The records desk, the 6-foot triangle, opened from the back into the records storage area, so that the medical records clerks could go directly to retrieve the records. Their return was not always speedy.

The appointment patients sometimes got their files and proceeded to the appointment desk area, where patients waited to be screened by a nurse or physician's assistant—sometimes. In some cases, the files would have been pulled by the appointment desk's clerk. Patients were then told that they should have gone straight to the appointment desk. However, if patients gambled on going straight to the appointment desk, they frequently stood in line for a long time and then were told that their records weren't there. They were then sent to stand in line at medical records.

If patients did not have appointments, they were told to go to medical records, get their files, go to another window at the appointment desk, stand in line, give their files to the nurse or clerk, sit and wait, and be screened by a health care provider. The walk-in clinic involved very long waits. Some people would come at 7:00 a.m. At noon, the clinic would shut down until 1:00 p.m. Patients who had not yet been seen by the medical staff at closing time, 5:00 p.m., were told to come back the next day. There was, however, no guarantee that such patients would be seen the next day. Their files were returned to medical records, with the patients having to begin the ordeal by queue the next day.

If patients were seen, they carried their files to screening. Patients returned to the large waiting room and waited to be called to see the doctor, still carrying their files. They carried them to laboratories, to radiology, to physical therapy, sometimes back to the doctor, and, finally, to the pharmacy. They returned their files to medical records desk and then left the clinic.

As a further complication, each of the specialty clinics, such as optical, dental, and audiology, had different rules about when one could get appointments and who could get appointments; they also had different hours. For instance, in 1984, the dental clinic was severely underfunded. Adult patients were seen only every 2 years; children under 18 years of age were seen once a year. All appointments were made between 7:00 a.m. and 8:00 a.m. on the first Monday of each month. After the first 50 patients had signed up, people were told that no more appointments would be given that month, although a cancellation list was kept. Hopeful patients were told to return the next month. The line began as early as 5:00 a.m. most of those first Monday mornings.

In sum, the clinic in 1984 was very similar to private health care facilities in appearance, but procedures were more difficult and complex. The process of obtaining health care was based on patients standing in long lines, moving with their records from one waiting place to another, doing without food and drink for at least 2 hours, and up to all day. The signs "spoke" to the patients and gave some needed information, but more important, the signs set the tone for the organization's expectations of the behavior of the patient within the organizational boundaries.

Limited access to certain representatives (e.g., receptionists, appointment secretaries, medical records clerks, and nurses) of the organization was possible. This contact was difficult and the process was slow. Interaction with the doctor took more time and was more difficult.

## CHANGES TO THE CLINIC, 1991

### *Architectural Design, 1991*

The changes to the clinic in 1991 were significant in that major architectural changes were made. The argumentative communication process negatively affected the patients and the process of obtaining health care. The building did not change in its basic appearance. New carpet was installed, which was light gray with a print pattern and with maroon pathways to various clinics. No changes had been made in the furniture since 1984. The televisions had been taken out of the front waiting area and out of all other areas except for the pediatric clinic.

The snack bar was still the only source of food and drink, but the restrictions on where to eat and drink were more strictly enforced. The women's rest room had undergone a change. All the doors had been taken off their hinges for the individual stalls, and there were signs stating "I told you so," referring to the threatened sanctions that had been imposed.

The medical records triangle desk and the appointment desk had changed. The medical records desk had closed windows, and the glass was completely covered with paper. The appointment desk glass areas were now, like those of the medical records desk, covered by paper except for the two small windows, again making interactions very difficult.

The most dramatic change was in the first part of the large waiting room. When patients entered the facility, they were faced with a series of modular, maroon-colored, carpet-covered booths, rather like telephone booths with solid walls. Large professional signs directed patients to step into the booths; the signs further read, "Do Not Go to Medical Records in Person." Inside each booth, the patient was faced with a series of four signs. Each had a set of instructions regarding the use of a no-dial telephone:

1. Pick up the telephone.
2. If you hear a busy signal, do not hang up. Someone will answer the telephone.
3. When someone answers the telephone, read your clinic card number and hang up.

4. Remain where you are until the telephone rings; you will be told what to do next.

No provision was made for a problem with the system, human error, or a very ill person who did not feel well enough to stand and wait for the busy signal to stop or for a telephone to ring. To listen to a busy signal without hanging up is counterintuitive. The uncertainty of waiting for a telephone to ring added to the stress of the health care search process. In the three times that the first author used the system, no person ever answered the telephone. On each visit, the researcher had to go against the instructions, knock on the closed and locked medical records door to arrange for her medical file, make apologies and justification for her request, and then stand in line to wait for her file before beginning her search for health care.

The changes did not speed up the process of health care. Rather, these changes resulted in the patients' being isolated from additional strata of the organization. Through the architectural changes, the organization's argumentative communication process said to the patients that their interactions with receptionists and medical records personnel demanded too much of the organization's resources. The nonphysician staff employees and their services became almost as inaccessible to the patients as the physicians and other health care providers had been. The overelaboration of the rhetorical perspective of the organization was intolerable to the clients. After a few months, which were difficult and unpleasant for both patients and employees, the 1991 changes were modified, and the "telephone booth" structures were removed.

### *Constraints on Interpersonal Communication, 1991*

Because the televisions had been removed, more conversation was possible among and between patients. However, because of the loss of the courtyard (see "Ways in Which Clients Were Funneled, 1991"), the patients and family members did not have a place to take breaks from the waiting room.

### *Documentary Communication Directed at Clients, 1991*

More specific signs discouraging "outside" food and drink were posted with sanctions threatening loss of health care. Permanent signs were more emotional in their messages: "Your misuse of this rest room has resulted in the doors being removed. Continued abuse of this facility will result in its being closed." Permanent signs regarding control of children replaced the handwritten signs in 1984.

## *Ways in Which Clients Were Funneled, 1991*

The building no longer had smoking areas. The former smoking area in the courtyard had also been an area where people sat and talked and where they took restless children. The doors to the courtyard were locked. The benches were removed. The pleasant area used as a rest area away from the medical setting was no longer available.

Prior to the architectural changes, patients walked their records from place to place in the clinic (e.g., from records to a specific clinic, from the clinic to the pharmacy, etc.). This process was time consuming, but the system did allow for patients to have more than one item on their agenda in their use of the clinic facilities. In the new system, patients were told that employees would carry the files. On the telephone, patients were told to go to their appointment, the walk-in clinic, pharmacy, and so forth. Under the new system, employees walked the files to an assigned destination. Although on the surface, the change appears to be better for patients, it had just the opposite effect.

Indians who use the federal clinics generally do not go to the doctor for one problem. They generally "save up" reasons to go to the multifaceted clinics because they cannot afford time off from work, child care, or transportation for frequent visits to a clinic many miles from their homes (Dixon Glenn, 1990/1991). Because the patients need to accomplish many goals (e.g., refill medicine, make future appointments, see a doctor, have laboratory work done, etc.), the changes in access to one's records had a negative effect. Carrying their records allowed patients to pursue their various needs in the various clinics. The change resulted in patients not having access to their files; therefore, they were unable to use different health stations easily. With reduction in staff and an increase in tribal affiliation, which resulted in more patients, the clinic did not have enough staff to quickly and efficiently move files from a clinic to a laboratory to X-ray to pharmacy. For instance, an aide would send a file to the laboratory, and the patient would then not be allowed to get medicine on that trip to the Indian clinic because the file was not available.

## DISCUSSION

Dixon Glenn (1990/1991) and Shaver and Dixon (1998) discuss the self-declared mission of the federal Indian clinics—the delivery of health care for an aggregate population, that is, members of federally recognized Indian nations. This mission is in central opposition to the perception of American Indian patients toward their reasons to be at the clinics—to obtain health care appropriate to their individual needs, which are multiple.

In rhetorical terms, this central opposition—the site of conflict—can be seen as enabling the positive and negative terms that organize the cultural language of this health care facility. Such enabling discourse structures the perceptions of participants by composing master metaphors that are agonistic (i.e., contesting and combative; Burke, 1969). In Lotman's (1990) terms, the rhetorical "text," a succession of independent signs, is "transformed into a semantic whole with its semantic content 'washed over' the entire space which bears the [integrated] meaning" (p. 48). The argumentative communication process is created and sustained by (a) the architectural design (including fixed and semifixed spaces), (b) constraints on interpersonal communication, (c) the documentary communication directed at clients, and (d) the ways in which clients are physically funneled through the organization.

The experiential effect of this process is described by Hummel (1994), who discusses bureaucratic language in these terms:

> Bureaucratic specialized language is specifically designed to insulate functionaries from clients, to empower them not to have to listen unless the client first learns the language. For a client who has learned the language is a client who has accepted the bureaucrat's values. Language defines both what problems we can conceive of and what solutions we can think of. Once a client uses the bureaucracy's language, the bureaucrat may be assured that no solutions contrary to his [*sic*] interests and power will emerge. (p. 181)

Hummel goes on to say that from the recognition of the "mind-changing function of language" (p. 181), the next step is to understand that the bureaucracy's language hides the questionability of that bureaucracy's own existence. In the case of the architectural changes at the clinic, the rhetoric through the architectural change was so clear that the reactions from the patients made the changes intolerable, even for the organization.

Although implicitly dilemmatic, oppositional messages are received and absorbed continually by patients at the clinics. The blatant message of the 1991 change resulted in normally passive patients objecting to the situation. Indian patients rarely complain about service or health care because they have nowhere else to go for health care, and the explicit and implicit messages threaten the withdrawal of health care privileges. The patients protested through informal means—the grapevine—and occasionally directly to caregivers. In addition, the staff was inconvenienced by the problems with the changes. Whether the architectural changes would have been reversed without complaints from the staff is not known. However, so great was the negative response that in less than 3 months, the booths were removed .

The argumentative communication process of the clinic revealed its culture, a culture that discounted the needs of the patients and protected its resources through gradual changes in procedures and physical space made from 1984 to 1991. However, no change was as dramatic or as negative as the telephone booths. The move to the booths was so clear a statement about the desire to isolate patients from the staff and so direct a message about the inferior role of the patient in the organizational culture that the normally passive patients expressed their unhappiness.

The concept of architectural rhetoric is yet another aspect of the analysis of language. Because architectural language, interpreted through ethnographic descriptions, can be directly examined and documented photographically, it provides data allowing expansion of organizational studies into rich areas of empirical data. In many instances, analysis of architectural language can provide the initial insight that facilitates the comprehensive analysis of organizational perspectives. In this instance, the organization eventually retreated from these architectural changes in the clinic, thus responding to the negative conflict encountered between organization and clients. Bureaucratic rationalization determined that the changes would increase efficiency. The clients perceived that the organization had discounted their needs.

## NOTES

1. The common usage in the state of Oklahoma among Native Americans is *American Indian*. Because this study is set in Oklahoma, we have chosen to use this term.

2. The number of tribes is disputed. There are tribes who retain their heritage, but who are not recognized by the federal government. Others, like the Pokagon Band of the Potawatomi Tribe, received federal recognition in the early 1990s. The Missouri Cherokees, not included in the Dawes Commission Indian Census (General Allotment Act, 1887), have begun their efforts to receive legal status.

3. The Woodland tribes Chickasaw, Creek, Seminole, Cherokee, and Choctaw were forcibly removed to Indian Territory (now Oklahoma) in 1838 (Woodward, 1963). The Osage (Missouri and Kansas) were forced to live in northern Oklahoma in the late 1800s. The Plains tribes Comanche, Apache, Kiowa, and others were made to live in Oklahoma Territory (the western portion of the state; Wright, 1951/1986).

## REFERENCES

Bantz, C. (1993). *Understanding organizations: Interpreting organizational communication cultures.* Columbia: University of South Carolina Press.

Billig, M. (1987). *Arguing and thinking: A rhetorical approach to social psychology.* Cambridge, U.K.: Cambridge University Press.

Billig, M., Condon, S., Edwards, D., Gane, M., Middleton, D., & Radley, A. (1988). *Ideological dilemmas: A social psychology of everyday thinking.* Beverly Hills, CA: Sage.

Brandon, W. (1961). *The American heritage book of Indians.* New York: Dell.

Burke, K. (1966). *Language as symbolic action.* Berkeley: University of California Press.

Burke, K. (1969). *A rhetoric of motives.* Berkeley: University of California Press.
Cherwitz, R., & Hikins, J. (1986). *Communication and knowledge: An investigation in rhetorical epistemology.* Columbia: University of South Carolina Press.
Deloria, V., Jr., & Lytle, C. (1983). *American Indians, American justice.* Austin: University of Texas Press.
Dixon Glenn, L. (1990/1991). Health care communication between American Indian women and a White male doctor: A study of interaction at a public health care facility (Doctoral dissertation, University of Oklahoma, 1990). *Dissertation Abstracts International, 51,* 2722B.
Eco, U. (1990). *The limits of interpretation.* Bloomington: University of Indiana Press.
General Allotment Act, 119, 24 Stat. 388 (1887).
Hall, E. (1973). *The silent language.* New York: Anchor.
Hummel, R. P. (1994). *The bureaucratic experience: A critique of life in the modern organization* (4th ed.). New York: St. Martin's.
Indian Health Service. (1990). *Indian health service regional report—1990.* Washington, DC: Indian Health Service.
Key, W. B. (1973). *Subliminal seduction.* New York: Signet.
Lotman, Y. (1990). *Universe of the mind: A semiotic theory of culture* (A. Shukman, Trans.). Bloomington: Indiana University Press.
Pratt, S. B. (1998). Razzing: Ritualized uses of humor as a form of identification among American Indians. In D. Tanno & A. González (Eds.), *International and intercultural communication annual: Vol. 21. Communication and identity across cultures* (pp. 56-79). Thousand Oaks, CA: Sage.
Shaver, L. Dixon. (1998). The cultural deprivation of an Oklahoma Cherokee family. In D. Tanno & A. González (Eds.), *International and intercultural communication annual: Vol. 21. Communication and identity across cultures* (pp. 80-99). Thousand Oaks, CA: Sage.
Shaver, P., & Shaver, L. Dixon. (1998). "Icons" of bureaucratic therapy: An application of Eco's semiotic methodology in a public health care facility. *Intercultural Communication Studies, 8*(2), 115-130.
Shaver, P., & Shaver, L. Dixon. (1992). Applying perspectival rhetorical analysis in intercultural consulting: The chromosomal bivalency model. *Intercultural Communication Studies, 2*(2), 1-22.
Solomon, J. (1988). *The signs of our times: Semiotics: The hidden messages of environment, objects, and cultural images.* Los Angeles: Jeremy B. Tarcher.
Weisman, L. K. (1992). *Discrimination by design: A feminist critique of the man-made environment.* Urbana: University of Illinois Press.
Woodward, G. S. (1963). *The Cherokees.* Norman: University of Oklahoma Press.
Wright, M. (1986). *Indians of Oklahoma.* Norman: University of Oklahoma Press. (Original work published 1951)

# IV

**FORUM ON DEVELOPING
FRAMEWORKS FOR
INTERCULTURAL
RHETORICAL ANALYSIS**

# 12

# On the Intersection of Rhetoric and Intercultural Communication

## A 25-Year Personal Retrospective

WILLIAM J. STAROSTA • *Howard University*

The path that winds through the early years of intercultural communication study eventually reaches a place and time 2 hours south of Indianapolis, Indiana, where the first dissertation formally designated as "intercultural communication" was defended on Groundhog Day, 1973. The author of said document had earlier applied to several doctoral programs in speech by setting two preconditions for admission: (1) that the degree be termed "intercultural communication," and (2) that the student be permitted to conduct dissertation research in India. The University of Wisconsin and Indiana University accepted these terms, and graduate work ensued in 1968 in Bloomington, Indiana.

The dissertation that followed these overtures was meant to be directed by Michael H. Prosser; it should have been conducted in India; it ought to have been a study of political rhetoric. Instead, it was none of these. The Fulbright-Hays program proposed that the author consider Ceylon instead of India for a 1971 doctoral fellowship. There, an aborted revolution rendered it impractical and politically hazardous for the author to inquire into Ceylonese campaign rhetoric. Consequently, his topic was scrapped in favor of another on information theory and village development, adopting the only theoretical framework that was supportable using books from the United States Information Agency library in Colombo. Then, before the author could return from the field with a self-directed work on how information of development structurally reached some villagers before others, Prosser left Indiana for the University of Virginia to attempt the building of a PhD program in intercultural communication. Given the rigid disciplinary walls surrounding Mr. Jefferson's "academic village," Prosser might as well not have tried.

If Rome was founded by children who were abandoned in the wilderness to be reared by wolves, the first dissertation to be defended in the field of intercultural speech was almost abandoned in the mountains of Ceylon following a failed coup. The writer—white, U.S. American, Asianist, male—returned with a draft of the work to be "reared" by Raymond G. Smith, an early experimentalist. Smith, with characteristic compassion, declared the quantitative work in critical theory written by an intercultural rhetorician to be defense-ready during the summer of 1972, with the concurrence of political scientist and China specialist Ronald Montaperto.

These personal reflections help the author to deconstruct his 25 years as a rogue intercultural rhetorician. This account makes the case that intercultural communication, as first practiced within the field of speech, was inspired by rhetoricians such as Prosser, Robert T. Oliver, John C. Condon, Jr., and Richard L. Johannesen. Although intercultural communication qua speech communication began with a critical and quantitative dissertation, the early study of intercultural communication was largely a study of rhetoric and culture.

Three considerations guide me as I self-reflexively reflect on a quarter century of my work. First, I repent some of my mistakes in perspective over 25 years of studying rhetoric and culture. Second, I stand by others of my conclusions and perspectives. Finally, I see in reviewing my work through 1999 eyes that some of my past work provides important leads for future inquiry.

## I. RURAL DEVELOPMENT RHETORIC

My earliest work on rhetoric and culture springs from a context of rural development in the "third world." In this work, I portray how folk communication forms may be used to promote social change campaigns and how government functionaries serve as rhetoricians in the cause of rural uplift. I also look at major national leaders as they initiate social change campaigns, and I unearth questions of ethics that accompany change campaigns.

I see now that I supposed that most messages initiated by change agencies and governments promoted the authentic needs of the villagers of the world. My taken-for-granteds—that the agency knows best, that innovations should be adopted by all villagers for the benefit of the nation, and that the public's task is to listen carefully and to enact, not to question and to initiate messages—corrupt much of what I wrote in my early years. I also worked within the construct of the *third world,* a place that must be penetrated and uplifted with messages of change so as to bring it "up" to a place alongside more primary worlds. I may have acquired my errant perspectives from the literature of political scientists and sociologists.

Simultaneously, though, my work offered some rich research leads that went largely unnoticed. Unesco, many years after my article on the use of traditional entertainment media to stimulate social change (Starosta, 1974), became concerned with achieving a "coalition" of folk and modern media. Today government units in India and Ethiopia, among others, use traditional entertainment forms to instill the idea of nationhood or to promote family planning. Further, published analyses of whether village drama, puppetry, or storytelling can promote women's health in Ouagadougou or Ghana continue to appear in the literature (Morrison, 1995; Riley, 1995). I still maintain that utilizing the properties of familiarity and credibility of traditional media for rural uplift remains worthy of study, although the use of such media could hardly be considered to be problem-free (Starosta & Merriam, 1986).

In my better moments, I anticipated current literature on tapping the indigenous knowledge of the villager in launching programs of social development (Starosta, 1976). My model of urban-rural communication from my dissertation remains insightful and heuristic, though it was first penned in 1971. My model concerns urban or foreign communicators ($A$), rural recipients ($B$), mass or interpersonal communication channels that link them ($C$), and populations that are usually not reached by such channels ($D$). The model exists in a universe of "messages about development" ($X$). Thus, *AB, AC, ABC, BD,* and the like represent messages about development that take place among the noted populations. When I offered the model, I carelessly focused on a top-down model of development communication. However, by identifying a communication function of persons who serve as channels between rural and urban populations, I promote a channel function that operates in two directions. I recognize that urban messages and rural needs can be misrepresented by a particular $C$ because that communicator is incompetent, or because she or he does not endorse the messages that are communicated. At the same time, this allows for a two-way flow of development communication, and it problematizes the channel function as an interpreter of "development" meanings.

My model heuristically led me to see that *CB* messages and *BC* messages represent the site of significant intercultural interpretation. However, my early, elitist orientation blinded me to many implications of this insight. The potential for channels to distort messages from urban agencies to rural areas and the reverse, and the necessity for someone to translate development messages with a risk of accidental or deliberate distortion, remain significant concerns. Further, my documentation of information "privilege" that was enjoyed by rural elites in even the most remote villages was unique in that it went beyond mass media to include interpersonal communicators, and also because the analysis was based on extended field interviews.

Writers now wonder if they were premature in believing that "a good five-cent transistor radio" is enough to bridge the gap between the world of technology and the village mind. This was a challenge posed by my early work on "the village-level worker as rhetorician" (Starosta, 1976), where I maintained that the then-current model of "knowledge" equating with new practice might work for some topics but not for others. At some point, the task of rural development moves from providing "information" to providing "persuasion," especially for selected topics. My chapter in a book on communicating for development that was edited by Moemeka (Starosta, 1995) revisits this problematic issue by tracing changes in family-planning communication policy and strategy in India. My chapter concludes with fieldwork findings from northern India that anticipate concerns of hermeneutics and culture: Words that had one meaning for communication planners in the city had different significations for villagers.

A collateral analysis explores the dilemma of Prime Minister Indira Gandhi, who considered whether she might need to add "a little compulsion" to her "persuasion" to promote family planning in India (Starosta, 1987). After considering philosophy and ethics along with the literature on compliance gaining, I characterized India's family-planning rhetoric as "de facto coercive." In making this argument, I weighed the power of a central communicator to carry out threats against the power of rural populations to downplay or to resist threats. The model that I developed to display these dynamics appeared in a political science journal. Therefore, my insights about elements of coercion that may accompany two-thirds world messages of change mostly remain unknown to speech communication researchers.

My concern that research reported in a political science journal may not reach those in speech communication highlights a recurrent concern for my writing over the years. I have turned to journals in black studies, educational technology, philosophy, interethnic relations, ethnohistory, and political science, among others, to provide outlets for research that my home discipline of speech communication did not always understand or appreciate. Moreover, some of my cocultural associates report a similar disrelish within the discipline that also devalues their work. Researchers who deal with rhetorical aspects of interethnic communication, then, must be prepared to contend with disciplinary gatekeepers who employ set perceptions as to what represents suitable methods and what size $N$ warrants the interest of their respective readerships. When writers despair of prospects for converting or convincing such gatekeepers about the worth of their research, they turn to extradisciplinary outlets to present their work. The use of such outlets may be devalued by some tenure committees and lessens the ability of writers on interethnic rhetoric to dialogue with key associates within their parent discipline.

## II. PHILOSOPHICAL QUESTIONS
## ABOUT CULTURAL RHETORIC

My second rhetorical study of an urban, two-thirds world, elite rhetorician addressing rural populations is that of Mohandas Karamchand Gandhi's convincing rural Indians to produce their own salt in defiance of a British ordinance (Chaudhary & Starosta, 1992). Anju Chaudhary provided me with historical materials about Gandhi's salt march to which I added comparisons to Western counterparts such as Thoreau and a characterization of Gandhi's rhetoric. Gandhi's rhetoric involved the fusion of ends and means, holism, and of ecological-systems advocacy. When published, though, the analysis felt incomplete. We could not answer the question, "Did Gandhi act as an Indian or as a Westerner in his campaigns of Satyagraha (truth force)?" Therefore, I conducted a secondary analysis to address this question for the readers of a philosophy journal. When our subsequent article appeared (Starosta & Chaudhary, 1993), we still had not reached agreement as to whether Gandhi acted as an Indian or as a Westerner.

This East-or-West paradox appealed to the philosophy journal's editors. More important, it raised the question as to which is the "real" person for any speaker who straddles genders, cultures, religions, nations, linguistic communities, cosmologies, or ontologies. When either of two independent interpretations explains the work of a speaker who straddles two identities, analyses of interethnic rhetoric must explore both interpretive systems to exhaust the hermeneutical possibilities. A move toward "double-emic" criticism, in which the critic makes a case for the operation of multiple interpretive perspectives, seems imminent. The reader is then left to decide how to "read" the "text" in view of its inherent "multilexicality" (see Starosta & Hannon, 1996).

My thoughts on ethical considerations for intercultural communication researchers (Starosta, 1981) began before those in the field routinely asked such questions, and it anticipated some current concerns of axiology among postcolonial writers. I see now that I should have viewed the person who provides data as co-owner of the data and should have realized that a researcher "privileges" that which she or he decides to investigate. I also should have seen that a researcher has a responsibility to listen to all voices, to the exclusion of none. My early writing on intercultural communication researcher ethics did not usually contradict these current understandings: It simply did not anticipate them. Possibly, my concern for disempowered rural peoples placed me in a postcolonial research mode before I even knew this to be a research option.

Three years later (Starosta, 1984a), I argued the case that interethnic rhetoric almost always tends to be disruptive, that it measures its success by the death of some existing order. This extreme ethical position is probably not sustainable in every case, but it provides a provocative counterweight to persons and agencies who introduce messages of change willy-nilly. Also, I wrote an analysis of "roots for an older rhetoric" that generalized about characteristics of two-thirds world rhetoric (Starosta, 1979). In this instance, I see considerable overgeneralization, but I would probably still write a similar article today. In my view, the hazards of having no guidelines for the criticism of two-thirds world rhetoric exceed the hazards of having overstated guidelines.

Finally, on the subject of ethics and culture, I interrogated one case of racism training "gone bad" (Starosta, 1989). A particular trainer used psychodrama to arouse strong feelings in his audience while he spoke on his "ism's" training method, but then he did nothing convincing to channel these passions into a prosocial direction. He arguably left unhealed psychological scars for many in his audience. I wonder, in retrospect, if many trainers and developers opportunistically promote interventions that sound appealing but that do more damage than good. This is a line of inquiry that urgently requires investigation at a time when "diversity training" proliferates and collides with "majority resistance." In terms of rhetoric and culture, this question might be rephrased as, "Are some or many changes that are promoted among two-thirds world, rural peoples administratively beneficial to sponsors but detrimental to program recipients?"

## III. INTERETHNIC RHETORIC

The process of "blind review" for journal manuscripts gives me no way to directly acknowledge the reader who asked me to explicate the contours of Mahatma Gandhi's rhetoric or to elaborate on the generic features of the criticism of interethnic rhetoric following an analysis of an apology by Jesse Jackson for his use of ethnic slurs to refer to the Jewish community in New York. Nevertheless, these manuscript revisions and others helped to advance my thinking in numerous areas of rhetorical inquiry.

A colleague, Larry Coleman, had researched in depth some aspects of the historical relationship between the African American and Jewish communities in the United States. He was at a loss, though, to find an appropriate critical framework to interpret Jackson's apology before a synagogue. Two rhetorical tasks seemed to me to be preeminent for Reverend Jackson: to deal with a political "gaffe" and to "apologize" for his characterizations of New York Jews as "Hymies" and of New York City as "Hymietown." Also striking, to me, was Jackson's use of Old Testament metaphors about wrestling with angels to establish common ground with the audience as joint believers in the Bible. But for an unnamed reviewer, we would have stopped here. Instead, we went on to draw out generic guidelines for every case of the analysis of interethnic rhetorical criticism:

1. The critic should delineate historical relations between the speaker's culture and that of the audience.
2. The critic should identify those elements of a speaker's culture that normally determine the speaker's style of discourse.
3. The critic should specify any prior image the speaker may have among those of the audience's culture.
4. The critic should enumerate public expectations regarding the address.
5. The critic should adopt interethnic rhetoric as the level of analysis. (Starosta & Coleman, 1986, p. 118)

This set of considerations for the critic of interethnic rhetoric was endorsed and extended by Hammerback and Jensen (1994), and the extended model of interethnic criticism was tested by R. A. Fernandez and R. J. Jensen on a speech by Tijerina before an Anglophone audience in Colorado (1995). Their expanded framework elaborates critical tools appropriate for the consideration of speech making in a society that moves increasingly toward multiethnicity, multilingualism, and multiculturalism:

6. The particular rhetorical form should be examined in relation to its rhetorical legacy in its ethnic culture.
7. The role of the specific rhetorical medium in that culture should be examined.
8. Any enumeration of the expectations should proceed from an understanding of cultural presuppositions as well as the rhetorical legacy of the form of communication.
9. The rhetor's or speaker's style of discourse should be viewed broadly to include the various structures, images, content, strategies, and appeals of a rhetorical piece.
10. In some cultures, the "speaker's" image might not require much attention, both because speeches are not the primary means of rhetorical communication and because the speaker is in reality a group that wishes to remain unobserved. (Hammerback & Jensen, 1994, p. 67)

Any analysis of rhetoric that neglects diversity must be problematized and interrogated by those who serve on journal editorial boards, lest readers believe that any U.S. American rhetorical event can exist in a cultural, ethnic, or gender vacuum.

Speakers wittingly or unwittingly represent a community or social grouping; they speak to those for whom some social identity is salient; their group and the Other's group may have a smooth or strained history of interaction; the two groups may or may not share a common first language; power relations may have placed one party's group above the other; and recent events may or may not have transpired that acted as irritants between the two communities. Speech criticism that offers only a monocultural view of a speech text carries a burden of proof to demonstrate its ecological validity and cultural relevance for a multicultural society.

An analysis of the newspaper coverage of the declaration of a national holiday for Dr. Martin Luther King, Jr., discloses an additional dimension for the analysis of interethnic rhetoric (Starosta, 1988b). A qualitative content analysis of stories (see Starosta, 1984b) about a King holiday displayed nearly no negative references to King, his character, his stature, or his private life for as long as the declaration of a national holiday appeared improbable. Only when the passage of such legislation started to appear likely did negative references in the press come to rival in frequency references that supported such a holiday.

If African Americans are commonly supposed to carry a "mask" that shields their feelings about racial issues from the general public, my findings on the King holiday suggest that some whites also wear masks to hide their racial feelings. Beyond my King findings, I recall that white voters said they would vote for Wilder, Gantt, Bradley, Dinkens, and other African Americans politicians, only to pull the voting lever for the opposing candidate roughly 11% of the time. As many as one of every five or six white Americans of voting age wears a mask for racial matters. Such a mask might become visible by using tools for the "close reading" of texts by David Duke or Pete Wilson, at the public level, or from the reading of archived letters to governors or from speeches by citizens to local councils, at other levels. If present tools do not see beneath such masks, then new rhetorical tools must be developed to disclose racial dissembling and to subject it to interrogation.

Another question of rhetoric and culture is raised by my study of United Nations resolutions regarding South African apartheid (Starosta, 1971, 1984a). For purposes of the study, I closely read speeches made by world delegates who came to establish the United Nations. I found that four value constellations or "myths" dominated their speech making. I then went through a chronological list of resolutions against apartheid to determine that first one myth and then another was used to condemn apartheid. When no more myths were available to add to the mix in the condemnation of South African racial policy, the United Nations then turned to condemnations of South Africa based on the disrespect that South Africa showed the United Nations, because the resistance to UN resolutions could only serve to weaken the United Nations Organization. South Africa's most heinous crime increasingly seemed to be that it acted as if the United Nations were unimportant.

Future students of organizational rhetoric in international organizations and other organizations will want to corroborate my UN findings. The ultimate condemnation of an organizational member may be not that she or he has transgressed against an organizational myth, but rather that she or he has acted in a way that leaves the organization weaker. At that stage, when the member is accused of acting in a way that weakens or undermines an organization's authority, perhaps no more can be said against the member.

## IV. MULTILEXICALITY

Early in my research I discovered that "truth" is seldom discernible in human affairs, especially in international relations, where few persons directly witness world events and where alliances render criticism of an ally unlikely. Two studies in particular increased my understanding of how different accounts of truth may be reported in person or through the media for matters of international or interethnic conflict. My first venture into polysemy examined the way the world press variantly describes international events. One paper would place blame on one party, a second on the other, whereas a third would opine that the situation was "one where matters were unclear to begin with, and did not seem to be getting any clearer" (Starosta, 1971, p. 245). The notion of "truth" that emerged from the paper was Chaim Perelman's, whereby competent observers with access to available facts decided an interpretation not worthy of further argument.

A second study took an avowedly postmodern turn. It deliberately searched out all available voices to furnish possible narrative accounts of an interethnic conflict between Francophone Quebecois policy and Canadian Mohawks. In all, through field ethnographic interviews coconducted with Sandra Wills Hannon, 13 distinct ways were encountered to coherently explain the events at "Oka" (Starosta & Hannon, 1996). Most of these events were at least partially incompatible with other accounts. Most of these accounts privileged one or another party to the dispute.

At this stage, we realized the interaction between interethnic rhetoric and journalistic reporting: The story recounted by the media in one's language or in organs designed to speak to one's community is likely to exert a disproportionate influence on whether certain accounts of reality came to be regarded as true and complete within that community. Such slanted understandings, once obtained, serve to "authorize" public actions regarding the conflict.

That existing media (including journals) privilege some methods and topics over others (Starosta, 1992/1993) represents a crucial rhetorical concern within a multiethnic, multicultural society. Gatekeepers, by choice or by habit, promote some accounts and methods over others, and they exclude some topics from consideration as being of little potential "value" to "the readership." In several rejection letters over the years, I was informed that interethnic rhetoric represents, at best, an "*N* of one," and that nothing of significance can be learned from a rhetorical analysis. In my own turn as gatekeeper, as a panel critic for a speech convention in New York City, I was requested by a quantitative intercultural researcher not to comment on the necessity to strictly account for the chronological order of variables in order to perform a path-coefficient analysis of data. What process of scholarly review admits elegant but flawed statistical analyses of a large $N$ but then rejects rigorously performed, culture-close analyses of cultural public discourse?

Because we were aware of claims that "mainstream" journals excluded topics and methods that commonly were employed in studies of culture and rhetoric, among other topics, Orlando L. Taylor as dean and I as editor founded *The Howard Journal of Communications* in 1988. Although we produced over 30 quarterly issues of about 7 articles each with featured topics including "hate speech," "English First," "(de)constructing meaning across cultures," "communication and marginalization," "communication and domestic cultures," "women communicating," "persuasion and culture," and "African American rhetoric," the most prominent indexing source declined to index the journal. Their letter ironically opined that theirs was a "mainstream" index that "must appeal to a diversity of users." The hegemony here in evidence ran opposite to the judgment of 14 other indexes—in women's studies, Latin American studies, political science, sociology, psychology, film, or African American studies—who opted to include *The Howard Journal of Communications.* Hegemonic gate keeping by scholarly journals too often drives analyses of culture and rhetoric to extradisciplinary publication outlets.

## V. OTHER REFLECTIONS ON RHETORIC AND CULTURE

An early chapter in Prosser and Starosta's *Intercommunication Among Nations and Peoples* (Starosta, 1973) gave me the chance to consider unintended and deliberately ambiguous communication in an international context. When a message is received that was not sent or that was sent ambiguously, how can it best be interpreted? When was it probably a message, and when not? When should a message be expected? Who stands to gain or lose from deliberate noncommunication? Further, are ambiguous or unintended messages more problematic within an intercultural context than a cocultural one, given the inherent difficulty of attaching meanings to messages that originate from an unfamiliar context? These questions remain as critical for intercultural communicators and rhetoricians now as they were 25 years ago. Now, finally, I see they apply to interpersonal communication as well as to diplomatic interaction.

Future work in rhetoric and culture may take directions pursued by me with Anthony Olorunnisola (Chen & Starosta, 1998) or as laid out in a

*Communication Yearbook* critique (Starosta, 1988a). We may speculate, for example, that the building of a relationship among those of differing cultures moves from an intracultural stage, through an interpersonal stage, through an intercultural stage, through a rhetorical stage, and on to a new intracultural stage. The rhetorical stage is one where variant values are negotiated and adjusted among parties so as to render them mutually palatable. This model of building a third culture should be put to the test of empirical research to further understand its dynamics.

Twenty-five years spent pondering matters of rhetoric and culture have provided me more questions than answers. Partly because the speech communication discipline has not always provided outlets for my work, dialogue with kindred spirits within the profession has been difficult for me to maintain. For this reason, I relish the chance to share my ideas with the readers of the *International and Intercultural Communication Annual.* A conversation may begin here that will bare strengths and weaknesses of my work that once went uninterrogated. From this conversation may grow a new generation of questions and lines of rhetorical inquiry concerning culture-rich discourse.

As researchers continue to probe matters of culture and rhetoric, I ask them to test five premises:

1. Language is a set of formal rules and relationships. Once used, though, language reflects the cultural experience, the region, the gender, and the ethnicity of the user. The cultural use of language cannot be a taken-for-granted in the critical analysis of domestic rhetoric.

2. The speech-oriented thrust of Aristotelianism must be tempered by attention to listening between cocultures (Chen & Starosta, 1998; Starosta, 1997). Because national cultures represent a collection of voices, only active, willing, open listening to those of other socializations can lead the rhetorical critic to culturally sensitive analyses.

3. Because the meaning of a text dwells in context, collaboration among persons of varying contexts proves necessary for the double-emic analysis of rhetoric. That is, researchers with insight into one context for the speaker's message likely lack insight for meanings from other cocultural perspectives.

4. Questions of privilege must be interrogated in future rhetorical criticism. Journal editors and others must reconsider what it is that renders an analysis of Winston Churchill "significant and newsworthy" but relegates the weaving of Tlinglet baskets by a woman in defiance of an attempt by authorities to erase her culture (Wolfe, 1992) as unrhetorical. Rhetoric must expand from the study of texts presented in public forums to include the texts of ordinary persons who tell their life stories in private places, with far less fanfare.

5. Rhetorical criticism must expand beyond the application of preset formulas for interpretation to the negotiation of culturally sensitive tools stemming from a view of the speaker as coresearcher.

## REFERENCES

Chaudhary, A. G., & Starosta, W. J. (1992). A case study of Satyagraha: Gandhi's 1939 salt march. *World Communication, 21*(1), 1-12.

Chen, G. -M., & Starosta, W. J. (1998). *Foundations of intercultural communication.* Boston: Allyn & Bacon.

Fernandez, R. A., & Jensen, R. J. (1995). Reies Lopez Tijerina's "The Land Grant Question": Creating history through metaphors. *Howard Journal of Communications, 6*(3), 129-145.

Hammerback, J. C., & Jensen, R. J. (1994). Ethnic heritage as rhetorical legacy: The Plan of Delano. *Quarterly Journal of Speech, 80,* 53-70.

Morrison, J. F. (1995). Feminist theatre in Africa: Will it play in Ouagadougou? *Howard Journal of Communications, 5*(3), 245-253.

Riley, M. (1995). Indigenous resources in a Ghanaian town: Potential for health education. *Howard Journal of Communications, 4*(3), 249-264.

Starosta, W. J. (1971). United Nations: Agency for semantic consubstantiality. *Southern States Speech Journal, 36*(3), 243-254.

Starosta, W. J. (1973). Non-communication as game in international relations. In M. Prosser & W. J. Starosta (Eds.), *Intercommunication among nations and peoples* (pp. 316-325). New York: Harper & Row.

Starosta, W. J. (1974). The use of traditional entertainment forms to stimulate social change. *Quarterly Journal of Speech, 60*(3), 306-312.

Starosta, W. J. (1976). The village level worker as rhetorician: A critique of diffusion theory. *Central States Speech Journal, 27*(2), 144-150.

Starosta, W. J. (1979). Roots for an older rhetoric: On rhetorical effectiveness in the third world. *Western Journal of Speech Communication, 43*(4), 278-287.

Starosta, W. J. (1981). An axiology for cross-cultural research in social change and communication. In W. G. Davey (Ed.), *Intercultural communication: Theory and practice* (pp. 37-41). Washington, DC: SIETAR.

Starosta, W. J. (1984a). On intercultural rhetoric. In Y. Y. Kim (Ed.), *International and intercultural communication annual: Methods of intercultural communication research: Vol. 8* (pp. 229-238). Beverly Hills, CA: Sage.

Starosta, W. J. (1984b). The qualitative content analysis of materials drawn from an international organization: A Burkeian perspective. In Y. Y. Kim (Ed.), *International and intercultural communication annual: Methods of intercultural communication research: Vol. 8* (pp. 185-194). Beverly Hills, CA: Sage.

Starosta, W. J. (1987). "A little compulsion with our persuasion?": "De facto coercion" in Mrs. Gandhi's family planning communication campaign. *Political Communication and Persuasion, 4*(2), 123-134.

Starosta, W. J. (1988a). *Ceteris Paribus* in the global village: An agenda for intercultural communication research. In J. A. Anderson (Ed.), *Communication Yearbook: Vol. 12* (pp. 310-314). Newbury Park, CA: Sage.

Starosta, W. J. (1988b). A national holiday for Dr. King?: A qualitative content analysis of arguments carried in the *Washington Post* and *The New York Times. Journal of Black Studies, 18*(3), 358-378.

Starosta, W. J. (1989). Thinking through intercultural training assumptions: In the aftermath. *International Journal of Intercultural Relations, 14,* 1-6.

Starosta, W. J. (1992/1993). Re-centering culture in intercultural communication. *Arizona Communication Journal, 19*(Fall/Winter), 19-26.

Starosta, W. J. (1995). Communication and family planning: The Indian experience. In A. Moemeka (Ed.), *Communicating for development: A new pan-disciplinary perspective* (pp. 244-260). Albany: State University of New York Press.

Starosta, W. J. (1997, February). Listening between co-cultures. Paper presented at the la Comunicaciùn Conferencia de las Americas, Speech Communication Association & Federaciùn Latinoamerica de Facultades de Comunicaciùn Social, Mexico City, Mexico.

Starosta, W. J., & Chaudhary, A. G. (1993). "I can wait 40 or 400 years": Gandhian Satyagraha east and west. *International Philosophical Quarterly, 33*(2), 163-172.

Starosta, W., & Coleman, C. (1986). Jesse Jackson's "Hymietown" apology: A case study of interethnic rhetorical analysis. In Y. Y. Kim (Ed.), *Interethnic communication: Current research* (pp. 117-135). Newbury Park, CA: Sage.

Starosta, W. J., & Hannon, S. W. (1996). The multilexicality of contemporary history: Recounted and enacted narratives of the Mohawk incident in Oka, Québec. In A. González & D. Tanno (Eds.), *The international and intercultural communication annual: Politics, communication, and culture: Vol. 20* (pp. 141-165). Thousand Oaks, CA: Sage.

Starosta, W. J., & Merriam, A. (1986). Appropriate media technology in peasant societies: The case of India and SITE. *Educational Communication and Technology Journal, 34* (Spring), 39-46.

Wolfe, E. (1992, October/November). The Tlingit basket as a rhetorical alternative form. Paper presented at the meeting of the Speech Communication Association, Chicago, IL.

# 13

## Future Research on Rhetoric and Intercultural Communication

### Moving Forward From Starosta's "Intersection"

JOHN C. HAMMERBACK • *California State University, Hayward*

William Starosta's review of his own career as a scholar and leader working in the "intersection of rhetoric and intercultural communication" for the past 25 years documents an extraordinarily focused and productive professional life. Yet, as a pioneer who persistently sought to establish and advance the interests of intercultural communication, he experienced low as well as high moments. He recounts his frustrations with editorial boards that have not sufficiently valued his work or intercultural studies. Especially discouraging were gatekeepers in speech communication who understood neither the effect of culture on rhetoric nor the contributions of rhetorical studies to an area dominated by scholars schooled in quantitative social-science methods. The sources of his frustrations, frustrations perhaps inevitable for someone who sees himself as a "rogue intercultural rhetorician" in an academic world controlled by firmly entrenched and often unfriendly forces, have shaped his scholarly research and professional activism. To establish a body of knowledge in undeveloped, albeit important, areas, he employed both field and rhetorical methods to investigate a wide range of topics. When communication journal editors did not appreciate his work, he published in journals outside of communication and founded our first scholarly journal devoted to intercultural communication. To provide guidelines for systematic study where none existed, he occasionally proposed models and posited conclusions that he realized were overstated or lacked precision.

As a pathfinder, Starosta inevitably made mistakes, which, to his credit, he acknowledges. For example, he initially adopted the prevailing elitist perspective that viewed uncritically the motives of those few people and institutions in control of channels of communication and the messages they carry. However, whatever his mistakes, they seem insignificant when compared to the valuable contributions noted in his chapter. In addition, there are other contributions, such as his teaching and encouragement of his own students and other scholars.

Starosta concludes his retrospective with five premises for "those who probe culture and rhetoric." His five premises compose only the beginning of what I believe should be a much longer list. In an attempt to help move our scholarship beyond the intersection described by Starosta, I will add four additional premises that I have discovered during my own career as a teacher, scholar, and administrator.

The first premise is that the rhetor must be considered—even in our postmodern age. Postmodernists have provided many important insights into communication and its effects on audiences, for example, by showing that our discourse is constrained by the messages we have received. Some of its devotees, however, unduly de-emphasize the rhetor. I recently reviewed a postmodern interpretation that treated César Chávez as a text but ignored the texts of Chávez (Hammerback, 1997). A combination of historical research and rhetorical analysis of Chávez and his public-address texts tells a different story—one determined far more by Chávez himself—than did the postmodern approach. The labor organizer had carefully analyzed his audiences of Mexican Americans and others and had often recorded their reactions to his public address. On the basis of his experiences, he developed a set of clearly expressed principles for effective rhetorical discourse. These principles of rhetoric shaped his speaking, writing, and nondiscursive communication throughout his long career and can explain how he became such an extraordinarily effective rhetor (Hammerback, 1994b; Hammerback & Jensen, 1980, 1988, 1998; chapter on Chávez in Hammerback, Jensen, & Gutierrez, 1985).

One such principle of rhetoric that can also account for the workings of the discourse of the African American civil rights activist Robert Parris Moses is that first and second personae are appropriate and maybe indispensable sources of invention when the goal is to convert audience members into activist organizers (Jensen & Hammerback, 1998). Effecting such a conversion may require the rhetor to change the character or reformulate the identity of an audience. Furthermore, rhetorical identification through a combination of substantive message and personae possesses the potential to achieve such a change or reconstitution—a rhetorical dynamic I initially outlined in an article on Spanish fascist José Antonio Primo de Rivera (Hammerback, 1994a). Both Chávez and Moses understood this principle well, wrote about it, and demonstrated it in their public address.

To understand Chávez's discourse, and to uncover principles, qualities, and maybe even theories that account for the workings of his rhetorical communication with Mexican American farmworkers specifically and Mexican Americans and others in general, a communication critic will profit from taking into account what the labor leader observed and understood about his own discourse. He saw himself not as an object formed by the texts of others but as a subject who could—and did—change audiences, institutions, and history through his communication. To discount his experiences, as well as those of others in groups that have been marginalized, can be especially painful to those whose history and voices have too long been ignored. Because neglecting the rhetor can seal off a source of insight into the communication and culture of groups we study, a better approach would be to merge insights from postmodernism with a close examination of the rhetor and his or her texts.

The second premise is that history must also be considered. A lack of historical context in some behavioral-science studies of ethnic or cultural groups can render those studies not only unreliable but in some cases dangerous. The danger extends past our academic world of words to the material world of the groups we study and particularly of marginalized groups. An example of this danger is supplied by Mexican American scholars and activists during those years (e.g., Gómez, 1973; Límon, 1973; Romano-V, 1971a, 1971b). These authors discovered the many problems caused by social-science studies whose impenetrable language, scholarly approach, and presumed rigorous scientific methods conferred an insidious unassailability and legitimacy upon their conclusions. Thus, for example, when research indicating that Mexican Americans were fatalistic and passive found its way into the knowledge base of social workers and others who created and carried out social policies, *fatalistic* and *passive* were sometimes translated into "unambiguous" and "lazy," a translation that influenced perceptions, policies, and programs, thereby directly harming Mexican Americans. Such stereotypes influence the self-image of members of the minority group, serve to justify debilitating discriminatory behavior toward them, and support negative stereotypes.

When history enters the research questions, the rendition of reality is transformed. It becomes clear that Mexican Americans had long been denied opportunities and had been treated unjustly and therefore could be expected to respond rationally by eventually acknowledging the inevitable, for example, that well-paying jobs were often unavailable, proper housing frequently unattainable, and fair treatment by the legal system sometimes impossible. Yes, perhaps some Mexican Americans accepted the restricted possibilities for their lives in the world they experienced and understood, and yes, perhaps many eventually acknowledged the impossibility of surmounting some of the barriers they encountered. However, such "traits" that are portrayed as ethnic deficiencies can be seen from a historical perspective as a response to material conditions rather than a product of ethnicity. By erasing a group's past, researchers increase the risk of not understanding that group's lived-out bases for behavior, beliefs, attitudes, and values and of not realizing that such behavior, beliefs, attitudes, and values can and do change when historical and material circumstances change.

My own experience of living twice in Mexico with Mexican families as I prepared to write a book about Mexican American discourse was that Mexicans as a group worked far harder than did my fellow Anglos in the United States. *Lazy* and *passive* certainly did not describe them, and these traits were not a part of any Mexican American heritage I witnessed. Moreover, Mexican Americans' rhetorical legacy from Mexico as well as their cultural orientation—largely products of their history—are vital to penetrating beneath the surface meanings of their discourse (Hammerback & Jensen, 1994). To ignore history invites a distorted interpretation of research; such distortion, in turn, can justify unfair treatment of groups.

The third premise is that mass media and visual, material rhetoric must be included in our studies. Rhetorical messages ever more frequently travel through mediated channels, and physical artifacts function as rhetorical texts. We must increase our study of how these media and artifacts influence responses and audiences representing particular groups and cultures. Most lacking are studies of new technologies of communication. Who among us, for example, explores the Internet's relationship with Mexican Americans or other cultural groups? The Internet is reaching and influencing larger and larger audiences, but in what ways, for what purposes, and with what effects?

Lastly, we need centers for the study of intercultural communication. After serving as assistant vice president for research and faculty development, I became convinced that centers possess advantages for obtaining money for research, teaching, and program development; for focusing our attention on our programs, professors, and contributions; for allowing scholars to reach communities outside of academia through mass media and consulting; and for facilitating interdisciplinary work to resolve the questions of concern to the communities we serve. At California State University, Hayward (CSUH), Gale Young won a $200,000 grant from the Annenberg Foundation to link media, cooperative learning, and intercultural communication. If she had not been director of CSUH's Center for the Study of Intercultural Relations, she almost certainly would not have received the grant. In our present political climate, which features efforts to elevate awareness of multicultural issues, and as our demographics shift to a more multicultural population and bring an accompanying set of pressing challenges and promising payoffs, centers of communication and culture are well placed to receive attention and support.

The quality and quantity of scholarship in the intersection of rhetoric and intercultural communication has grown considerably during Starosta's 25-year career. Ethnographers and rhetoricians are joining quantitatively oriented behavioral scientists in identifying and investigating research questions that promise to expand our understanding, define our academic boundaries, and contribute to the communities we serve and study. Yet much remains to do. The importance of intercultural communication has undeniably grown as our demographics have changed and our world has shrunk. Because the intersection that frustrated Starosta continues frequently to be blocked, the time seems right to bring together our scholars and leaders—perhaps at a conference sponsored by the National Communication Association or the International Communication Association—for a focused discussion of the research agenda for rhetoric and intercultural communication as we enter a new century.

## REFERENCES

Gómez, D. F. (1973). *Somos Chicanos: Strangers in our own land.* Boston: Beacon Press.

Hammerback, J. C. (1994a). José Antonio's rhetoric of fascism. *Southern Communication Journal, 59,* 181-195.

Hammerback, J. C. (1994b). The words of César Chávez, Teacher of Truth. *San José Studies, 20,* 10-14.

Hammerback, J. C. (1997). [Review of the book *César Chávez: A triumph of spirit*]. *Quarterly Journal of Speech, 83,* 398-399.

Hammerback, J. C., & Jensen, R. J. (1980). The rhetorical worlds of César Chávez and Reies Tijerina. *Western Journal of Communication, 44,* 166-176.

Hammerback, J. C., & Jensen, R. J. (1988). "A revolution of heart and mind": César Chávez's rhetorical crusade. *Journal of the West, 27,* 69-74.

Hammerback, J. C., & Jensen, R. J. (1994). Ethnic heritage as rhetorical legacy: The Plan of Delano. *Quarterly Journal of Speech, 80,* 53-70.

Hammerback, J. C., & Jensen, R. J. (1998). *The rhetorical career of César Chávez.* College Station: Texas A&M University Press.

Hammerback, J. C., Jensen, R. J., & Gutierrez, J. A. (1985). *A war of words: Chicano protest of the 1960s and 1970s.* Westport, CT: Greenwood Press.

Jensen, R. J., & Hammerback, J. C. (1998). "Your tools are really the people": The rhetoric of Robert Parris Moses. *Communication Monographs, 65,* 126-140.

Límon, J. E. (1973). Stereotyping and Chicano resistance: An historical dimension. *Aztlan, 4,* 257-258.

Romano-V, O. I. (1971a). The anthropology and sociology of Mexican-Americans. In O. I. Romano-V (Ed.), *Voices: Readings from El Grito, a journal of contemporary Mexican-American thought* (pp. 26-39). Berkeley, CA: Quinto Sol.

Romano-V, O. I. (1971b). Introduction. In O. I. Romano-V (Ed.), *Voices: Readings from El Grito, a journal of contemporary Mexican-American thought* (pp. 16-24). Berkeley, CA: Quinto Sol.

# 14

## A Response to William Starosta's "On the Intersection of Rhetoric and Intercultural Communication"

RAKA SHOME • *Arizona State University*

I have been invited to respond to Professor William Starosta's chapter in which he reviews his own theoretical and personal engagements with intercultural communication. Indeed, it is an honor to respond to Professor Starosta's assessment of 25 years of his work in the field of intercultural communication. Starosta's contributions to the field of intercultural communication, including establishing the much needed *Howard Journal of Communication,* are well known. At a time when intercultural communication in our field was dominated by the scientific and objectivist model of studying culture, Starosta's work pushed (and challenged) those boundaries and, in so doing, opened up spaces for alternative paradigms to enter into the study of culture.

Starosta's chapter takes us down a long road that provides glimpses of his changing intellectual engagements with the understanding of "culture" in an intercultural and international setting; it highlights the struggles of doing intercultural work in a field that largely leans toward a depoliticized empirical model of studying culture and that continues to be informed by hegemonic gatekeeping mechanisms of what counts as "worthy" scholarship on culture. This is a field that has done little to theorize issues of power and ideology in the study of culture, as though culture could exist outside the relations of power and ideology that produce it as a site of struggle.

At a time when complicated and sophisticated approaches to the study of culture that foregrounded issues of power and ideology were already being pursued in several other disciplines, such as anthropology, English, women's studies, cultural studies, film studies, and more, the field of intercultural communication remained insulated from these critical challenges—challenges that have changed the face of academic work in several disciplines. Starosta rightly emphasizes that this methodological "hegemony" marginalizes perspectives that emphasize issues of privilege, power, and domination or that employ a nonsocial scientific paradigm for studying culture. In so doing, it perpetuates a peculiar avoidance of issues of power struggles that are central to any study of racism, ethnocentrism, and imperialism. Although some recent works, such as González, Houston, and Chen's (1997) *Our Voices* and Nakayama and Martin's (1998) *Whiteness: The Communication of Social Identity,* are breaking new grounds, the larger hegemonic model of studying culture that Starosta identifies continues to sustain itself.

As I was reading Starosta's chapter, I remembered my initial engagement with intercultural communication as a first-year master's student in 1990. Being an international student, I had hoped this might be an area of the field that would appeal to me. With this impulse, I went to the library to hunt out some "key" textbooks in intercultural communication. Much to my disappointment, what I found were works in which issues of ideology, power, and privilege were glaringly absent. Much of the work that I found seemed largely application oriented and primarily interested in theorizing (and offering "hypotheses" and "rules") on what people need to know to get along with "Others," where Others were typically assumed to be the "nonwhite" subject. The unmarked whiteness of the books, the ways in which whites were constructed as the "norm" against which the nonwhite Others were positioned, and a lack of acknowledgment of the privileges—racialized, gendered, sexualized, and classed—of the authors and how those privileges informed and limited their perspectives both surprised and dismayed me.

Titles such as *Communicating With Strangers* or *Bridging Differences* seemed to be informed by an assumption that "strangers," and those with "difference," were those from another culture or nation, and that intercultural theory could be a route through which to "master" the Other and her or his difference. Rarely were the "voices" and experiences of pain, struggle, and disempowerment of Others represented; rarely were issues of systemic racism, neocolonialism, and imperialism that inform the ideologies embedded in various communicative interactions between Anglo Americans and those from "Other worlds" addressed. Although the field has indeed changed since then (but not as much as it should have) with the emergence of critical perspectives that do focus on power and ideology, the struggles that Starosta allows us glimpses of are important to note. Indeed, they are symptomatic not just of the state of intercultural communication but of the larger field of communication in general.

In the field of intercultural communication, as Starosta suggests, the prevailing methodology becomes even more problematic, for it leaves unexamined the very power-laden cultural norms and privileges that have traditionally sustained the field and determined what can and cannot count as worthy intercultural scholarship. As González, Houston, and Chen (1997) have noted, through privileged forms of scientific inquiry, intercultural scholars have often displayed "unfamiliarity with the specific practices that lend significance or dimensions that are created. *Furthermore, we rarely hear any single cultural participant's voice in the abundant intercultural work that has been produced by various researchers* [italics added]" (p. xii).

In this review of Starosta's retrospective look at his own work, I want to especially address one particular issue that Starosta raises at the end of his chapter. I choose this issue because it encourages us to recognize some of the challenges that we are faced with in any intercultural work. One of the premises that Starosta offers at the end of his chapter has to do with the importance of examining issues of privilege. Starosta states that "journal editors and others must reconsider what it is that renders an analysis" scholarly. Although Starosta does not spend too much time on this issue, I believe this is a thread worth picking up and extending. This issue of privilege is important not only for challenging the Eurocentricity that informs gatekeeping mechanisms of our field but also for examining the researcher's own subject position, a point that is not adequately developed in Starosta's chapter.

Intercultural researchers must examine issues of their own privilege (whether racialized, nationalized, sexualized, gendered, classed, etc.) in relation to the cultures they study and claim to "speak for." For instance, although there is a strong thread of reflexivity in Starosta's own work, it is significant, however, that he does not mark his own subject position as a white, male, American citizen studying the "third world" and how his ability to spatially move to another world and study it is itself enabled and produced by larger neoimperial relations of capitalism and geopolitics.

In much postcolonial work, the issue of the positionality of the researcher has become an important aspect of recognition. At a time when intellectual work, caught in the circuits of capitalism that so mark the academy, begins to function as "commodity" to be "consumed," it becomes important to examine how and in what ways our subject positions as cultural critics are enabled and inscribed by the imperialism of a "new world order" that allows some of us in the "West" to move as scholars to study Other worlds, that enables some of us to be "heard" but not Others. As Mohanty, Russo, and Torres (1990) have suggested, a question that intercultural researchers must face is "who produces knowledge about colonized peoples and from what locations?" (p. 3).

At issue here is an argument that invites a self-reflexive examination of our subject positions as researchers that would entail recognizing how racialized and nationalized privileges inform our work in our attempts to "represent" Other worlds. Such an examination would also urge us to confront how our desire to "speak for the Other" and the conceptual maps through which we name and produce the third world itself can be limited by our socio-cultural-national locations and can consequently result in a peculiar fetishization of the third world. This is the much-debated problem of speaking for the Other that has occupied so much space in debates in feminist and critical race literature.

The argument being posited here is not that only third world scholars can write about third worlds; rather, the issue is that as we research Other worlds we need to examine our own nationalized, racialized, gendered privileges that inform our subject position and our intellectual constructions of the worlds we claim to study. To be sure, there is no easy way out of this critical dilemma, but there is something to be gained from situating ourselves and our works within larger geopolitical relations and to ask the following questions: What is it that allows me to even "represent" the Other (instead of vice versa)? What is it that allows my representation of Other worlds to enter a certain institutionalized circuit in the Western academy? How can I reflexively negotiate between my own privileged subject position as a scholar in the West and the worlds that I want to study? How is the knowledge that I am producing about Other worlds being consumed in the West and in what ways is that consumption reinforcing what postcolonial feminist critic Gayatri Spivak (1990) elsewhere has called the "epistemic violence" of imperial knowledge structures? If the goal of intercultural work is to empower the voice of Others, then a serious examination of our histories, geographies, locations, and positionalities that inform the politics of our research must be taken into account. These are important issues, for they highlight how in the process of producing knowledge about Others we may too often find our knowledges ending up reinforcing the very systems that we want to destabilize.

This issue of postcolonial reflexivity is thus more than an issue of pointing out the privileges that inform gatekeeping mechanisms in the academy. It is an issue, first and foremost, of seeing how our ability to represent the "oppressed" itself might be caught in larger geopolitical relations of imperialism that might allow a white American to easily move to some third world country to study it, but that do not allow a parallel movement of someone from the third world to come to the West. This issue of reflexivity, despite occupying a central space in much current literature on culture and cultural studies, is yet to be significantly taken up by intercultural work in our discipline. Recent works in cultural studies such as Deborah Gordon and Ruth Behar's edited collection *Women Writing Culture* (1995), Trinh Minh-ha's *Woman, Native, Other* (1990), and Gayatri Spivak's *The Postcolonial Critic* (1990) have urged intercultural scholars to address these issues in order to recognize how a certain intercultural project and the position of the researcher is frequently enabled by, and inescapably complicit in, the larger structures of imperialism.

One may ask here, "So what is the way out? If we are always already caught up in these larger imperial structures, what do we do?" The issue, I believe, is not so much to seek a "way out" but rather to recognize this tension and to keep this tension alive in our work—a tension that, if seriously considered, will force us to be reflexive about our subject position as researchers and enable more reflexive renditions of Other worlds. This would be a rendition in which the researcher remains acutely aware of the privileges of her or his subject position in relation to the worlds being studied and in which the researcher always recognizes that the "knowledge" she or he may produce is by necessity incomplete. Such a process is also therefore one that invites us to begin the process of what Gayatri Spivak (1990) called "unlearning our privileges." This process of "unlearning" recognizes that the relation between the (white) researcher in the West and the culture of Other worlds being studied is already caught in, and enabled by, the violence of larger imperial relations. Research on intercultural communication, if it is to be truly responsive to the neoimperial relations of our times, must foreground this issue of positionality. Spivak (1990) phrased this problem as a problem of learning to negotiate with structures of imperial violence, a negotiation that makes the scholar more than an intellectual producing knowledge for knowledge's sake; rather, it makes the intercultural scholar a politically responsible subject who is constantly negotiating with her or his own privileges in relation to those she or he claims to name and to give voice to.

## REFERENCES

González, A., Houston, M., & Chen, V. (1997). *Our voices.* Los Angeles: Roxbury Press.

Gordon, D., & Behar, R. (1995). *Women writing culture.* Berkeley: University of California Press.

Mohanty, C., Russo, A., & Torres, L. (1990). *Third world women and the politics of feminism.* Bloomington: Indiana University Press.

Nakayama, T., & Martin, J. (1998). *Whiteness: The communication of social identity.* Thousand Oaks, CA: Sage.

Spivak, G. (1990). *The postcolonial critic.* New York: Routledge.

Trinh, T. M. (1990). *Women, native, other: Writing postcoloniality and feminism.* Bloomington: Indiana University Press.

# 15

# Response to Commentaries by Hammerback and Shome

WILLIAM J. STAROSTA • *Howard University*

I welcome John Hammerback's extension of my "reflections." I especially endorse his view that something is lost when authorship of cultural texts is de-emphasized. Although postcolonial critical analyses place diminished emphasis on authorship of a text, John Hammerback and Richard Jensen restore an emphasis on the crafting of messages by rhetors of another cultural heritage. In a postmodern era, the audience influences or even creates the text, yet so do the rhetor and the rhetor's cultural traditions. The rhetorical tradition seeks to restore the author of the text, in the belief that message intent and the culture of the message crafter remain essential elements to fully interpret the message.

Nor do I contest Hammerback's stress on history. The rediscovery of ethnic differences in eastern Europe, the persistence of racial antipathies at home, and the cultural repression of Native Americans and First National peoples all vividly demonstrate that memories of strained historical relations find their way into particular rhetorical acts. Behavioral scientists will never furnish the satisfying richness of detail that is needed to fully appreciate actors in a historical context.

Hammerback's stress on media and on material rhetoric and his suggestions for the creation of centers to study intercultural communication speak for themselves. I applaud his call to "unblock" the "intersection" that selectively denies publication access to those who write on culture and rhetoric.

Raka Shome has offered her wonderful eloquence on matters of the giving of voice to women in postcolonial society. Except for my intensive field study of family-planning communication in South Asia, I have paid far too little heed to women's perspectives in my quarter century of writing. That I founded a journal that regularly deals with issues of concern to women, including those of the two-thirds world, will have to stand as my mea culpa. Though I sensed that I lacked the perspective to deal with some topics, I facilitated authentic, scholarly discussion of such issues.

Shome's concern for "power and ideology" reminds me of Hammerback's reference to "history." Historical relationships privilege some persons and classes of persons over others, and such power is relinquished slowly, if at all, through ongoing struggle. Admittedly, culture is ever a center for conflict, a "site of struggle."

Why were early texts so very slow to acknowledge the influence of power and ideology? My years as an editor have convinced me that to talk about culture, ethnicity, and gender inherently marks the researcher as a revolutionary and, in "scientific" circles, an outcast. I wonder if authors of early intercultural texts were simply naive, or if they were fearful of nonacceptance? Yes, early intercultural communication texts do a dismal job on questions of power and privilege.

Shome proposes that I have not overtly interrogated my "position as a white, male, American citizen" who studies "third world" affairs. This is striking to me, because I credit myself with being acutely conscious of my privilege during the several decades I have deliberately spent among those of other cultures and ethnicities. Perhaps my identity as a white male has become so obvious to me while teaching at a historically black university, while taking an Asian studies graduate minor, or from thirty-plus years of dual-cultural marriage that I imagined it must be equally apparent to others as well. This shortcoming I "own," and I hope my coming chapter on "dual.consciousness@USAmerican.white.male" may help to clarify my position on matters of my privilege.

# Index

# About the Authors

VANESSA BOWLES BEASLEY (Ph.D., The University of Texas, 1996) is Assistant Professor in the Department of Speech Communication at Texas A&M University, College Station, Texas. She studies rhetoric and public address, focusing on the historical and contemporary impact of diversity on political communication in the United States. Her research has been published in *Political Communication, The Presidency and Environmental Policy,* and *The Encyclopedia of Television.*

DONAL CARBAUGH (Ph.D., University of Washington, 1984) is Professor of Communication at the University of Massachusetts, Amherst. He is author of the books *Situating Selves* and *Talking American,* and he is editor of *Cultural Communication and Intercultural Contact.*

LYNDA DEE DIXON (Ph.D., University of Oklahoma, 1990) is Associate Professor in the Department of Interpersonal Communication at Bowling Green State University. She is an Oklahoma Cherokee, and her research interests include culture and gender issues in health, education, and organizational contexts. Her publications include books, chapters, and, most recently, coauthored studies on Native People's issues in *Human Communication Research, Canadian Journal of Native Education,* and *Intercultural Communication Studies.*

ELIZABETH GAREIS (Ed.D., University of Georgia, 1992) is Associate Professor at Baruch College. She is author of *Intercultural Friendship: A Qualitative Study* (1995). She has produced instructional materials for foreign language education that have been published by the University of Michigan Press. Her work specializes in the use of film in language education.

MARY M. GARRETT (Ph.D., University of California, Berkeley, 1983) is Associate Professor in the Department of Communication at Wayne State University. She teaches rhetorical theory, rhetorical criticism, and cultural studies, and her current research interests center on argumentation and on comparative studies. Among her recent publications is "Chinese Buddhist Religious Disputation," in *Argumentation* (May, 1997).

ALBERTO GONZÁLEZ (Ph.D., Ohio State University, 1986) is Professor and Chair in the Department of Interpersonal Communication at Bowling Green State University. He teaches and writes on intercultural communication and rhetoric.

JOHN C. HAMMERBACK (Ph.D., Indiana University, 1970) is Professor of Speech Communication at California State University, Hayward. He teaches and writes about public communication, rhetorical theory, and rhetorical criticism. His scholarly contributions include authoring or coauthoring more than 30 essays in journals and books, and a CD-ROM. He is coauthor of *A War of Words: Chicano Protest in the 1960s and 1970s* (1985) and *César Chévez: The Rhetorical Career of a Teacher of Truth* (1998).

RONALD L. JACKSON II (Ph.D., Howard University, 1996) is a cultural communicologist specializing in identity construction and negotiation. His research areas accent identity by exploring Africalogical communication theory, critical White studies, cultural masculinities, and cultural identity as negotiation. He is the author of *The Negotiation of Cultural Identity Interrogates Whiteness as Cultural Space* (forthcoming). His work appears in a variety of academic publications, including *The Howard Journal of Communication* and *The Journal of Black Studies.*

RINGO MA (Ph.D., University of Florida, 1987) is Associate Professor of Communication at State University of New York, Fredonia. He has taught in Canada and the United States and has guest-lectured at eight universities and colleges in the People's Republic of China. His major research area is communication and culture in East Asia and North America. He has contributed articles to *Communication Quarterly, Southern Communication Journal, World Communication, Journal of Pragmatics,* and *Journal of Asian and African Studies.* He is also the winner of the 1997 Distinguished Scholarship Award from the International and Intercultural Communication Division of the National Communication Association (for the best article published in 1996).

RAYMIE E. McKERROW (Ph.D., University of Iowa, 1974) is Professor in the School of Interpersonal Communication at Ohio University. His research and teaching interests revolve around the history and theory of rhetoric, argument, and persuasion. His most recent work involves the articulation of a "critical rhetoric."

KATHI LYNN PAULEY (M.A., Texas A&M University, 1994) is Assistant Professor of Communication Arts and Sciences at Calvin College and a doctoral candidate at The Pennsylvania State University. Her research focuses on environmental rhetoric and the use of landscape in narrative film.

TARLA RAI PETERSON (Ph.D., Washington State University, 1987) is Associate Professor in the Speech Communication Department at Texas A&M University. Her research focuses on the relationship between environmental rhetoric and the public sphere. In 1997, she published *Sharing the Earth: The Rhetoric of Sustainable Development.* Her research appears in *The Quarterly Journal of Speech, Environmental Values,* and *Agriculture and Human Values,* and as chapters in several books.

PAUL M. SHAVER (Ph.D., University of Oklahoma, 1991) is Vice President of Sabine Telecommunications Services, Inc., in Conroe, Texas. His research, consulting, and publications focus on organizational communication processes in media, medical, intercultural, and business settings.

RAKA SHOME (Ph.D., University of Georgia, 1996) teaches at Arizona State University. She specializes in feminist cultural theory with a focus on postcolonial and critical race studies. Her work has appeared in *Critical Studies of Mass Communication* and *Communication Quarterly.*

ROBERT SHUTER (Ph.D., Northwestern University, 1973) is Professor and Chair of the Department of Communication Studies at Marquette University in Milwaukee, Wisconsin. A leading scholar in the area of intercultural communication, he has published in such journals as *Journal of Social Psychology, Communication Monographs,* and *Journal of Communication.* His intercultural research has been published in the *New York Times* and *Wall Street Journal.*

WILLIAM J. STAROSTA (Ph.D., Indiana University, 1973) is Professor of Intercultural Communication at Howard University. He is founding editor of *The Howard Journal of Communications.* He conducted sponsored research in India, Canada, and Sri Lanka. His most recent research concerns media coverage of interethnic conflict, double-emic rhetorical criticism, listening across cultures, and third culture building. His work appears in *International Philosophical Quarterly, Communication Yearbook, Political Communication and Persuasion, The International and Intercultural Communication Annual, World Communication, Intercultural Communication Studies, The International Journal of Intercultural Relations, The Journal of Black Studies, The Educational Communication and Technology Journal,* and *The Quarterly Journal of Speech,* among others.

DOLORES V. TANNO (Ph.D., University of Southern California, 1990) is Professor of Communication at the University of Nevada, Las Vegas. Her research and teaching interests focus on the intersection of intercultural communication, rhetorical criticism, and communication ethics.

KAREN WOLF (Ph.D., University of Massachusetts, 1998) is Assistant Professor at Oregon State University, where she specializes in cultural analyses of rhetoric and the ethnography of communication.

AEP- 3080 /636269

Emerson College Library

Emerson College Library
100 Beacon Street
Boston, Ma  02116